CHICAGO POLICE

An Inside View – The Story of Superintendent Terry G. Hillard

ABOUT THE AUTHOR

Dr. Jurkanin serves as executive director of the Illinois Law Enforcement Training and Standards Board, a position he has held since 1992. He is also founder and director of the Illinois Law Enforcement Executive Institute and is senior editor of the *Law Enforcement Executive Forum*, both at Western Illinois University. Dr. Jurkanin has 30 years of experience in the policing field and has authored and coauthored a number of books and journal articles. He is a long-time member of the Education and Training Committee of the International Association of Chiefs of Police and serves on the Governor's Law Enforcement Medal of Honor Committee. Jurkanin holds a Ph.D. from Southern Illinois University in education and social justice.

A Project of the Illinois Law Enforcement
Executive Institute at Western Illinois University

CHICAGO POLICE

An Inside View – The Story of Superintendent Terry G. Hillard

By

THOMAS J. JURKANIN, Ph.D.

and

TERRY G. HILLARD

CHARLES C THOMAS • PUBLISHER, LTD.
Springfield • Illinois • U.S.A.

Published and Distributed Throughout the World by

CHARLES C THOMAS • PUBLISHER, LTD.
2600 South First Street
Springfield, Illinois 62704

© 2006 by CHARLES C THOMAS • PUBLISHER, LTD.

ISBN 0-398-07610-3 (hard)
ISBN 0-398-07611-1 (paper)

Library of Congress Catalog Card Number: 2005050554

Printed in the United States of America
UB-R-3

Library of Congress Cataloging-in-Publication Data

Jurkanin, Thomas J. (Thomas Joseph), 1955-
    Chicago police : an inside view – the story of superintendent Terry G. Hillard / by Thomas
J. Jurkanin and Terry G. Hillard.
        p. cm.
    Includes bibliographical references and index.
    ISBN 0-398-07610-3 – ISBN 0-398-07611-1 (pbk.)
    1. Police administration – Illinois – Chicago. 2. Chicago (Ill.). Police Dept. 3. Hillard,
Terry G. 4. Police chiefs – Illinois – Chicago – Biography. I. Hillard, Terry G. II. Title.

HV8148.C42J87 2005
363.2'09773'11 – dc22

                                                                                    2005050554

This book is dedicated to my wife, Terri, and to Elizabeth and the Coach. I love you all.
— THOMAS J. JURKANIN

This book is dedicated to my wife, Dorothy; my children, Terri Lee and Dana; my granddaughter, Danaé; my mother, Lelia Mae Drew; and my stepfather, Alfonso Drew, Sr. I would also like to thank my brothers and sisters for their support and being there for our mom when I was unable to be there for her care. Last but not least, the folks who are forever on my mind and in my thoughts and prayers, a salute and thanks to the police officers who have given me their support and loyalty while I was the superintendent of the Chicago Police Department.
— TERRY G. HILLARD

PREFACE

The following article was written by *Chicago Sun-Times* columnist Michael Sneed and appeared in the April 18, 2003, edition of the *Sun-Times*. Michael Sneed is a long-time friend of Terry Hillard and, as a columnist, followed his rise to the top of the Chicago Police Department. When Hillard decided to retire after five and one half years as superintendent of the nation's second largest police department, he first talked to his family, then to the Mayor, and then to his good friend Michael Sneed. What follows is Sneed's tribute to Terry Hillard.

* * * * * * * *

In 1979, a police officer named Terry Hillard stepped quietly into my life.

His cadence was reserved; his comments measured. He was one of Mayor Jane Byrne's bodyguards, when I was her press secretary . . . and his reserve was a contrast to the flamboyant personalities of Byrne's security staff.

My brief tenure with Byrne was tortured; my brief acquaintance with Hillard was blessed.

And years later, when Mayor Daley chose Terry to become police superintendent, I was stunned by Daley's ability to choose so wisely.

Hillard's sudden decision Thursday to pull the plug on his 35-year career was not a surprise to those of us who knew him best.

But you might be surprised why this man – this elegant, kind, almost saintly man – abruptly decided to call it a day and will be leaving office in August.

It's true Hillard has an 8-month old granddaughter, Danae, he wants to spend more time with as well as an 80-year old mother, Lelia, who has a number of medical problems. And it's true he has been cancer-free for 10 years and was just given a clean bill of health.

And it's equally true the average tenure for big city police superintendents is less than three years and he's been at the grindstone for more than five years.

But what really was Hillard's epiphany was the sudden, unexpected death recently of his beloved friend, First Deputy John Thomas.

"His passing was a wakeup call," said Hillard.

"His death hurt me a lot. . . . We didn't go to dinner and hang out. But we talked together three or four times a day and every night . . . and at 4:15 every afternoon, we'd chat in my office and talk about work and our families."

"I tend to walk to clear my head," said Hillard. "And when John Thomas died I walked a lot the next day. I walked alone. I walked by the lakefront . . . and I remember how he'd always tell me, 'Soup, we are two country boys who came up here and were blessed in our work. When you quit, I'll leave one week after you and then we are both going to teach. We're going to teach criminal justice.' John was from southern Illinois, and I am from South Fulton, Tennessee, and we just hit it off even though we'd only known each other for about eight years. And he always said, 'We will get through this.'"

"He believed what I believe. That everyone has to be heard. That you have to listen. That we have to take care of our police officers," said Hillard, who has made this philosophy the center of his administration.

Hillard, who had become legendary for doing what his predecessors did not – showing personal concern for the private agonies many police families face when alcohol, drugs, finances, or illness hits – carries a special African poem in his pocket.

"It's old and orange and full of wisdom," said Hillard. It's tattered from use. It says . . .

"Every morning in Africa, a gazelle wakes up and knows it must outrun the fastest lion or it will be killed. Every morning in Africa, a lion wakes up and knows it must run faster than the slowest gazelle or it will starve. And it doesn't matter whether you are a lion or a gazelle. When the sun comes up, you better be running."

Said Hillard, "In essence, this is the profession we are in. You better have your game together and be progressive in your thinking and listen to folks from the bottom to top; otherwise you are not going to be a good leader."

Hillard joined the police department March 11, 1968, after spending four years in the Marine Corps and 13 months in Vietnam, "where you learned to obey orders and dig a foxhole if someone said to dig one!"

"In other words, you have to operate as a team to survive, and I hope that's the legacy I will leave behind. That we were a team."

The man who decided not to join the State Police and became a Chicago cop instead was following his mother's orders to come home.

The man who lost a close friend was following a pal's orders to follow your bliss while still healthy.

The man who adores his wife, Dorothy; two children, Dana and Terri; twin brother; sick mother; and seven other siblings will continue to keep that African shard of wisdom in his pocket signaling him to keep running.

But this giant of a man will prefer to walk in order to keep his head clear.

– Michael Sneed, *Chicago Sun-Times*, April 18, 2003

INTRODUCTION

In macro-style, this book examines crime, criminal activity, and police response. More specifically, the book focuses on the City of Chicago, which has a long history of and association with crime. The purpose of this book is to get inside the Chicago Police Department so that the reader might gain a better understanding of police operations not only in Chicago but in other major city police agencies. Although every big city police department is similar in many respects, each is also unique, having its own operating and management style. Police agencies often reflect the culture of the city and the people they serve.

Chapter One provides an overview of the history and cultural characteristics of the city of Chicago. Chapter Two summarizes the history of crime in Chicago in the twentieth century by focusing on five infamous crime episodes: Leopold and Loeb, Capone, Dillinger, Speck, and Gacy. Taken together, the first two chapters provide a backdrop for a better understanding of events that, for better or worse, have influenced the City of Chicago and its police force.

In large part, this book is centered on the life and career of Terry G. Hillard, who served as a Chicago police officer for 35 years and retired as superintendent of police. Hillard's early life and career is examined to gain perspective on how his childhood and experiences on the job contributed to his rise to the top of the nation's second largest police agency. The balance of this book focuses on the five and one-half years in which Hillard served as superintendent of police.

Police administration and management is an ever-developing field. By examining the challenges, problems, and issues that Superintendent Hillard faced in his tenure, future police administrators will be forewarned concerning possible pitfalls and better informed about effective management techniques. This book examines how the Chicago Police Department battles gangs, guns, drugs, and murder; how Hillard exhibited leadership in good times and in bad times; how Hillard dealt with politicians, the community, cops on the street and the media; how the department handled difficult crimes and their investigations; and how Hillard led, what he learned in the process, and what he accomplished. The final chapter examines the reasons why Hillard chose to retire as superintendent of Chicago Police.

This book examines contemporary police issues including police corruption and brutality, use of force by police, police pursuits, police shootings and deaths, community policing, police accountability, and the use of emerging technologies in the fight against crime.

It is important for citizens to understand their police. Too often, law enforcement officers are criticized by those who do not have a complete understanding of what police do and the innumerable problems that they face on the job. Police do make mistakes, and they are justifiably held accountable for their actions; however, the life of a cop is not a walk in the park. It is the hope of the authors that, after having read this book, readers will have gained a more complete understanding and appreciation for the police and the difficult job they perform in striving to protect us all.

Proceeds from this book will be used to further educational and training opportunities for police officers.

ACKNOWLEDGMENTS

The authors would like to thank the team of researchers who methodically worked to document and record facts contained within this book and provided moral support and encouragement throughout the process. Dr. Vladimir Sergevnin, Susan Nichols, and Jennifer Wooldridge were invaluable in shaping the content and structure of this book. Sheila Albright typed draft after draft of the manuscript and was patient and encouraging throughout.

Also, the authors thank the Chicago Police Department and the Chicago Fraternal Order of Police, Lodge 7, for their assistance and support of this project.

The authors also wish to acknowledge the Chicago news media for the excellent job they do in reporting on crime, especially the *Chicago Tribune*, the *Chicago Sun-Times*, and the *Chicago Defender*. Many of the facts contained within this book came from news articles appearing in these publications.

CONTENTS

CHICAGO POLICE

An Inside View – The Story of
Superintendent Terry G. Hillard

Chapter 1

THE CITY

She is always a novelty, for she is never the Chicago you
saw when you passed through the last time.
— Mark Twain

Among American cities, Chicago might best be characterized as dynamic and alive. The beauty of the skyscrapers reaching toward the sun and casting their reflections upon the rough blue waters of Lake Michigan reveals the glitter, gleam, and energy of this metropolitan masterpiece.

Rich in history, culture, tradition, and folklore, Chicago has emerged and rebuilt itself a hundred times over since that fateful night on Sunday, October 8, 1871, when, according to legend, Mrs. O'Leary's cow kicked over a lantern in her barn and the city burned. It was never documented that the fire was started in this manner, nor was the theory eliminated as a possibility, and so the story lives on. The night was dry and windy, and Chicago's buildings and structures had been built much too close together. When the fire finally tired and the flames burned out, more than 17,000 buildings were destroyed, and 100,000 people lost their homes, businesses, or both. Such a devastating loss would cripple any city and cause its people to despair about their future – but not Chicagoans. John Stephen Wright, speaking on behalf of Chicago, immediately and confidently proclaimed, "Five years will give Chicago more men, more money, more business, than she would have had without the fire. Chicago is not burnt up, only well blistered for bad ailments, to strengthen her for manhood" (Chicago Historical Society and the Trustees of Northwestern University, 1996, p. 1). He was right; the people and the city would quickly rise again, and the city would develop into world-class status.

The people originally drawn to Chicago came for the promise of a more prosperous life fueled by commercial and agricultural trade, the union stockyards, and the industrial revolution. The completion of the Illinois Michigan Canal in 1848 opened Chicago up as a world shipping center. The first railroad, the Galena and Chicago Union Railroad, was completed just a few years later, and many other railroads were soon built. In 1840, the population of Chicago was less than 5,000; by 1850, the population was nearly 30,000; by 1870, the city boasted a quarter of a million people; and, by the end of the nineteenth century, the city population had reached 1.7 million (Chicago Public Library, 2004). Chicago had indeed become a world hub for the transportation of goods.

As the city continued to grow building by building, street by street, and neighborhood by neighborhood, the pavement, stone, and glass came to visually represent the city's prosperity. However, those who best know Chicago, while appreciating its impressive structural girth, recognize that Chicago's people are what best define the city.

Chicago folks are friendly, robust in spirit, hard working, and generally represent and embrace the wholesome values associated with the Midwestern lifestyle. Many of the families that now live in Chicago are primarily descended from Polish, Irish, German, and Italian immigrants and are now second and third generation. Chicago's predominantly African-American families migrated from the southern states to work in the city's stockyards and the many emerging factories in the 1920s, 1940s, and 1950s. Most recently, in the 1980s and 1990s, large populations of Hispanic and Mexican-born immigrants relocated to Chicago. Retaining and respecting the best cultural traditions of their ancestors, today's "born and raised" Chicagoans and recent immigrants have created their own culture and their own identity. As stereotyped by the popular *Saturday Night Live* television show, "Da Bears" comedy skit portrays language usage, loyalty to sport, and a love of food (bratwurst and other fat-rich delights) as central to Chicago culture. Chicago sports fans still love Mike Ditka, "Da Coach," genuinely appreciating his brashness, toughness, loyalty, and no-nonsense approach to life and the game of football. The Chicago stereotypes can be amusing, but we all know that the people of Chicago are so much more interestingly diverse.

The 2000 U.S. Census indicates that Chicago's population is just under 3 million. Included in the Chicago metropolitan area are 8.2 million people, with hundreds of thousands of people commuting to the city daily for work or flocking to the city for entertainment, shopping, dining, and fun. Within the city of Chicago, the population is diverse and comprised of 36% African-American, 31% Caucasian, 26% Hispanic, 4% Asian and Pacific Islanders, and 3% other or combined races (City of Chicago, 2003). The neighborhoods in Chicago reflect the cultural and ethnic diversity of its people. It is a fact that Chicago's Polish population is second only to that of Warsaw. While the city continues to develop and reinvent itself, many of the ethnic and cultural neighborhoods have been largely maintained. The museums, restaurants, watering holes, and traditions of established ethnic communities continue to thrive and offer every richness that such diversity brings. Race and ethnicity may define Chicago's individual citizens, but the city's inhabitants are irrefutably "Chicagoans" through and through.

Chicagoans' passion for their city may best be illustrated by their love of local sports teams. One need only sit between a White Sox and Cubs fan at a ballgame at ivy-walled Wrigley Field or "The Cell" on the city's South Side to appreciate the fierce loyalty Chicago baseball fans have for their teams. And who could forget the dominance of the Chicago Bulls, Coach Phil Jackson, and the team led by Michael Jordan in the 1990s? The Bulls, with Jordan, won six National Basketball Association World Championships, putting together a "three-peat" from 1991 through 1993 and another "three-peat" from 1996 through 1998. With the world's greatest player on the world's greatest team, mania prevailed. The United Center stands in tribute to the Bulls of the 1990s – referred to as the "House that Michael built." A bronze statue of Michael Jordan in an athletic pose forever welcomes visitors to the United Center and reminds everyone of a reign in sports that will never be forgotten. The Bulls, the Monsters of the Midway, the White Sox, the Cubs, the Blackhawks – they all have the support of their loyal Chicago fans. Work is important, but the sport, spirit, and camaraderie associated with rooting for Chicago teams are integral to the city's lifestyle.

Chicago is also well known for its politics and strong political characters. The father and son duo of Mayors Richard J. Daley and Richard M. Daley has guided the city for 37 of the past 50 years. The Daleys' reign in the mayor's office, featuring their acute political savvy and powerful presence, has led Chicago to prosperity. Chicagoans elect and re-elect their mayor based upon trust, loyalty, and the belief that the mayor knows, and will absolutely do, what is in the best interests of Chicago and its people. In February 2003, Mayor Richard M. Daley was elected to his fifth consecutive term and received an astonishing 79% of the vote. *Time* magazine recently named Richard M. Daley as one of the most effective and powerful mayors in the nation, saying, "He wields near imperial power and most of Chicago would have it no other way. . . . He speaks with a blunt, blue-collar brio that Chicagoans find endearing. . . . He's used [his power] to steer the Windy City into a period of impressive stability, with declining unemployment and splashy growth" (Thigpen, 2005). It is widely assumed, if not acknowledged, that Daley could well be mayor for life if he so chooses. He is currently the longest-serving big city chief executive in the nation. His father, Richard J. Daley ("The Boss"), died in office at 75 years of age, after serving as Mayor for nearly 21 years. Put in contemporary terms, "The Daleys rule in Chicago." Their election and re-election upon re-election demonstrate once again the core traditional values of Chicago people: loyalty and trust. While mantras and city slogans are often created to represent symbolic as opposed to substantive affect, Chicago truly is "The City That Works" – a tribute to the mayor, to the people who elect him, and to their almost sacred bond of respect and mutual trust.

Frank Sinatra loved Chicago, hanging out at the Ambassador East Hotel's "Pump Room" and popularizing the well-known song "Chicago, (is) My Kind of Town." As the lyrics so aptly proclaim,

This is my kind of town, Chicago is
My kind of town, Chicago is
My kind of people too
People who smile at you
And each time I roam, Chicago is
Calling me home, Chicago is
Why I just brim like a cloud
It's my kind of town
My kind of town, Chicago is

My kind of town, Chicago is
My kind of razzmatazz
And it has, all that jazz
And each time I leave, Chicago is
Tuggin my sleeve, Chicago is
The Wrigley Building, Chicago is
The Union Stockyard, Chicago is
One town that won't let you down
It's my kind of town

Chicago was indeed Sinatra's kind of town – full of life, music, dance, beautiful women, and wine. Rush Street once was known as a party district where "anything goes," where revelers could indulge themselves in personal predilection and overconsumption of alcohol until the sun rose over the city. While the seedier elements of prostitution, gambling, and vice are now less evident, the music, dance, libations, and "all night" parties continue on Rush Street, Division Street, and throughout the city. Contemporary piano bars like The Red Head on Ontario with patron sing-alongs led by Lisa McClowry and Thomas Linsk, harken back to the days of old and introduce a new generation to the music, fun, and frolic of years past. It is said that Sinatra's ghost still wanders Rush and is present at Jilly's, the popular drinking and dance establishment named after Sinatra's long-time bodyguard Jilly Rizzo.

If New York is "the city that never sleeps," Chicago is "the city that never goes to bed." The distinction is significant. "The city that never sleeps" may imply an underlying anxiety and restlessness, but "the city that never goes to bed" connotes a choice not to shut down. Chicagoans often choose not to go to bed, to stay out and enjoy the town, and to combine last call with sunrise. Chicago is where "all nighters" and "early risers" meet in transition on the sidewalks, trains, and cafes. Again, it was Sinatra who knew Chicago the best:

Chicago, Chicago, that toddlin town
Chicago, Chicago, I'll show you around – I love it
Bet your bottom dollar you'll lose the blues in Chicago
The town that Billy Sunday could not shut down
On State Street that great street, I just want to say
They do things that they don't do on Broadway – say
They have the time, the time of their life
I saw a man and he danced with his wife
In Chicago, my home town

The Chicago blues began to emerge as a distinctive and popular form of entertainment around the same time that Sinatra was celebrating the city. In the late 1940s and 1950s, Chicago became known as "the home of the blues." African Americans had migrated in large numbers from the south and had brought with them their beloved music, culture, and style. Musical influences that were prevalent in the Mississippi Delta, Memphis, and St. Louis were transported to Chicago. The "Chicago Blues" added voice amplification as a new and distinctive musical genre – and included an ensemble of harmonic, piano, drums, and electric guitar. Such legendary blues artists as Muddy Waters, Howlin' Wolf, Buddy Guy, T-Bone Walker, and B. B. King could be heard "singing the blues" on the sidewalks and clubs down on Maxwell Street, on the South Side of Chicago (Baker, 2004, p. 1). The longing for Chicago is forever echoed in the lyrics of the classic blues tune "Sweet Home Chicago":

> *Come on, now baby, don't you wanna go*
> *Come on, baby, don't you wanna go*
> *Back to the place I love so, sweet home Chicago.*

The blues are still an important part of Chicago night life, and the night-clubs specializing in the blues, like House of Blues, Blue Chicago, and Kingston Mines, offer the best example of integration of black and white. Race is unimportant; a love of the blues brings folks together. Chicago hosts an annual, outdoor, summer Blues Festival in beautiful Grant Park, just off Lake Michigan, to honor the music and its historical and enduring influence on the city, its people, and culture.

Individual businesses do their share to enrich Chicago's vibrant, multicultural atmosphere as well. For example, the Billy Goat Tavern is known for serving up two of Chicago's basic food groups: hamburgers and beer. The original tavern located on Michigan Avenue at lower level is still a popular hangout for Chicago newspaper reporters, and the walls are covered with blown-up articles and bylines of years past. The Billy Goat Tavern also receives renewed annual attention because of its link to the Chicago Cubs and what is known as the "Billy Goat Curse." The Billy Goat Tavern's original owner was Bill Sianis, who was an immigrant from Greece and started the restaurant in 1934. Sianis sported a goatee beard and had a long narrow face – he resembled a billy goat – thus, the name was born. The "Billy Goat Curse" was cast on October 6, 1945, when the Cubs were playing the Detroit Tigers in the World Series, and Bill Sianis bought a box seat for himself and his mangy pet goat named "Murphy." Sianis and Murphy showed up at Wrigley Field to watch the fourth game of the World Series and were turned away because Murphy's grooming habits were determined to be sub-par.

Disappointed and angered, Sianis stood in front of Wrigley Field, raising both of his hands and proclaiming in his heavy Greek accent: "Cubs, they not gonna win anymore! They never gonna be another World Series played at Wrigley Field!" The Cubs went on to lose the next three games of a series they had led 2–1 when the curse was cast. The Cubs have not played in the World Series since (Hedley, 2004, pp. 1–2). The fans of Chicago's two baseball teams dislike each other with a fierce intensity, but one thing they share is frustration. Cubs fans have been waiting to win the World Series since 1908, and White Sox fans since 1917.

The Billy Goat Tavern was also the inspiration for the now famous *Saturday Night Live* quick-order grill comedy sketch, starring John Belushi, Dan Akroyd, and Bill Murray, where orders were yelled out, "cheeseborger, cheeseborger; no fries, cheeps; Pepsie, no Coke!" The Billy Goat Tavern is indeed a Chicago institution.

Chicago is also known for its food and most notably the distinctive style in which Chicago restaurants prepare hot dogs and pizza. Chicago- style hot dogs are boiled, never grilled. They are pure beef and placed in a steamed poppy seed bun. The condiments include mustard, chopped onions, green pickle relish, small pickled (sport) peppers, tomato wedges, cucumbers, and a spear or two of dill pickle. They are topped off with a dash of celery salt. When ordering a Chicago-style hot dog, one simply says "the works," and everything is automatically included. One warning to out-of-towners: to avoid embarrassment, never, never order ketchup on a hot dog. This is considered a major faux pas, an offense which could immediately place one's reputation in serious jeopardy and cast one as an uninformed outsider.

Chicago is also well known for "deep-pan" or "deep-dish" pizza. The Chicago-style pizza is prepared with a thick olive-oil coated crust that extends up the side and to the top of the baking pan. The pizza is prepared in layers, much like lasagna. Ingredients of choice usually include large amounts of Italian sausage with chopped onion, green peppers, pepperoni, garlic, basil, oregano, and tomato sauce, topped with heaping amounts of mozzarella and grated Parmesan cheeses. One large slice of Chicago-style deep-dish pizza could well constitute a meal for those visitors unaccustomed to Chicago-style dining and the hearty appetite that defines the city.

While Memphis may be heralded as the barbeque capital of the world, Chicago holds its own. Lem's Bar-B-Q is located on 75th Street in the heart of the city's black South Side. "Like Jazz and the blues, barbeque rode the rails north from Louisiana and Mississippi on the Illinois Central and took root in black neighborhoods. The meat-laden pork ribs, charred black on the outside, still rosey pink underneath the crust are best eaten with a mixture of Lem's hot and mild sauces while leaning over the hood of your car outside" (Apple, 2004, p. 18).

The opulence of Chicago can best be seen along the lakefront and most significantly along the Magnificent Mile (otherwise known as Michigan Avenue) where pricey stores, shops, and boutiques offer the finest in trade from throughout the world. The Gold Coast houses the richest of the rich in luxurious multimillion-dollar townhouses, Brownstones, condominiums, and apartments while offering a beautiful view of the city, Lake Michigan, and Lake Shore Drive. The Gold Coast is home to national and worldwide entrepreneurs, business moguls, and celebrities, including Oprah. Chicago is blessed with 31 miles of lakefront property, 550 parks, and 15 miles of beaches. Lake Michigan serves as the city's front yard.

The Sears Tower, built in 1973, is among the tallest buildings in the world, rising a quarter of a mile into the Chicago sky and providing 110 stories of business and commercial office space. The Sears Tower, the John Hancock

Center, the Merchandise Mart, the Aon Center, McCormick Place, and hundreds of corporate headquarters located in downtown Chicago leave no doubt of the international presence of Chicago in the world market. The skyline of Chicago shoots majestically upward, worn like a crown of diamonds and gold atop the proud Prairie State of Illinois. Chicago's O'Hare International Airport is the busiest in the world, handling nearly one million flights annually as it transports business travelers to and from the city. Chicago is indeed an international hub for business, finance, and tourism. The world's largest cookie and cracker factory, Nabisco; the world's largest candy factory, Brach and Brock; the world's largest ice cream cone factory, Keebler; and the world's largest gum factory, Wrigley's, all originated in Chicago.

Chicago is also renowned for its eclectic and interesting museums, of which there are 54, including the Museum of Science and Industry, the Adler Planetarium, the Art Institute of Chicago, the Shedd Aquarium, and the Field Museum. Tourists travel from around the world to study culture, art, and science in Chicago's museums. In addition, nearly 200 theaters of the performing arts bring dance, music, Broadway, and cultural entertainment to the city.

The latest addition to the ever-evolving landscape and culture of Chicago is Millennium Park – a private-public initiative that boldly announces Chicago's prominence as a worldwide player in the Second Millennium A.D. Situated on a 24.5-acre parcel of reclaimed land between the Chicago skyline and Lake Shore Drive, the park is a jewel of architectural design. At a cost of $475 million, Millennium is a collection of outdoor public art and cultivated gardens. The Jay Pritzker Pavilion is both intriguing and practical, providing a venue for outdoor music concerts with a seating capacity of 11,000 people. There are an outdoor skating rink, bike rentals, and paths for long leisurely walks. Perhaps the most intriguing aspect of Millennium Park is a giant sculpture, designed by London's Amish Kapoor, titled "Cloud Gate." The sculpture resembles a giant bean, as if it were mysteriously dropped to earth from an alien planet. This shining bean, made of polished stainless steel, symbolically reflects the multidimensional character of Chicago and its people. It is at once beautiful and nonsensical. At a cost of $11.5 million and weighing 110 tons, this 33-foot-tall bean is a testament to Chicago's appreciation of art; a statement that Chicago is unique, if not offbeat and eccentric; and proof that Mark Twain was on point in proclaiming that Chicago is "always a novelty."

Chicago is irrefutably a beautiful and fascinating city. Its people are good-hearted and kind. Strangers to the city are welcomed warmly with open arms, but, while the face of Chicago may embrace visitors with a kind and welcoming smile, Chicago in other respects is like any other large American city: all that glitters is not gold. Like other cities, Chicago struggles with problems of crime and social disorder and suffers from inadequate and substandard housing, poverty, unemployment, gangs, guns, drugs, and a murder rate that is alarmingly high. While well-positioned business folks may typically spend $300 to $400 a night to rent a single room at an upscale downtown hotel, blocks away, entire families live in poverty in tiny spaces and considerable filth. Pre-dinner drinks, steaks, dessert, coffee, and nightcaps for two will cost $200 to $300 at an upscale restaurant in downtown Chicago while Chicago residents working in that same restaurant would have to work at minimum wage for weeks, if not months, to pay the dinner bill. Nearly 20%, or 556,791 Chicagoans, report an annual income below the federal poverty level ($13,290 for a family of three), and 28% of the city's children and youth live in poverty (Chicago Housing Authority, 2004).

It is a short walk from the Gold Coast to the Cabrini Green government housing complex, but the standard of living, the money, the opportunity, the access, the promise, and the hope of the two neighborhoods are so diametrically opposed that an understanding and appreciation of one culture would seem to prohibit an understanding of the other. Chicago can be an extreme example of the "haves" and "have nots" inexplicably existing in the same community yet living distinctly different lives.

On a visit to the city, one is also struck by the considerable number of homeless people, sleeping in doorways of businesses and on heated grates, begging for money, and subtly, by their presence, reminding us all that life can be cruel. Again, Chicago is no different than other large American cities that have been unable or unwilling to effectively manage the problems of economic diversity. San Francisco, Denver, New York, Miami, Los Angeles, and others also struggle to hide the painful reality of citizens who do not fit within the accepted culture and style of the city. The following poem is offered as a call for reflection upon this forgotten segment of society.

The Street People

From their faces you can't tell
but their eyes seem to yell
that the things that they have seen
have made their souls real mean
those bitter grins that they hold
make them look so old
they're not dangerous you know
they've just no where to go
They're the street people

The clothing that is worn
is dirty, old and torn
and their bodies shiver so
as they shuffle through the snow
the shelter that is found
is a clearing on the ground
so they suffer through the night
laying curled up there in fright
They're the street people

The urban streets where they live
seem to take and not to give
and they wander through the night
as city lights shine bright
their lives are filled with despair
as they stand alone and stare
their bodies without thought
as their spirits slowly rot
They're the street people

With their bellies seldom fed
it's to the garbage pails they head
searching hungry through the trash
for a meal of rotten hash
whiskey will sometimes sooth the pain
of nourishment not sustained
but whiskey won't make them well
or deliver them from this hell
They're the street people

They will ask you for a dime
as you walk pressed for time
they're confused and alone
on the streets where they roam
battle scars have left them weak
life is tough and they are meek
they have strayed off now so far
that they don't know who they are
They're the street people

It's easy not to care
not a burden here to bear
these people so depraved
too helpless to be saved
and this life they live they choose
it's the good life they refuse
so we watch them slowly die
and it's them alone who cry
They're the street people

But these people are people first
who have only experienced the worst
when human dignity is lost
society pays the cost
you see it's we who are to blame
we must all feel their pain
we must take these people in
let them one more time begin
They're the street people

From their faces you can't tell
but their eyes seem to yell
that the things that they have seen
have made their souls real mean
those bitter grins that they hold
make them look so old
they're not dangerous you know
they've just no where to go
They're the street people

– Thomas J. Jurkanin

To a large degree, all major cities in the United States are models of what is best about American life and, at the same time, what is worst about American life. For those who have made the grade, all is well, but for those who have yet to attain the American dream, freedom is restricted, opportunities are limited, and poverty is a reality. Because skyscrapers coexist with ghettos and CEOs walk the streets with the homeless, there is a blending of the masses, and this vast range of social and economic inequity leads to numerous social problems. Crime is one such manifestation.

Chapter 2

INFAMOUS CHICAGO CRIMES

Chicago is well known for infamous crimes and criminals. Al Capone's escapades during the 1920s and 1930s still captivate a worldwide audience. For example, visitors to Russia need only name Chicago as their home to elicit an immediate recognition of crime, gangster Al Capone, and machine-gun fire. Deserving or not, Chicago and crime are synonymous. The city of Chicago has seen its fair share of shady, unscrupulous, and deranged characters. It has witnessed the shooting death of John Dillinger outside a Chicago theater; the bloody, gangster-style shootings known as the St. Valentine's Day Massacre purportedly orchestrated by Capone; the notorious serial killings of John Wayne Gacy; the brutal, murderous rampage of Richard Speck; and the cold, calculated murder of an innocent young boy at the hands of brilliant University of Chicago students Leopold and Loeb. Each of these crimes is fascinating in its own right. Each documented crime story reminds us that although this magnificent city of 2.9 million people harbors a mostly decent, God-fearing, and loving population, it is also home to a small minority of people who represent the most despicable, violent, and depraved individuals that could ever be imagined on the face of the earth.

These infamous and spectacular cases of murder and criminal activity associated with the city of Chicago overshadow the thousands of murder cases that are not famous and that occur as frequently as 600 times per year, nearly twice daily. Most crimes, in fact, are *not* notorious and are often forgotten the next day. These crimes are solved at a rate of less than 50% and involve people who are rarely remembered; the names of both the murderer and the murdered are often lost in the statistics, never to be recalled again. Still, each of Chicago's infamous crimes has left its indelible mark upon the city. Documented in this chapter are five of Chicago's most famous crime stories.

Leopold and Loeb – 1924

One of the most fascinating crimes ever to be committed in the city of Chicago was the murder of 14-year-old Bobby Franks. Like many murder victims, Bobby was an unsuspecting victim who happened to be at the wrong place at the wrong time. The year was 1924 when, inexplicably, two brilliant graduate students who were enrolled at the academically prestigious University of Chicago conspired to commit the perfect crime. Eighteen-year-old Richard Loeb was handsome, talented, and smart. He was the youngest student to have ever graduated from the University of Michigan. Loeb had a fascination with crime and would read detective stories incessantly. He had been raised in a home of wealth and privilege – his parents were multimillionaires. Nathan Leopold was a 19-year-old law student whose scholarly interests were wide-ranging, including ophthalmology and philosophy. He was particularly intrigued by the writings of Friedrich Nietzsche and the book *Beyond Good and Evil*, but Leopold's predominant interest, and the object of his obsession, was Richard Loeb. Leopold admired and idolized Loeb both as a friend and as a lover.

Leopold and Loeb conspired to make a game of kidnapping and murder as if engaging in casual sport. The crime was nothing more than an intellectual exercise fueled by Loeb's fascination with crime and Leopold's total willingness to please Loeb. On May 21, 1924, Leopold and Loeb coaxed young Bobby Franks into their rented car as he was walking home from school. The two knew Bobby casually and knew that his parents possessed considerable wealth. Once in the car, it is believed that Loeb stabbed and beat Bobby to death with a chisel; it is unclear whether or not Bobby was sexually assaulted as well. The body was then disposed of under a concrete culvert near the Illinois/Indiana border. The body was stripped naked, and acid was poured over it to cause disfigurement and to impede identification. Young Franks' clothes were burned in the basement of an apartment building. Leopold and Loeb thought they had committed the perfect crime, and the only unfinished business was to collect the $10,000 ransom that they had already demanded from Bobby's parents.

Before the money was to be delivered, a laborer working near the culvert where Bobby was dumped discovered his lifeless body. Near the body lay a pair of distinctive eyeglasses, which had apparently fallen out of Nathan Leopold's pocket when he and Loeb dumped the body. The glasses had a unique hinge that was traceable to a single Chicago optometrist, who had only written three such prescriptions for that design. Other evidence against Leopold and Loeb mounted quickly, including a match between the typeface on the ransom note and the typewriter Leopold used in his law study group. In light of the overwhelming evidence presented by police, both Leopold and Loeb confessed to the crime under separate interrogations.

Clarence Darrow, one of the most prominent defense attorneys of the time was hired to defend Leopold and Loeb. Presented with the culpable evidence against his clients, Darrow convinced the boys to plead guilty to kidnapping and murder. He would argue an insanity defense designed to spare the two young men from receiving the death penalty. In what some say was one of the most brilliant arguments ever to be made against the death penalty,

Darrow presented an impassioned 12-hour presentation. Based upon Darrow's plea, the Judge spared the lives of the defendants and sentenced each to life in prison plus 99 years.

During the four-week trial, the most prominent psychiatrists of the time, many from the East Coast, were enlisted by both the state and the defense to examine and provide opinions on the mental health of Leopold and Loeb. The question was, were these two brilliant and promising young teenagers insane? How else could such a cold and calculated criminal act be explained? The numerous psychiatrists studying the two could not agree on whether they were insane or simply cold-blooded murderers.

Leopold and Loeb were convicted of murder and sent to the Joliet Correctional Center. Loeb was killed in a prison fight in 1936. Leopold spent 33 years in prison and was released in 1958. Upon release from prison, Leopold relocated to Puerto Rico where he died in 1971. While in prison, Leopold earned a master's degree, wrote several books, and taught himself to speak 27 foreign languages. Whether he was insane could not be determined by science, but the fact that he was a genius is indisputable.

Al Capone and the Gangster Era – 1925 to 1931

Al Capone is notoriously associated with Chicago as a gangster and mob leader; however, Capone was not originally from Chicago. In fact, he was raised in New York City after his birth in 1899. Capone dropped out of school following the sixth grade and learned his trade – crime – as a member of "New York's Five Points Gang." As a young apprentice, Capone studied under the tutelage of such experienced gangsters as Johnny Torrio and Lucky Luciano. Despite his lack of formal education, Capone learned the business well and was considered to be a smooth operator with a lot of potential.

In Chicago in 1920, "Diamond Jim" Colosimo was a very successful crime boss. He had firmly established a crime business that included prostitution, gambling, and other vice in a "wide open" area of the city known as "the levee." He also had a direct connection to Mayor "Big Bill" Thompson and other influential politicians. Colosimo was politically involved as a precinct captain and a union organizer, and he controlled the Italian community's vote. He collected "kickbacks" from brothels and delivered the money to crooked politicians. In 1920, Colosimo was in trouble and needed help because he was being extorted for money. His enterprise and life were being threatened by the Black Hand Gangs. At this time, Colosimo called upon his cousin, New York's Johnny Torrio, and asked him to come to Chicago to protect his operation and run his business. When he arrived in Chicago, Torrio brought Al Capone as his right-hand man.

Torrio was an astute businessman who was meticulously organized and very ambitious. He knew how to promote new enterprises, both criminal and legitimate, to turn a profit. With the passage of the National Prohibition Enforcement

Act of 1920, Torrio immediately saw the enormous opportunity and potential for selling bootleg liquor. Colosimo, on the other hand, was comfortable with his current business and resisted Torrio's suggestion to move into bootlegging. On May 11, 1920, Colosimo was shot in the head. It was speculated that Torrio, Colosimo's cousin, ordered Capone to commit the murder. So much for close family ties. Torrio and Capone immediately took over Colosimo's operation and moved aggressively into the bootlegging business.

Various reform movements had been initiated in the early 1900s to clean up the mob-connected Chicago government. William Dever, elected Chicago Mayor in 1923, directed police to vigorously enforce prohibition. "Within weeks of taking office, Dever's police shut down 7,000 soft-drink parlors and restaurants operating as speakeasies" (Wendt & Kogan, 1953, p. 239). It was at this time that Torrio and Capone relocated their operation to Cicero, a small town west of Chicago. There they quickly corrupted politicians and opened a number of gambling, prostitution, and bootleg liquor establishments. It was in Cicero that Frank Capone, Al's brother, was killed in a shootout with Chicago police officers.

During the years of prohibition, there was a enormous opportunity to make huge profits from selling bootleg whiskey and beer, and gangster organizations jockeyed for market territory. The competition for control of neighborhoods and politicians was intense. Dion O'Banion's operation was located on Chicago's North Side and controlled the Irish neighborhoods, while the "terrible" Genna brothers worked on the West Side and served the needs of Italian and Sicilian neighborhoods. It was only a matter of time before bloody battles between the gangs would erupt. On November 10, 1924, O'Banion was gunned down for double-crossing Torrio; on January 24, 1925, Torrio was shot by O'Banion's guys. Although Torrio survived the shooting, he soon turned his operation over to his top assistant, Al Capone, and returned to New York.

Al Capone had to prove himself as a formidable crime boss. From 1925 through 1929, gang wars became commonplace. The battle was for power, profit, and control. The Genna brothers were the first to go; several were murdered, and the others were forced out of town. Joey Aiello and his family soon took over the North Side and put a hefty cash bounty on the life of Capone. In the most notorious attempt to kill Capone, rival gangs fired hundreds of machine gun rounds into a restaurant where Capone was dining in the city of Cicero. Capone was not hit. Between 1925 and 1929, countless gangsters were gunned down by rival gangs, and bombing of property and personal intimidation were commonplace. On Valentine's Day, February 14, 1929, the gangster wars of Chicago culminated in what is now known as the St. Valentine's Day Massacre. Seven members of the Aiello and "Bugs" Moran gang were lined up inside a garage and machine-gunned to death by rival gang members posing as police. Although no one was convicted of the crime, it was clear that Capone and those loyal to him had orchestrated the murders.

The St. Valentine's Day Massacre was a turning point in Chicago gang history, and Al Capone had clearly established himself as the crime boss of Chicago. He was only 30 years of age at the time. The *Chicago Daily News* ran an article in 1930 which, according to one researcher, estimated that Capone controlled over 6,000 speakeasies and 2,000 handbooks for betting on horseracing. Furthermore, the combined revenue from these enterprises, plus prostitution and racketeering, was estimated to be $6.2 million a week, or $322 million annually (Lombardo, 2004, pp. 12–13).

In 1929, President Herbert Hoover, at the calling of the Chicago Crime Commission, "ordered a full-scale attack on the Capone syndicate by the Prohibition Bureau and the Internal Revenue Service" (Lombardo, p. 13). Under the supervision of Elliot Ness, prohibition agents led a raid of several of Capone's distilleries and breweries, seizing and destroying alcohol, trucks, and other equipment. Meanwhile, the Internal Revenue Service and the U.S. Department of the Treasury continued to investigate Capone for tax evasion and brought charges against him in 1931. Capone was sentenced to 11 years in federal prison on October 24, 1931, and served his sentence at U.S. penitentiaries in Atlanta and at Alcatraz. He was released from prison after serving 7½ years and moved to his long-time home in Palm Island, Florida. Capone never returned to Chicago. Afflicted by a condition of brain deterioration brought on by syphilis, Capone degenerated to a point where he had the mental capacity of a 12-year-old child. He died at home on January 25, 1947, at the age of 48. Although Capone was born and raised in New York City, spent just under 12 years in Chicago, and was boss of organized crime for only six years, he will be forever remembered synonymously with Chicago and crime.

John Dillinger – 1933 to 1934

John Dillinger became a national folk hero in 1933 and 1934 as a handsome, well-dressed gangster. His gang of thugs robbed banks throughout the Midwestern states of Illinois, Indiana, Ohio, Michigan, Minnesota, Wisconsin, and South Dakota. As John Dillinger's crime spree flourished, he traveled in and out of Chicago on a frequent basis. Toting machine guns, driving a Packard, wearing suits and ties and straw hats, Dillinger and his gang were hungry for money and notoriety, and they seemed to enjoy killing anyone who got in their way. Dillinger's crime spree would last just one year, but his legend would last much longer.

John Herbert Dillinger was born in Indianapolis, Indiana, in June 1903. His father was a hardworking man who was employed as a grocer. The family enjoyed a comfortable, middle-class lifestyle. Dillinger's mother died when he was just three years old, and although his father remarried, John never cared for his stepmother. As an adolescent living in the city of Indianapolis, he began to get in trouble frequently. His father became so concerned about his son's wayward behavior that he relocated the family to a farm in Mooresville,

Indiana. Although his father had hoped that life would be better for John away from the temptations of the city, the move made little difference. Dillinger continued to get into trouble and soon dropped out of school.

Although Dillinger worked for a short time in a machine shop, where he was described as a good worker, his rowdy and deviant lifestyle outside of work would soon cause him to lose his job when he was arrested for auto theft. Dillinger also spent some time in the Navy, but while his ship was docked in Boston, he deserted and returned to Mooresville where he married a 16-year-old girl by the name of Beryl Hovious. Beryl and the 21-year-old Dillinger soon moved to Indianapolis.

Dillinger's first attempt at committing a major crime for profit came on September 6, 1924, when he and a friend attempted to rob a grocery store in his hometown of Mooresville. The two were quickly apprehended and later sent to prison. While in prison, Dillinger met several inmates who would later become members of his gang. He became an angry man in prison and would conspire incessantly with his prison pals to commit crimes on the outside once they were released. Dillinger was paroled from the Indiana State Correctional System in May 1933; he was 31 years old.

Almost immediately after being released from prison, Dillinger began his new career as a bank robber. In the summer of 1933, he and his partners robbed a bank in New Carlisle, Ohio, on June 10; the Commercial Bank in Daleville, Indiana, on July 17; the First National Bank in Montpelier, Indiana, on August 4; the National Bank in Bluffton, Ohio, on August 14; and the Massachusetts Avenue State Bank in Indianapolis on September 6. Sixteen days later, Dayton police caught up with Dillinger, arrested him, and transported him to the Allen County Jail in Lima, Ohio, to face charges for the Bluffton Bank robbery.

After three weeks of being held in the Allen County Jail, Dillinger's prison buddies from Indiana, who had orchestrated their own jail break, came to break him out. They approached the jail and told Sheriff Jesse Sarber that they were officials from Indiana and had come to return Dillinger to Indiana State Prison for parole violations. When the sheriff asked to see their credentials, they shot and beat him; he later died. The gangsters stormed the jail and freed Dillinger.

With the gang together in full force, the crime spree continued. In order to amass weapons, Dillinger and his gang robbed police station arsenals. They robbed police stations in Auburn and Peru, Indiana, stealing caches of machine guns, rifles, revolvers, ammunition, and bulletproof vests. The bank robberies and killings continued. The gang moved from Greencastle, Indiana, to Racine, Wisconsin, to East Chicago, Illinois. In the East Chicago robbery, the gang shot and killed another police officer, their third law enforcement official. The second was a Chicago Police Sergeant, named William Shanley, who was shot and killed on December 14, 1933, during an attempt to capture a member of Dillinger's gang. This murder prompted the Chicago Police Department to form a special unit called the "Dillinger Squad." As a result, in January 1934, the heat was on, and it was then that Dillinger and his friends decided to retreat to Florida and later to Tucson, Arizona, until things cooled down. Dillinger and his gang members were hiding out at a hotel in Tucson under assumed names when a fire broke out and the hotel was evacuated. A fireman recognized Dillinger and summoned the police. Dillinger and his gang were arrested. They were later extradited to the county jail in Crown Point, Indiana, to stand trial for the murder of the East Chicago police officer.

The county jail in Crown Point was said to be "escape proof," and the sheriff made it clear to all who would listen that Dillinger would not escape from his jail. The sheriff was wrong. Dillinger fashioned a fake gun and forced guards into opening his cell. He then locked the guards and the jail trustees in a cell, stole several machine guns, and drove the sheriff's car to Chicago where he left it abandoned. Despite all of the crimes he had committed, the FBI only now became actively involved because by stealing a car and crossing state lines, Dillinger had violated the National Motor Vehicle Theft Act. Dillinger would soon become the FBI's "Public Enemy Number One."

Dillinger quickly left Chicago with his girlfriend, Evelyn Frechette, and relocated to St. Paul, Minnesota, where he teamed up with other gangster buddies including Lester Gillis, a.k.a. Baby Face Nelson. Dillinger and his gang continued robbing banks in Sioux Falls, South Dakota, on March 6, 1934, and Mason City, Iowa, on March 13, 1934. Dillinger and his girlfriend were living in an apartment in St. Paul in March of 1934 when the FBI got a tip and moved in. The couple escaped through a back entrance of the apartment building in a barrage of gunfire. The two then retreated to Dillinger's hometown of Mooresville, Indiana, and lived with his father while Dillinger's leg healed from a wound he received in the escape. On April 13, 1934, Dillinger robbed the police arsenal in Warsaw, Indiana, to replenish his supply of ammunition, weapons, and bulletproof vests.

Dillinger and his gang then retreated to a summer resort in Wisconsin called the Little Bohemia Lodge. The owner of the lodge became suspicious of the influx of shady characters and notified the FBI. Dozens of FBI agents traveled from Chicago with plans to surround the lodge in the early morning hours of April 23, 1934. As the agents quietly approached the lodge, dogs began to bark, alerting the gang, who opened fire in the direction of the agents using machine guns. They were able to escape through the back windows of the lodge and flee on foot and in cars.

J. Edgar Hoover, embarrassed by the botched capture attempt in Wisconsin, sent Special Agent Samuel A. Crowley from headquarters in Washington, D.C., to Chicago with orders to capture Dillinger and his gang. Crowley and Melvin Purvis, Special Agent-in-Charge of the Chicago FBI office, made Dillinger their top priority. The FBI worked with local police to track down all leads as to the whereabouts of Dillinger.

On July 21, 1934, a woman named Anna Sage contacted an East Chicago police officer she knew with important information on Dillinger. Anna Sage, whose real name was Anna Cumpanas, was a madam at a brothel in Gary, Indiana. She was originally from Rumania, and the federal government had initiated proceedings against her for deportation because she was considered to be an undesirable alien. Sage wanted to make a deal with the FBI. She would give them information on Dillinger's whereabouts if they would intercede on her behalf so that she would not be deported.

A meeting was set up with Sage and FBI bosses Crowley and Purvis, and a deal was struck. Sage told Crowley and Purvis that Dillinger had visited her brothel with a girlfriend of hers by the name of Polly Hamilton. Sage said that she, Polly, and Dillinger were making plans to go to a Chicago theater the next night, which would have been Sunday, July 22, 1934. Sage identified the theater as the Biograph Theater. She offered to wear an orange-colored dress (which appeared red under lights) to the theater so that police could identify her and her party. The plan was put into action, and dozens of FBI agents and undercover police officials were stationed outside the Biograph Theater on Sunday evening. Anna, Polly, and Dillinger arrived at the theater, as promised, at 8:30 PM. The three entered the theater to watch a movie starring Clark Gable entitled *Manhattan Melodrama*.

Crowley immediately telephoned J. Edgar Hoover to get instructions. Hoover told him to wait until the movie ended and then to capture Dillinger as he exited the theater. Hoover did not want any innocent people to get hurt. Dillinger and his two companions left the theater at approximately 10:30 PM. Purvis was standing in the doorway of a store with an unlit cigar. Once Purvis identified Dillinger, he lit his cigar to signal agents and police to move in. Dillinger, sensing the trap, reacted immediately, grabbing for his gun as he ran toward a nearby alley. Five shots were fired at Dillinger by FBI agents. Three of the bullets struck him, and one lethal shot entered the back of Dillinger's neck and exited through his eye. Dillinger was killed instantly, falling face down on the darkened Chicago streets. Crowds of people gathered to see the fallen gangster. The one-year crime spree of John Dillinger was over in an instant. Dillinger was dead, and the Chicago gangster era would soon be over as well.

Richard Speck – 1966

By all accounts, the life of Richard Speck was a failure from the start. Speck was a sociopath and a psychopath. Crime, sex, alcohol, and drugs were his primary interests; this combination of addictions led to the brutal murder of eight student nurses on a summer night in Chicago, Illinois, in the year 1966.

Richard Speck was born in small-town Kirkwood, Illinois, in 1941. He was the seventh of eight children. Speck's father died when Richard was six years old. After his father's death, Speck's mother relocated the family to Dallas, Texas. She soon remarried a Texas man by the name of Carl Lindberg. Lindberg had an arrest record and was a chronic alcoholic, and he would often physically abuse Richard. Unsuccessful in school, the teenaged Speck started hanging out with a bad crowd of boys known for fighting, drinking excessively, and generally getting into trouble.

Speck married a 15-year-old girl named Shirley Malone when he was 20 years old. At the time Speck was working as a garbage collector. Not surprisingly, the marriage ended in divorce for various reasons, including Speck's alcohol and drug use. Shirley Speck recounted how Speck had raped her at knife point and reported that his need for sex was insatiable – he claimed to need sex four or five times a day.

By the early 1960s, Richard Speck had a long arrest record in Texas. He had dozens of arrests for crimes like public drunkenness, disorderly conduct, and burglary. In 1963, Speck was convicted of theft and check forgery and spent two years in prison. His was a hapless life spent in and out of jail. In 1965, Speck was charged with assaulting a Dallas woman at knife point during a robbery. Before being sentenced to prison, Speck fled Texas. He later moved to Monmouth, Illinois, a town where he had once lived as a child. Monmouth was a quiet little town located about 200 miles southwest of Chicago and 40 miles south of the Quad Cities. Although Speck worked there a short time as a carpenter, his main activity was drinking at local bars, the sleazier, the better. His favorite hangout was the Palace Tap.

On April 2, 1966, a 65-year-old Monmouth woman was attacked and raped at knife point in her home. Then, on April 13, a barmaid at Frank's Place, another of Speck's hangouts, was found dead behind the tavern. Speck was the primary suspect in both crimes. As evidence linking Speck to the crimes mounted, he packed up and quietly left town on a bus bound for Chicago.

When Speck arrived in Chicago, he sought and was promised a job with the Merchant Marines. Upon reporting to the union hall, he was told that the job had already been given to another man. Speck spent some time working on an iron-ore ship on Lake Michigan, but he was fired for drinking on the job. Unemployed and without a place to stay, he turned to what he knew and liked best: hanging out in sleazy bars; becoming intoxicated on alcohol and drugs; and pursuing his interests in burglary, kinky sex, and other scandalous activities. Accounts of what led up to the mayhem that occurred in the early morning hours of July 14, 1966, are not clear.

The morning of July 14 was sweltering hot. Investigators speculate that Speck drank heavily at a strip of bars located in a South Side Chicago district that was a known hangout for alcoholics and society rejects. The strip was less than a mile from 2319 East 100th Street, an apartment building that housed a large number of nursing students from South Chicago Community Hospital. Sometime in the early morning hours, Speck entered a two-story apartment, and, in a fit of unimaginable debauchery, he murdered eight young student nurses ranging in age from 20 to 24 years: Gloria Jean Davy, Patricia Ann Matusek, Nina Jo Schmale, Pamela Wilkening, Suzanne Farris, Mary Ann Jordan, Valentina Pasion, and Merlita Gargullo. All eight were victims of the depravity of this 25-year-old drunken derelict. The women were alternatively tied, strangled, stabbed, and raped. One was found naked on a couch with her hands tied behind her back and a strip of cloth tied tightly around her neck; she had also been anally raped. Another was found with a nurse's white stocking tied around her neck; she had been stabbed 18 times. A third victim was gagged and stabbed through the heart. A fourth victim was stabbed three times in the chest, once in the neck, and once in the eye. Yet another was stabbed repeatedly in a ritualistic pattern and left with her legs spread and her breasts exposed. As fate would have it, one of the student nurses, an Asian girl named Corazon Amurao, hid undetected under a bed and witnessed the murders. Speck had apparently lost track of the girl during his murderous rage. Once Speck left, Corazon ran screaming from the apartment. Police were immediately summoned to the scene. Police officers and an experienced crime reporter who were first to arrive at the scene were so shocked and appalled upon entering the apartment that they had to retreat outside to vomit. The apartment and the bodies were soaked in blood. Each room in the apartment looked like a battlefield.

Several days following the murders, Richard Speck was picked up at a flop house by Chicago police after a failed suicide attempt. The manager of the flop house called police, and the police transported Speck to the hospital. The police did not recognize him as the killer. The attending physician saw a tattoo on Speck's arm that read "born to raise hell," an identifying characteristic that had been linked with the murderer and had been widely publicized in the daily news. After the attending physician alerted police, Speck was arrested and charged with the murders.

When the story of the eight murdered nurses and subsequent arrest of Speck was published in newspapers throughout the nation, police authorities from Benton Harbor, Michigan, and Indiana contacted Chicago police and asked to interview Speck. Four females had been murdered in Benton Harbor at the same time that the iron-ore boat on which Speck was working was docked in the harbor; also, three missing girls, presumed dead but never found, disappeared when Speck's boat was docked in an Indiana harbor. Speck was never arrested for any of these murders.

Richard Speck was found guilty in Cook County Circuit Court on eight counts of murder and was originally sentenced to death, but the sentence was overturned in 1972 when the U.S. Supreme Court abolished capital punishment. The court then sentenced Speck to 400 to 1,200 consecutive years in prison. Speck died in prison of a massive heart attack on December 5, 1991. He was 49 years old. In 1996, more than four years after Speck died, crime reporter Bill Kurtis uncovered a home movie that had been taken by a prisoner in Statesville Prison that showed Speck in his cell wearing women's panties and engaging in sex with a fellow inmate. Speck had developed breasts from a regimen of hormones he had been taking. Other segments of the video showed Speck using cocaine. In one memorable quote captured on the video,

Speck said, "If they [Illinois Department of Corrections] knew how much fun I was having in here, they would turn me loose."

John Wayne Gacy – 1971 to 1978

In early May 1994, John Wayne Gacy was flown by the state of Illinois from Menard Correctional Center in southern Illinois to Statesville Penitentiary in Joliet. Just after midnight on May 10, 1994, Gacy was put to death by lethal injection, bringing to a close a dreadful life that had distinguished the 52-year-old man as the most renowned serial killer in history. He was known to have kidnapped, sexually abused, tortured, and killed 33 young men.

John Wayne Gacy was born in Chicago in 1942. He had two sisters, one older and one younger. His childhood was fairly normal, although his father was known to be physically and verbally abusive to him and his sisters. Gacy attended high school but failed to graduate. Later he enrolled in and completed business college and was hired as a management trainee by the Nunn-Bush Shoe Company. By all accounts, Gacy did very well, both for himself and the company, and he was quickly promoted to a management position and transferred to Springfield, Illinois. In Springfield, he operated a men's clothing store. He stayed in Springfield for about a year.

Gacy was married in 1964 to Marilyn Myer. Marilyn's family was from Waterloo, Iowa, where her family owned a popular and profitable restaurant specializing in chicken. In 1966, Marilyn's father requested that John and Marilyn relocate from Springfield to Waterloo so that John could run the restaurant and Marilyn could come home and spend time with her family. From 1966 through 1968, Gacy became very active in the Waterloo community. All who knew Gacy at this time claimed that he was gregarious and outgoing, even charismatic.

From the outside, John Wayne Gacy, now 27 years old, appeared to be a productive, well-adjusted member of the Waterloo community. He was married, ran a business, participated in community organizations, and was raising two young children. Everything would change that year. In 1968, John Wayne Gacy was arrested on a felony charge. The charge stemmed from an incident wherein Gacy forced a young male employee who worked at the restaurant to have sexual relations with him. The young man was chained and choked by Gacy while Gacy raped him. Gacy pled guilty to sodomy and was sentenced to serve ten years in the Iowa State Prison System. The arrest and subsequent conviction were a shock to the Waterloo community and to Gacy's family and friends. Gacy's wife soon filed for divorce, and he abruptly stopped communicating with his children upon entering prison.

Gacy was released from prison on October 18, 1971, after serving 18 months of his ten-year term. He returned to Chicago to rebuild his shattered life. After securing a job working in construction for a few years, Gacy started his own construction business called PDM. He soon remarried, bought a home in Des Plaines (just outside the Chicago city limits), and pretty much settled in. In Chicago, Gacy once again became active in the community, helping in political campaigns, joining the Jaycees and Junior Chamber of Commerce, and, step by step, gaining respect as a smart businessman. His contracting business became quite successful. Instead of hiring experienced laborers who had families to support, Gacy would hire teenage boys who were looking to earn extra spending money. As a result, Gacy was often in a position to underbid many of his competitors on various jobs.

John Wayne Gacy also enjoyed being a clown – literally. He would dress up in a clown costume and volunteer to entertain at children's parties and local hospitals. He called himself Pogo the Clown. This activity made him a popular friend of neighborhood kids, their parents, and the entire community. At home, Gacy was less popular. His second wife divorced him because of his wild and unpredictable mood swings and his incessant fascination with the volumes of homosexual pornographic magazines he collected and cherished.

In December 1978, Des Plaines police were investigating the disappearance of a young school boy named Robert Piest, who had worked at a local drug store. Gacy had been seen talking to the boy on occasion and, in fact, was the last person to be seen with him. Piest, an ambitious young man who knew that Gacy had a construction business, was just interested in finding a better job. While conducting a criminal history and background check on Gacy, the police found out about the sodomy conviction in Iowa. They sought and were granted a search warrant based upon Gacy's history as a sexual predator and the fact that Gacy had been seen talking to Piest.

During the search of Gacy's house, numerous items were packaged and seized by police to be examined as possible evidence. The police also noticed an unpleasant smell emanating from the house but assumed it was related to sewage problems. When examining the items confiscated at Gacy's home, the police discovered a ring that was linked to another young boy who had disappeared a year earlier. The police also discovered a payment receipt for a roll of film that young Piest was given by a fellow drug store employee the same day that he disappeared. With the new evidence, police sought and were granted a court-issued warrant to search the house a second time.

Sensing that the police were on to him, Gacy walked into the Des Plaines Police Department on December 22, 1978, and confessed, not only to the murder of Robert Piest, but also to the murder of all the boys he could recall killing during his maniacal killing spree. Documentation of the murders would be easy to substantiate, because a large majority of his victims' bodies (29 in total) were buried in a crawlspace under his house and garage. Other victims' bodies were dumped in the Des Plaines River. All of the boys had died in a similar manner. Gacy had a well-defined, sexually driven, modus operandi.

Using charm and conversation, Gacy would easily befriend his victims and talk about his volunteer work as a clown and a magician. He would tell them that the handcuffs he used in his clown act had a trick release. He would handcuff them and challenge them to figure out how to release the handcuffs. Once they were handcuffed, Gacy would drug his victims with chloroform and take them to his home. There the boys were gagged and tortured while Gacy concurrently raped and strangled them, most often with a rope. The young men Gacy killed ranged in age from their early teens to their mid-20s. Many of them were homosexuals or prostitutes who hung out at an area called "Bughouse Square" in downtown Chicago, an area known for homosexual activity. Other victims, however, were chosen at random or had worked for Gacy in his contracting business.

One by one, authorities exhumed 29 bodies from beneath Gacy's suburban home at 8213 Summerdale Avenue. The world watched day after day as the house was dismantled and the bodies were exhumed. Gacy was tried and convicted in Cook County Criminal Court (Chicago) of murdering 33 young men. More than 108 witnesses were called to testify at the month-long trial, including two boys who had been raped, whipped, and tortured on separate occasions by Gacy at his home. Inexplicably, the lives of the two boys had been spared, and they did not report the crimes, presumably because they were too humiliated. Upon learning of Gacy's killing spree, however, the boys felt obligated to come forward in order to bolster the case against Gacy.

Gacy claimed to have multiple personalities, saying that the personality of Jack Hanley did all of the killings. Some believe that Gacy's claim of multiple personality disorder had to do solely with his attempt to avoid the death penalty. The jury did not find Gacy to be clinically insane, and they convicted him after deliberating for only two hours. On March 13, 1980, Gacy was sentenced to die. He spent 14 years in Menard Correctional Center before being put to death by the state of Illinois.

John Wayne Gacy's home, located in a family neighborhood, was a den of evil inhabited by a madman. The clown, the contractor, the friendly neighbor, and the insane killer all resided there with a collection of 29 dead bodies. One consulting psychiatrist wrote the following:

> Gacy could be sweet as Ronald McDonald in his clown outfit, treating kids to Hershey's kisses. And within a fraction of a second, he could become like an inflamed, incensed animal, thoroughly out of control. (Morrison & Goldberg, 2004, p. 108)

Leopold and Loeb, Capone, Dillinger, Speck, and Gacy were all ruthless and deranged murderers with Chicago connections. Even though their individual motives for murdering may have varied, each showed little compunction for taking a human life. Some murdered for money and power; some were driven by sexual perversion; and others considered murder a simple game or a way of life. Most, if not all, seemed to enjoy the act of murder.

Although theories of crime abound, criminologists are at a loss to definitively explain why individuals become involved in criminal activity. Some theorists believe that biological factors are at work (i.e., people are born criminals);

other theorists believe that cultural, psychological, and social factors conspire to nurture one into a life of crime. In all probability, crime is caused by a combination of all of these factors.

In a macabre and bizarre story recently reported in the *Chicago Tribune*, it was revealed that the brain of John Wayne Gacy has been preserved in the basement of Chicago psychiatrist Helen Morrison's home for more than a decade. Dr. Morrison had clinically assessed Gacy prior to his trial and had testified on his behalf, indicating that she believed Gacy to be legally insane. Upon his execution, Gacy's family had given the state of Illinois permission to entrust Gacy's brain to the care of Dr. Morrison for further study. According to reports, and Morrison's own book *My Life Among Serial Killers*, Gacy's brain was removed in a postexecution autopsy in which she assisted, and Morrison drove away with Gacy's brain in her car (Fritsch, 2004). The brain was preserved in a jar with a liquid known as Formalyn. Dr. Morrison wrote the following about the autopsy:

> As I assisted, the pathologist carefully opened Gacy's cranium with an electric Stryker saw and removed the calvarium (top of the skull). There, then, was this grey matter, the 1,300 gram organ that caused such misery and grief for so many. I was very excited to begin the search for what may have caused him to exist in his persecutory, murderous netherworld. After connections to the spinal cord and various membranes (dural reflections) were easily severed, the brain, soft, was removed with a kind of a "swoosh" sound. (Morrison & Goldberg, 2004, pp. 123–124)

In an interview on CNN, Morrison revealed that Gacy's brain had indeed been stored in her basement since his death a decade ago. She said, "[It's] the safest place it can be" (Fritsch, pp. 8–9). According to Morrison, studies of Gacy's brain revealed nothing remarkable: "They basically told us that there's actually nothing abnormal, so no tumor, no growth, no sign of injury; the ventricles are fine; no sign of hydrocephalus" (Fritsch, p. 8).

Notwithstanding Dr. Morrison's benign efforts, it seems highly unlikely that the field of medicine will contribute in any meaningful way toward an understanding of why people kill. If there is a "murder gene," or a pattern of biological pathology in individuals who murder, it will not be discovered anytime soon.

It is also interesting to observe how the media is quick to "parade out" the so-called "national crime experts" every time a high-profile murder or a series of murders goes unsolved. Forensic psychiatrists, psychologists, criminology professors, and retired agents of the FBI are always eager to express their opinions in front of a national audience on the type of person or persons the police should be looking for or to otherwise give a "criminal profile" of the likely offender. Take the case of the Washington, D.C. sniper, the so-labeled "Beltway Serial Killer," who in 2002, over a month's time, sporadically shot 13 people, killing ten, in Maryland; Virginia; and Washington, D.C. While police were busy working the case and following up on every single lead, the so-called "national experts" were on television daily giving their opinion and advice. Most of these experts were wrong. The fact is that "criminal profiling" is based on studies of statistical probability; so is shooting dice. While criminal profiling may be one tool for police to use in an investigation, in most cases, it is of limited use; and when criminal profiling is done by the media, it is often counterproductive to the ongoing investigation. One psychologist wrote a criminal profile report that was released on October 9, 2002, before the Beltway Sniper was apprehended providing the following "likely" portrait:

> In the absence of any specific criminal evidence, and based solely on the rational consideration of likely personality configurations consistent with the known behavior patterns of the individual responsible for the October 2002 shooting spree in the Washington, DC area, it appears most likely that the sniper has a sadistic personality pattern, possibly modulated by negativistic and paranoid tendencies. (Immelman, 2002, p. 1)

No shit, Doc. Thanks for the help. That narrows it down; now we can go arrest the son-of-a-bitch.

Crystal ball antics of solving serious crime have seldom proved useful. In years past, police have even called mystics with supposed extrasensory perception to gather clues on how a crime occurred and where the body could be found. In many cases, "criminal profiling" is more "crystal ball gazing" than science.

The fact remains that all but a small percentage of the 16,000 to 17,000 murders committed in the United States annually are investigated by local police, and such cases are solved by meticulous, good old-fashioned police work. If there were credible evidence that forensic psychiatrists, psychologists, criminologists, or ex-FBI agents had the answers to "who murders" and "why," local police agencies would surely find the money to bring them on staff in scores to close the backlog of cold murder cases that have never been solved.

Chapter 3

THE EARLY LIFE OF TERRY G. HILLARD

In his popular book *Everything I Needed to Know I Learned in Kindergarten*, author Robert Fulghum postulates in a simple, straightforward manner that lessons we learn early in life need to be remembered. They can largely dictate the success, happiness, and contributions that we realize in our adult lives. "Play fair"; "Hold hands and stick together"; "Clean-up your own mess"; "Share everything"; "Don't hit people"; and "When you go out in the world, watch out for the traffic" – these are but a few of the basic tenets and wise observations contained within Fulghum's book. In other words, in examining a life lived, it is critical to understand the formative years of situation and experience, environment and social context, and family. Chicago Police Superintendent Terry Hillard's childhood had a huge impact on the police officer, and the man, that he would become.

Terry G. Hillard and his twin brother, Jerry, were born on August 11, 1943, in South Fulton, Tennessee. Their mother's name was Lelia Mae. South Fulton is a small town of 2,500 people located in the northwest corner of the state, near the border between Tennessee and Kentucky. Terry and his twin brother had an older brother named James (nicknamed Denny), who was four years old at the time of their birth. Two sisters, Laraine and Diane, would soon follow. The family would eventually include ten children in what Terry refers to as "the first wave" and "the second wave." The first five children were born in South Fulton, and the second succession of five, Alfonso, JoAnne, Michelle, Michael, and Yolanda, were born after Terry's mother and stepfather moved to Chicago, Illinois.

Terry met his biological father only on a few occasions. Terry's stepfather was named Alfonso Drew, and Terry always considered him to be his dad.

While in Tennessee, Terry's mother met and married the man she would always refer to by his last name, Drew. Both worked for the Illinois Central Railroad. Drew was a hardworking man of slight build who was a cook on the trains that passed through South Fulton. Terry's mother was a hostess and went on the trains to serve refreshments to the passengers during short stops in South Fulton. After his mother's marriage, Terry took Drew as his last name.

He would be known as Terry Drew until he enlisted in the military, when he discovered that he would need a birth certificate. His birth certificate gave his legal name as Terry G. Hillard, so he took that name from that point forward.

Terry spent the first 13 years of his life in South Fulton, surrounded by a large extended family there – aunts, uncles, cousins, and, of course, his immediate family, who all lived in town. South Fulton was in the Bible-belt and was predominantly Baptist, so Terry's Sundays were taken up with church activities. Terry had Sunday school in the morning, church from noon until 3:00 or 4:00, a break to go home to eat dinner, and church again on Sunday night. As Terry says, "This was the South; religion was important; and that's the way it was. To me, I didn't know any different."

In the 1940s and early 1950s, South Fulton was also segregated. Blacks were prohibited from entering a number of public places and private businesses. Terry remembers a particular restaurant in town where ordering procedures were different for blacks than for whites. First of all, blacks could not go into the restaurant and sit down at a table to eat. They had to place their orders at a small window inside the restaurant to which they were directed by a crudely designed sign. Black people were allowed to order hamburgers, hot dogs, french fries, or pop at this window, but they could not order pizza, milk shakes, or malts. Terry says, "As a kid, you don't ask why; that's just the way it was."

Terry describes the movie theater in South Fulton as having a main level for whites and a second floor balcony "that was for the blacks." He says that he and a group of 30 to 40 other black kids would go in the side door of the theater and up the stairs to the balcony to watch the movie. Every now and then, a black kid, being mischievous, would drop some popcorn down on the white people sitting below. After two warnings for such behavior, all of the black children would be asked to leave the theater. "We didn't get to see the cartoons; we didn't get to see anything; we just left."

The all-black grade school that Terry attended from first through eighth grade was housed in a small building placed out in the middle of a field. In grammar school, Terry played basketball, which was the only sport offered for black students. In the South at this time, white and black children did not compete against each other. Sports were highly segregated, and athletes were allowed to compete only with others of their own race.

As a child growing up in Tennessee, Terry loved listening to the Brooklyn Dodgers on the radio, even though the St. Louis Cardinals were the closest major league team. Terry remembers, "The Dodgers had Gil Hodges, Pee Wee Reese, Roy Campannella, Billy Cox, and, of course, the legendary Jackie Robinson." In the evening, while his aunts and the women-folk would be doing what they were doing, the young boys and Uncle Flop would be around the radio, listening to the ball game. Jackie Robinson was an inspiration back then because he was the first black player to break into the major leagues. "We listened to [each] whole game; I don't care whether it got over at 11:00 PM, midnight, or 1:00 AM," Terry recalls fondly. "In the heat of the summer, the windows propped open wide, we'd sit with family members listening to the Brooklyn Dodgers baseball game." These games are particularly fond memories that Terry has of his boyhood.

In 1952, Terry's mother and stepfather moved to Chicago, Illinois. Because they both worked for the Illinois Central Railroad, they could easily transfer to Chicago, where there were more opportunities. It was also their belief that the children would eventually receive a better education in a large urban setting. Because the children were in school and accustomed to having family and friends around them in South Fulton, the five children stayed behind and lived with their two aunts and Uncle Flop for nearly two years. Terry's mother and stepfather would visit the children often, especially on birthdays, holidays, and other special occasions. They had free passes to ride the train, so the trips were easy and inexpensive.

Finally, the entire family relocated to 3616 South Park Drive in Chicago, and Terry enrolled at Wendell Phillips Grammar School. Later, the family would upgrade from that four-room apartment to a five-room apartment at 3702 South Park Drive. The new accommodations offered a living room, dining room, two bedrooms, and a kitchen. In the new apartment, the three boys slept on a roll-out bed in the dining room, and the two girls slept in one of the bedrooms. Terry's mother and stepfather shared the other bedroom.

Before moving to Chicago, Terry had never heard of the game of football; he had only played basketball and baseball. In his first year of high school, he decided to go out for freshman football. As he remembers, on his second day of practice, he saw a strapping young man named Marshal Loftin, who was about 6'3" and weighed roughly 200 pounds, take a massive hit from another player. The sudden and aggressive impact broke Loftin's leg. Terry said he immediately walked over and turned in his equipment. "I figured I would play baseball, a little basketball, and maybe run some track. I didn't think I wanted to play football. It was too brutal."

Terry did not have a lot of time for sports because he also worked while growing up in Chicago. His first job was as a paper boy for the now defunct *Chicago American*, from which he earned about $11.00 per week. He recalls that he was robbed of this money on about three separate occasions by older neighborhood kids who figured him an easy target on collection day. Each time he was robbed, his route manager, who was only about 19 years old, protected Terry from the thieves and gave him the support and encouragement he needed to continue his route.

Terry's second job was as an office aide for the National Association for the Advancement of Colored People (NAACP). An incident that occurred while he had that job caused him to be arrested. He went with a group from the NAACP to conduct a civil protest at Rainbow Beach, which was on Lake Michigan on the South Side of Chicago, and open to whites only. The police were called, and the protesters were arrested. In his first encounter with the Chicago Police, Terry was slapped around by a big white plain-clothed officer and then taken to the police station where he was detained for two or three hours. When Terry was released and returned home, his stepfather was waiting for him and said, "Terry, what were you doin' out there? You don't know how to swim. What are you doin' on the beach in the first place?" Terry said, "I went there to protest." Terry's stepdad said, "No, you stay away from there from now on."

As time went by, the family would expand from seven to 12 members – ten kids and mom and dad. Terry's stepfather would typically leave on a railway trip for five or six days, come home for two days, and then be gone again. This left "Mamma" to raise the kids and govern the home. Terry says,

> I'll tell you, she ruled with an iron hand. There wasn't a whole lot of what we called, back in those days, whoopings, or anything like that, but we had to do chores. On Saturdays, everything was stripped off the bed and cleaned. She had a routine, and that was the way it was done. Everyone participated, from sweeping, mopping, waxing the floors, doing the dishes, and going to the laundromat. There wasn't enough time to get into trouble. But, if you did find time to get into trouble, she would pile on extra chores just to make sure everything was fair and you would not get in trouble again.

Terry recalled that he was once required to wash all the dishes for six months following an act that had met with his mother's disapproval. It is clear that as members of their household, Terry and his siblings learned duty and responsibility.

Terry described both his parents as hardworking, humble, and low-key. Terry's stepfather would receive his paycheck from the Illinois Central Railroad and bring it home to his wife, who handled all of the bills. Terry says, "With my parents raising ten kids I wondered at times, how the hell did they do it? But they did. They instilled values in their kids and showed us by example how to work hard, . . . survive, and interact with the larger community."

Terry tells one story that is particularly illustrative of the home environment in which he was raised. One day during his first year of high school, Terry was suspended for getting into a fight. He remembers,

> Some guy said something about my mamma and pow, as fast as I could, I hit him. So when I arrived home from school, Mamma looked at me and said, "What's your problem?" I said, "This kid said something about you, Mamma." She said, "He said something about me? About what?" I forgot what this guy said, but I said, "I didn't particularly care for it, and I hit him." She said, "That's not the way you do things – you can't go around hitting people because you don't like what people say."

In reflecting upon his mother's reaction, Terry says she made her point.

> There wasn't no howling, no slapping you upside the head, nothing like that. It was just, "That's not the way you handle things like that, no matter what he said about me. He doesn't know me; you know that. Suppose someone else says something about me. Are you going to hit them too?"

Terry didn't know how to respond, but he thought quietly to himself, "Hey, I'm going to be suspended from school for five days, home by myself, watch television, cool out." He couldn't have been more wrong. Terry remembers those days as the days of his life when he worked the hardest. "Mamma had assigned something for me to do every minute of the day."

Terry worshiped his older brother, Denny, who was always someone who would take time to explain things to Terry and give him advice. In his humble way, Terry would later say, "Denny was older than me and smart, so I listened." During his last six months of high school and before entering the Marine Corps, Terry says that he was not very focused, was not listening to his mother and father, and was generally adrift. "At this point in my life, I could have gone either way – good or bad." Denny, on the other hand, was mature, reserved, and respectful. He always knew what was right and what was wrong. He always did the right thing. When Denny graduated from high school, he went to work for Kohler Laboratories. After four years, he was well established at work and had his own apartment. Terry says, "The last year of high school, I was a wild, wild kid. I liked to party, so my dad sent me to live with Denny my last six months of high school. I had no choice. My old man said, 'I'm tired of you. You're out of here.' He wanted me out of his sight." It was during this time that Denny led by example. According to Terry,

> When things would go wrong, and I would get in the doghouse, Denny would tell me, "Here's what you did wrong, here's what you need to do to get this squared away, and here's what you need to say to Mamma, say to the old man, if you expect to get your butt out of the doghouse." Eventually, I got to go back home.

Terry tells a story about being assigned to do dishes by his mother. A clean kitchen was very important to her. She worked all day at Illinois Central Station, and when she would come home and walk into her kitchen, she expected it to be clean, with no dishes in the sink. Everything had to be washed and put away; the garbage had to be emptied; there could be nothing on the stove; and everything had to be wiped up. She wanted a perfectly clean kitchen, so she would assign the children to "kitchen duty" on a rotating basis. Terry says,

> Well, me, when it was my turn, I'd come home from school, clean the kitchen, then I was out of there – go play basketball, baseball, strike-out, or just hang out with the guys. My siblings knew that it was my week to wash dishes, so when I left to go play, they would go use a cup or make a sandwich and mess up the kitchen. Mamma would come home, I'd be in trouble, and she would extend my rotation of kitchen duty. My brother Denny finally pulled me aside and said, "You don't get it do you? You don't get the message. You have to stay here, till Mamma gets home so that she can see that you are here and that the kitchen is clean, and then you can cut out."

Wise brotherly advice.

Terry describes his time growing up with ten children as disciplined but fun. He says that they didn't have a lot of material things, but they always had food, and both of his parents were excellent cooks. When dinner was served, the children were expected to be at the table. If they were late for dinner, everything would be put away. They would be allowed to fix leftovers but had to clean up the kitchen by themselves when they were done. Terry says that his brother Denny will not eat oatmeal to this day because sometimes, which seemed to be years, when things were tight, breakfast would be oatmeal and toast every morning.

Religion was always important, and attending Sunday services was a must. When the family moved to Chicago, Terry's mother told her children that she didn't care which church they attended, but they were going to go to church. Terry and his twin brother, Jerry, joined the Mt. Olive Baptist Church, and Denny and the two girls joined the South Park Baptist Church. Both churches were within walking distance of the house, but Terry and Jerry's church was about four blocks farther away, a decision they would later come to regret on cold, wintery Sunday mornings.

As Terry explains, "Mom's not one of these folks who says you have to go to church seven days a week, but on Sunday, you need to take your family to church." In later life, Terry converted to Catholicism.

> I'd go down to her house on Sunday, and she'd say, "Terry you didn't go to church today, did you?" I'd say, "Yeah, Mom, I went to mass last night." She'd look at me and say, "So I'm right. You didn't go." I said, "Mom, I went to mass on Saturday; mass is church for us, you know?" Then, later, one of the other kids would say, "Mom, you know, he went in his cowboy boots and jeans." I'd say, "Here we go." This was not acceptable to Mom. The way she sees it, church is on Sunday, and you go in a suit and tie, not on Saturday, in boots and jeans.

After graduating from Wendell Phillips High School, Terry went to work as an office boy for Seagram's Distilleries for about two years and then joined the Marine Corps. Terry says that the best decision he ever made was enlisting in the Marine Corps. He says that the Marine Corps gave him focus, taught him leadership, taught him the importance of teamwork, taught him how to establish goals and discipline, and generally taught him how to think and act like a productive young man.

Hillard was sent to the Marine Corps Recruiting Depot in San Diego, California, for basic training. It was the first time he had ever been away from home, and he was scared. He and the other Marine recruits were picked up by the Marine Corps at the airport and put in "cattle cars." He recalls them as actual trailers that were originally designed to haul cattle, which had been converted into troop transports by the installation of rough benches. The new recruits arrived at the base at about 1:00 in the morning, and after exiting the cattle cars, they were instructed to place their feet on the yellow foot imprints on the pavement. Hillard says he will never forget that moment.

> A 6'2", 190-pound specimen of a man named Sergeant Brophy walked up to me, and my eyes were wandering around, and Sergeant Brophy said, "If you

don't look straight forward with those big brown eyes, I'm going to put this size ten and a half foot up your doggone butt. Look straight forward and don't say a thing." He put his white nose on my black nose, and I said to myself, "Uh-oh, what have I gotten myself into?" And that was my introduction into the United State's Marine Corps. As a naive kid from Tennessee, via Chicago, I was scared out of my boots. The rest of boot camp, whatever this man said, I did. No hesitation whatsoever.

Following boot camp and a brief furlough spent in Chicago, Hillard was assigned to Charlie 1-5 – that's C Company, 1st Battalion, 5th Marine Regiment. After some additional training in advanced infantry at Camp Pendleton, Hillard was sent to Okinawa, Japan. This was the transition period before being sent to Vietnam. After receiving orders to go to Vietnam and arriving at DaNang, the company was quickly moved out into the field and issued live ammo, fragmentation grenades, and white phosphorous grenades.

This was the first time we realized that this was no longer a game. It was a war – the real thing. It was at this time that a lot of the guys started writing letters back home, guys who never wrote home, never had contact with their families before. They started writing home and telling their moms and dads, their girlfriends, sisters and brothers, and friends, that they were getting ready to go off into the rice paddies, getting ready to go fight a war. And, I'll never forget as we moved out, the first Marine I saw get killed. He was hit by a sniper; the bullet ripped right through his neck. Several weeks later, I saw a friend of mine get killed – Private First Class Bell, a black kid from Detroit. He was killed in a fire fight. That's when it hits you, seeing one of the young guys you went through boot camp with, laying lifeless. His life was over in the split second it takes to pull a trigger, or blink an eye.

Hillard describes his company's mission as "hunt and destroy." He was in a rifle unit that stayed on the move. There was one base camp, but the company would send out probing patrols every day and every night to initiate ambushes. The rifle squad had 13 men and was supported by Hillard's machine gun squad, which had nine men and two M-60 machine guns. His job as a machine gunner was to provide cover and support for the rifle team. The squad would go out at night, set up, and wait quietly for hour upon hour. There were mosquitoes, bugs, and other pests crawling all over their bodies, and they had to sit there and not move. The rice paddies were covered in rank, filthy water, and the soldiers had to dig foxholes for protection from the enemy. But when an ambush would begin, they had to move. Hillard says that one thing non-military people often do not realize about military strategy is that when soldiers get caught in an ambush or fire is coming in their direction, they are taught to move *toward* the gun fire, not take cover. The Marine Corps encourages providing as much superior fire power as possible, and that's what Hillard's company did.

After seeing that first Marine killed, Hillard made up his mind that he was going to get back home, and getting home meant adhering to his training. In his opinion, a percentage of those guys who did not make it home were the ones who did not follow their training or those who just did not take things seriously, and he wasn't going to make that mistake. He says, "I made up my mind the first day that I've got 13 months and that I would follow my training, follow commands – everything they told me to do – and I would get back to the states." In those 13 months, Hillard saw countless Marines die or become maimed for life.

Hillard recalls that the one thing the Marine Corps did not talk about or prepare him for was seeing people get killed and injured:

> These were young boys and men who were thrown into battle. We would see our friends from boot camp getting shot by a projectile that would hit them in the shoulder and tear the flesh from their bones in a devastating manner. Or guys would step on doggone punji sticks that would send bamboo spikes completely through their foot, leg, and thigh. Seeing this devastation and carnage leaves you with a different perspective, a different psyche – but you had no choice but to move on, for the sake of your own survival. I just remember thinking, "It's 13 months, and I am going to survive."

While in Vietnam, Hillard would receive four medals for his outstanding service, including the Presidential Unit Citation, which was presented to the entire unit for taking Hill 55. This operation was one of the first amphibious landings to take place in Vietnam. It was a search and destroy mission that lasted about 15 days. Hill 55 was an important strategic military site for the United States because it was just south of DaNang and located on the coastal plain. From its summit, one could see all the way to DaNang to the north, to the ocean to the east, to the "Arizona Territory" to the west, and to the Que Son Mountains to the south. In taking Hill 55, a number of Marines were killed or wounded. They were fighting not only the Viet Cong but also the North Vietnamese Army. Fortunately, the kill ratio was in the Marines' favor. The company Hillard belonged to was under the command of Captain Francis Xavier Ballard III. Captain Ballard was a small man, probably only 5'7" or 5'8", but he was an expert in general warfare and field strategy, and he was one tough Marine. He knew his job, and he did it well. He directed the taking of Hill 55, and Hillard reports that he was proud to have him as his leader.

When asked whether he experienced any form of racism in the military, Hillard said that it was there, but he didn't dwell on it. He indicated that the men he served with had a job to do. They were white, black, and Hispanic, but race just didn't matter. Hillard said he got promoted just as fast as anyone else.

> There were times I didn't agree with certain things that my squad leader, gunny sergeant, or staff sergeant said or did, but I didn't think they were singling me out or picking on me because of my race. It was just the Marine Corps. And, in the Marine Corps, there is order and rank that prevails.

Hillard says that when he was in Vietnam, his mother wrote him every day during his 13-month tour of duty. He didn't get a letter every day because mail call was irregular, sometimes coming around once every two or three weeks. Sometimes, he had 15 or more letters from his mother at one time. "The letters kept me informed about what was going on back home with my family and helped give me more of a reason to get back home. The letters kept my spirits up."

One story Hillard tells about keeping in touch with his mother had to do with a letter he sent to her just months prior to being sent stateside. In Vietnam, many of the young soldiers would buy motorcycles at drastically discounted rates and have them shipped back to the states so that they would be there upon their return. Hillard thought this was a good idea and found a motorcycle that he particularly liked. In his letter to his mother, he explained that in about four or five weeks, he was going to make a downpayment on a motorcycle and have it shipped to his mother's address. His instruction to her was to store the motorcycle in the basement of the apartment building until he got home from Vietnam. His mother replied to this letter in an expedited manner, and the message was clear. His mother told him to "save your money. If you send a motorcycle here, it isn't going to be here when you get back."

Hillard says that not only his mother, but his brothers, sisters, and friends would write to him and send him cookies and Kool-Aid care packages. He had a lot of support from back home while he was in Vietnam.

Hillard would see a lot of death in his lifetime, but in Vietnam, he never felt that he would be killed.

> Young people don't believe that they can die. Whether they are just naive, or feel that they are invincible, I'm not sure. I never felt that I was in a position where I would say, "Ok, within this next wave, or the next fire fight, there's a possibility that I'm going to be shot or step on a doggone booby trap" – I was always convinced I was goin' home.

Part of Hillard's strategy for surviving in Vietnam was taking care of himself and adhering to principles of teamwork. He said that during the entire 13 months he was in Vietnam, he probably drank two beers, and he never used drugs.

> When you mess with drugs over in Vietnam, you are taking away your ability to be alert, to be cognizant of your environment and what's going on around you. If I had taken that route, I might not be sitting here today, you know? I wanted my senses to be at 100% at all times.

When Hillard left Vietnam, he was sent to Camp LeJeune, near Jacksonville, North Carolina. In anticipation of his return home to Chicago after serving overseas, Hillard wrote to his mother to tell her that the first thing he wanted was for her to fix his favorite meal: fried chicken, greens, sweet potato casserole, corn bread, a pound cake, lemon meringue pie, and banana pudding. He explained that he probably would return during the middle of the week on Tuesday or maybe Wednesday. She said she would prepare the dinner the following Sunday. Hillard's family traditionally had fried chicken every Sunday, but Hillard wrote back and said, "No, this is what I want when I get there. The first night."

With the battles of Vietnam behind him, Hillard said he enjoyed his time at Camp LeJeune; he had a chance to wind down and readjust. It was during these months, while he was waiting to be discharged, that Hillard and his Chicago buddies took road trips from Camp LeJeune back home to Chicago in his 1966 fastback Volkswagen.

Hillard and four other young Marines could squeeze into the small car. One of Hillard's requirements for being selected for the trip to Chicago was that each passenger had to know how to drive a stick shift. The trip was just under 1,000 miles one way, and Hillard and his friends drove straight through. They would leave Camp LeJeune on a Friday at about 2:00 or 3:00 in the afternoon. The trip would take about 16 hours, so they would arrive in Chicago about daybreak, 5:00 or 6:00 AM on Saturday. The young men would sleep all day Saturday, and then go out in Chicago and party Saturday night and early Sunday morning. They would then sleep a few hours and leave at 5:00 AM sharp Sunday morning in order to get back to base on Sunday night. Hillard charged each passenger $25 for the trip, which included a special packaged "dinner to go" prepared for them by his mother for the trip back to Camp LeJeune. She would fry three or four chickens and pack bread, soda, and pound cake. Hillard recalls, "We would starve on the way to Chicago, but going back, we ate well. Tired and hungover, we'd eat Mom's fried chicken all the way back."

Hillard said that when he returned home from the military, he rarely discussed his war experience with any of his family or friends. He considered his time in Vietnam, what he saw and what he did, as personal and private. More than 50,000 young men lost their lives in Vietnam, and Hillard believes that that's not something one should be eager to think about, talk about, or remember. Life goes on and that chapter of his life was over.

The only problem Hillard had adjusting when he returned home was that he could not sleep through the entire night. He would fall asleep for two hours and then get up. He was conditioned to wake up in this manner because when he was in Vietnam, soldiers took turns standing watch for the enemy. Also during the night, he would wake up and think about those young men he saw get killed or wounded by bullets, grenades, and booby traps. It took him over a year to readjust to civilian life.

When Hillard was discharged from the Marine Corps, he moved back in with his family. The Marines had changed him in many ways, and he feels that most of those changes were for the better. He was more disciplined and independent. He tells the story that while he was growing up, his mother would always iron his clothes, even his tee shirts and underwear. After the Marine Corps, Hillard told his mother, "We don't do that in the Marine Corps. We just wash them, fold them, and put them in the drawer." When she continued this practice, he would stop her and say, "Mom, we don't do that anymore, you know?"

Following his honorable discharge from the Marine Corps and after taking a few months for himself, Hillard became an employee of the Chicago Transit Authority as a bus driver. The job was not a good fit for him and lasted only four to five months. On one particular day, Hillard had enough of dealing with the people riding his bus. He carefully parked his bus, walked over to a pay phone, deposited a dime, and called the dispatcher saying, "This is badge #6384; I'm just letting you know I've got a swinging load at Lawrence and Kimball, and I'm quitting." Hillard says,

> I took my little $10 of tip money out of the box, left the rest of the money, walked off the bus, got onto another bus, went back to my car, drove home, and slept for about three days. I just had it up to here dealing with the public as a bus driver, people gettin' on my butt. The machine says, "tokens are a quarter," and they would put in pennies and nickels and jam up the machine. Then people coming up cursing you, and I said I don't need this hassle. To this day, I regret quitting. For all I had learned in the Marine Corps, it hadn't taught me about the little temper I had, that there was another way I should have been able to deal with this situation, you know?

Just a few weeks after quitting as a bus driver, Hillard got a call that he had been accepted by the Chicago Police Department and would soon report to the police academy on O'Brien Street for basic training.

Chapter 4

UP THROUGH THE RANKS

Terry Hillard originally wanted to join the Illinois State Police, but his mother encouraged him to become a Chicago police officer because Illinois state troopers could be assigned anywhere in the state. Since Hillard spent four years away from home in the military, his mother wanted him to be close to her and family.

Hillard describes his experience at the Chicago Police Academy as nearly identical to Marine boot camp. The academy was placed in a city-owned building that dated back to the Civil War; the hardwood floors were immaculately polished; and without the convenience of air conditioning, classroom temperatures could reach 95 degrees. Hillard adjusted easily to the Chicago Police Academy. Police agencies are paramilitary by structure and design, so many of the same expectations, procedures, and adherence to structure and discipline were familiar and nonthreatening. Besides, Hillard was 25 years old when he joined the department, and was mature and responsible.

Fresh out of the police academy, Hillard was assigned to the 18th District. The first day on the job, looking as sharp as could be, he walked into the 18th District station house and said to the commander, "Officer Hillard reporting for duty, Sir." Hillard said the guy never even looked up at him. On the second, third, and fourth days, the same routine occurred. Finally, Hillard said to a fellow officer, "The watch commander won't even say 'hi' to me. He won't acknowledge that I'm alive." The officer said, "So, figure it out. He doesn't want to say 'hi' to you; he doesn't want to talk to you."

Years later, as superintendent, Hillard would preside over the dedication of a new 18th District station house. Phyllis Appelbaum, a member of the police board recalled that Hillard referred to his commander and first days on the job in his dedication speech. She made the following observation:

> If you go back all of those years, here's a young African-American guy in a big Irish police department coming in as an ex-Marine, spit-polished and clean; he knew from the very beginning that if he followed a certain path, did the right things, followed the high road, kept himself moving, that he would, in the end, make a difference. He did not allow a grouchy old commander to change his perspective.

As Appelbaum said, "Terry knew that you don't have to agree with the system, but you have to honor the system until you can make it better, and you don't make it better by spitting in someone's face. In the end, Terry would endure and make a hell of a difference."

Hillard was already a patrolman with the Chicago Police Department when he met and married his future wife, Dorothy. Dorothy, just a few years younger than he, was the younger sister of Jesse Brown, with whom Hillard had served in the Marine Corps. (Jesse later served as secretary of the U.S. Department of Veteran Affairs in the Clinton cabinet.) Hillard had seen pictures of Jesse's younger sister, but he also knew that Jesse didn't want any of the guys showing interest in his little sister. In the year or two following his discharge from the Marines, Hillard hosted many reunion parties for his old buddies from the military. They would come from Texas, New York, Ohio, and Florida to party for the weekend. The parties would start on Friday and go all the way through Sunday night. At the time, he was living in an apartment on 89th and Cottage Grove with a childhood friend.

Before one of the reunion parties, Hillard asked another friend to invite Jesse's sister to the party. As he recalls, the friend invited her, but she spent the party sitting in the kitchen talking to a guy named Steven Todd. When Hillard came in the kitchen and saw Dorothy talking to Todd, he asked her, "Why are you talking to him? This guy is married. You don't want to be talkin' to a guy who's married. I'm a single man."

After this initial meeting at Hillard's party, they had one date after another. About three months later, they were engaged, and in another 12 months, they were married.

From the beginning, Hillard never called Dorothy by her first name. He refers to Dorothy by the same nickname that her brother Jesse used. When Dorothy was born, her parents brought her home and said, "Oh, it's a girl." From that day forward, her brother Jesse called her "Girl." In the military when Jesse would talk about his sister, he would always tell his friend that "Girl" did this or "Girl" did that, so when Hillard met her, he called her "Girl" as well. Thirty-five years of marriage later, she is still "Girl." For her part, Girl calls her husband "Hillard," which is also thanks to her brother Jesse and his service with Hillard in the military, where soldiers often referred to each other by last name only.

Hillard says that for a marriage that started off so nerve-rackingly, his has lasted a long time. Hillard and Girl were married in Chicago at the Metropolitan Church at 41st and King Drive. On the day of the wedding, May 9, 1970, Hillard stood at the back of the church, thinking,

> "I'm waiting, I'm waiting" and everyone was there – my family, my friends, and my oldest brother Denny, who was the best man. I'm in the back of the church with Denny, and this thing was supposed to start at 1:00 PM. Now it's 1:35, 1:40 PM, and everyone's here, but Girl is no where to be found."

After an extended period of time, his mother walked to the back of the church, looked at Terry, put her hands on her hips while clutching her purse, and said,

"What is goin' on?" He responded, "I don't know." Denny spoke up and said, "It's supposed to be the other way around, Terry; you're the one who is supposed to be late." Mom was not impressed by Denny's humor. "You, young man, be quiet. Now what the hell is going on? Is Girl going to show up?" Hillard said, "Mom, she'll be here, she'll be here."

Sure enough, several minutes later, Girl arrived. It seemed that her three uncles had thought it would be a good idea for them to celebrate on the morning of the wedding. They all started toasting and celebrating with the bride, causing her to be late for her own wedding ceremony.

The ceremony itself went smoothly until the pastor asked the couple to exchange vows. He asked, "Do you, Terry Hillard, take this woman to be your lawfully wedded wife?" Terry replied, "Yes, I do." Then, the pastor looked at Dorothy and asked whether she took this man to be her lawfully wedded husband. There was silence. The pastor asked the question a second time, and Hillard thought to himself, "Jesus Christ, first you're late and now you're going to change your mind." He elbowed Girl, and she said, "Oh, yeah, yeah, yeah."

Hillard says it turned out to be a very nice wedding. The couple paid for it themselves. Although both of them had full- time jobs, neither of them had accumulated enough days to take a long honeymoon, so they were married on Saturday, had a reception that evening at Hillard's parents' house, and went back to work on Monday. The couple later honeymooned in New York City.

Once they settled into their new life together, Girl became very insistent that Hillard go back to college. She thought he should take a few courses at a time while continuing to work on the force because if he intended to move up in rank, education would be important. Girl knew the importance of education. She was employed by the Chicago School System, had bachelor's and master's degrees, and had pursued doctoral studies. Another influence on Hillard's decision to go back to school was his squad leader in the Task Force. John Tolley was a big Irishman who operated like a "darn drill instructor," according to Hillard. He was always on his squad members to go back to school. Hillard says, "We would go to work, make two or three gun pinches in a week's time, recover a couple of hot cars, make several felony arrests, and still the first words from his mouth were, 'You guys need to get back to school. You need to get your degree.'" Of the ten members on the squad, only Hillard and one other officer returned to college.

Hillard started taking classes in 1970 at Loop Junior College. Since he was a veteran, all of his schooling, books, and supplies were paid for by the GI Bill. Hillard received his associate's degree in criminal justice and then continued his studies at Chicago State University where he completed his bachelor's degree in 1976 and his master of arts degree in 1978 – all while working full-time. He tells the story of how he and fellow officers pursuing degrees would meet in the basement of his house to form "study groups" and assist each other in preparing for tests and course assignments. At the time when he completed his university studies, it was still quite unusual for police officers to have higher education degrees. The vast majority of Chicago police officers had only high school educations.

Hillard and Girl were married more than seven years before their first child, Terri Lee, arrived on September 10, 1977. Girl had difficulty becoming pregnant and consulted with a fertility specialist. Hillard says that he and Girl figured that Terri Lee would be their only child, but approximately three years later, Dana, their son, was born. Hillard remembers thinking, "Where the hell did he come from?" It was at this point that Hillard and Girl decided that two children were enough. He says, "I didn't want to be like my mom and dad with ten kids. Girl went back to work, and it's been like that ever since."

Hillard says he learned a lot about women during Girl's pregnancies – like getting up at 2:00 in the morning to try to find some watermelon and strawberry ice cream. He said he would call his mom and ask, "Why in the hell . . . ?" And she would say, "Just do it. Don't ask questions; just do it." So he would.

Hillard says that he and Girl had a lot of support in raising Terri Lee and Dana. His sisters, his mom, and Girl's mom all helped out so that the young parents never had to worry about finding babysitters.

Hillard and Girl spent the first seven years of their marriage living in a two-flat apartment building with the landlord living downstairs. She was an older lady who tended to be a bit nosey. Hillard recalls the situation as ironic when they were burglarized. The thief came in through the window, knocking out the air conditioner and taking most of his guns and clothes. The meddlesome landlord didn't hear a thing, but when Girl told Hillard that she was pregnant, the landlord heard her "loud and clear." She told the couple that they had to move out of the building and into the front house on the property. Hillard and Girl later bought their first house in 1977, and they still live at the same address.

Hillard's seventh year on the job would prove to be one of his most difficult. At the time, he was 32 years old and working undercover in a Gang's Crime Unit on the city's South Side. The squad was run by Sergeant Fred Miller and included Lovejoy Foster; Richard Peck; Marvin Pharr; Clarence Travis; Hillard; and his partner, Leon Allen. Hillard credits these guys with teaching him how to be a good cop. On Valentine's Day, 1975, Hillard's unit received information that an individual named Timothy Johnson had been involved in a domestic situation in the south suburbs. Johnson had allegedly brutalized his wife and shot four suburban police officers.

As more information became available, Hillard and the other members of his squad learned that the suburban police had responded to the domestic violence call and had attempted to arrest Johnson. After a 30- to 40-minute standoff with police, Johnson had shot his way out of the house and fled. He had shot four police officers in the process. The suburban police believed that Johnson might be in the city of Chicago, hiding out at his girlfriend's apartment on East 48th Street.

Hillard's unit called on a marked Chicago squad to meet them at the disclosed address, because they were all in plain clothes. Once everything was organized outside the apartment building, Hillard went upstairs to a third-floor apartment accompanied by Sergeant Miller and several other gang unit members. Hillard was armed with a pump shotgun. Two other officers stayed outside the building in back, and one officer, John Smith, covered the front of the building.

Sergeant Miller and Officer Foster knocked on the apartment door and were greeted by a pregnant woman identified as Johnson's girlfriend. Hillard remained a safe distance down the hallway behind the other officers and covered them with his shotgun. From his position, he could see that there were several young children running around inside the spacious apartment and that there were a number of closed and locked doors leading into and out of the apartment. Johnson's girlfriend was not being cooperative with Sergeant Miller, denying that she had heard from Johnson and stating that he was not in the apartment.

After a short period of conversation between the officers and the woman, Hillard heard a noise coming from one of the closed-off rooms. He yelled, "There is somebody in that room!" Officer Foster asked the woman to open up the room, and she replied, "We got roomers up here, and I don't have the key." "Roomers" referred to tenants who would sublet individual bedrooms in an apartment. The officer asked, "Who lives there?" And she said, "I don't know." Hillard then heard a window slide open in the blocked-off room, so he immediately ran back down the stairs. When Hillard got to the street, he saw Officer John Smith with his gun "drawn down" on a man who had jumped out of the third story apartment window. Smith had his service revolver pointed at the suspect, who was in a crouched position on the sidewalk and looking in Smith's direction.

Hillard, reaching street level and still carrying his shotgun, pointed the weapon at the suspect and said, "Don't move, police!" Hillard had a beard and an Afro, and in spite of his undercover status, he wanted the suspect to know that he was with the police.

The suspect didn't appear to be injured, so Hillard ordered him to get up and get over against the wall of the apartment building. The suspect complied, so Smith holstered his revolver and walked toward the suspect in an attempt to handcuff him. Hillard kept his weapon pointed toward the suspect and remained at a safe distance. As Smith began to approach the suspect, Hillard yelled, "John, wait until the rest of the crew gets down before we do anything else, you know? You got your pistol; I got my shotgun; let's wait until the rest of the crew comes down." Smith replied, "No, we can handle it, we can handle it."

As Smith approached, the suspect sprang toward him and went for his gun. Hillard moved in the direction of the struggle as Smith yelled out, "He's got my gun! He's got my gun!" Hillard jammed his shotgun directly against the hip of the suspect and pulled the trigger. His shotgun was loaded with a deer slug, which was the equivalent of a large-sized, single ball bearing. Hillard remembers "that the suspect let out a scream after being hit, and then, like some

Superman, the suspect threw Officer Smith off of him and into me, knocking us both down." The suspect, then in possession of Smith's service weapon, ran across the street, limping heavily. He then quickly turned back around and started firing in Hillard and Smith's direction. The first shot fired by the offender hit Smith's leather jacket, and the second round hit the heel of his shoe, but neither one of the shots actually hit the officer. The offender's third shot grazed Hillard in the left wrist, and the fourth struck him in the right elbow. Smith kept shouting, "He's got my gun, he's got my gun!" Hillard, now wounded in both arms, handed Smith his snub-nosed .357 magnum.

The offender turned and ran down the street with Smith in pursuit. Having heard the shots fired on the street, the officers still in the building and on their way down the stairs had called "shots fired" into police communications. Many police squads would soon respond. When Sergeant Miller reached Hillard, he said, "Come on, you're shot, we're getting you to the car, and I'm taking you to the hospital." Hillard said, "I don't want to go anywhere until this son-of-a-bitch is caught!" Miller said, "No, you've got to go to the hospital." The sergeant put Hillard in the car and headed toward Michael Reese Hospital.

On the way to the hospital, Hillard and his sergeant listened to the police radio. More police squads were being called. The offender had run about a block and a half from the shooting scene and was holed up in a second floor apartment. Two responding officers had followed the suspect into the apartment building, and the suspect again fired at the officers. The bullet splintered the wood of an upstairs porch and sent a sliver of wood into one officer's eye.

In a short time, police surrounded the apartment building. The offender, indeed identified as Timothy Johnson, suddenly jumped from the second floor apartment, attempting to flee the police once again. He was immediately swarmed by police and apprehended. Johnson was transported to Providence Hospital for treatment where he was later arrested and charged with multiple criminal offenses.

Hillard says that the thing people do not realize is how fast the chain of events surrounding a shooting incident occurs. The entire incident involving Hillard began and ended in a span of about 15 minutes.

It would take Hillard nearly one year to heal. Dr. Mitchell Krieger, an orthopedic surgeon, performed what is called a "wedge reduction surgery" to realign Hillard's radius bone. On his right arm, Hillard wore two casts, one on the upper portion of his arm and one on the lower, that were connected by a hinge. The combined casts weighed ten to 12 pounds and were carried in a sling. After several months off duty, Hillard was anxious to get back to work, but the police surgeon and the brass at the Chicago Police Department would not listen. Finally, the department agreed to let him come back on desk duty, and he was promoted to temporary sergeant. Hillard went through months of physical therapy and ultimately lost about 6% function in his right arm. Before being allowed to go back on the street where he wanted to be, Hillard had to complete tests at the police academy to prove that he still had the ability to perform all required police tasks.

Hillard says the shooting incident never caused him to reconsider staying in policing. A number of old timers in the Gangs Crime Unit kept saying, "You need to take a disability retirement and go get another job or go back to school." But Hillard replied, "You know, guys, I'm a young guy. I'm only 32 years old. I don't want to be on disability retirement. I want to be a police officer."

While Hillard was in the hospital and going to physical therapy, he realized that although he had been shot and was in pain, there were people in much worse shape than he. He saw many people in the hospital without legs or arms and some with no limbs whatsoever. "It's difficult to worry about losing some movement in an arm when you see people in these kinds of conditions." Seeing those patients gave Hillard a renewed perspective on "what is important in life."

Hillard also learned a lot about his family from his ordeal. On the night of the shooting, Hillard was asked about how he wanted his family notified that he had been shot. He asked Sergeant Miller to call his oldest brother, Denny, first, saying, "Denny will know how to break it to my mom." He also asked that one of his partners go back and pick up his wife, explain what happened, and bring her to the hospital.

Sometime after midnight, Officer Lovejoy Foster called Denny and said, "Terry has been shot; he is not in a life-threatening condition, but we think you need to get to the hospital." Denny then called Laraine, Hillard's oldest sister, who was living with her mother and father at the time. Denny told Laraine what had happened and said, "Quietly get dressed. I will pick you up in a few minutes; then I will wake Mom and Dad and tell them what happened."

What happened next was eerie. As Laraine was waiting for Denny to arrive, Hillard's mother came out of the bedroom and asked her, "How bad is he?" Laraine asked, "What do you mean?" She replied, "Don't play games with me; how bad is he?" Somehow Hillard's mother knew that he had been shot. Hillard explained that "the way the phones were arranged in the house, there is no way Mom could have heard Denny's call coming in. She was asleep in the back bedroom, and that room had no telephone." Furthermore, his sister took the call from her second floor bedroom. Hillard says, "It's unbelievable, but Mom woke up and knew that I had been shot – mother's intuition."

Hillard's mother commented very little about the shooting after that night except to say that Terry had survived 13 months in battle in Vietnam and didn't get a scratch but came back to Chicago and got shot twice in a short time on the job.

When Girl arrived at the hospital, she met Hillard as he was being taken to the emergency room. She approached his stretcher, grabbed his hands in hers, looked down at him and winked, and then whispered, "Have you got on clean underwear?" Hillard says that he was caught off guard by her reaction, but Girl did help to bring humor to an otherwise stressful night. Hillard also says that his wife did not dwell on the shooting, nor did she encourage him to get out of policing. She just told him, "Don't get shot anymore."

Hillard also remembered that the support he received from the Chicago Police Department and his fellow officers following the shooting was overwhelming. Hillard's mother did not come to the hospital as often as she wanted to because there was always a bunch of officers in the room and she could not visit with him in private. Hillard's friends from the department set up a schedule for someone to pick him up every day and take him to physical therapy, to the doctor, or wherever else he needed to go. Hillard says, "That's one thing about the Chicago Police. Those folks who are injured in the line of duty, or some other serious injury or illness, are taken care of with support from fellow officers. That's something the Chicago Police Department does very well."

Hillard received several police department awards for his brave and exemplary service in connection with the shooting, including the department's highest award, the prestigious Police Medal, the Award of Valor, and the Blue Star Award. Mayor Richard J. Daley and Superintendent James Rochford presented the awards to Hillard at the annual Police Recognition Ceremony. Hillard said he will never forget that night.

> They brought me into the back of McCormick Place, right behind the stage, where the mayor's big limo would drive up and let him out. Soon the mayor arrived and came up to me and said, "How you doin'?" Terry told him his name, and the mayor touched his arm and said, "How's the arm?" The mayor then put his arm around Hillard's shoulder and said, "Don't rush back. Be completely healed because we don't want you going back out there and getting hurt again. Take your time; be patient; do it right."

Hillard said both Mayor Daleys always cared a lot about police.

Timothy Johnson, the man who brutally beat his wife, shot four suburban police officers, eluded police, shot Hillard twice, and permanently injured the eye of another Chicago police officer, would spend less than three years in jail for his rampage.

If police are accused of becoming cynical from time to time, there may be good reason. Hillard, however, gives no indication that he harbors lingering resentment or ill will over the incident. He says,

> That's the system. The justice system had spoken. I had to continue to move on with my life – it just made me more determined that I was going to do what I was trained to do. I was going to continue to follow proper police procedure, so that in the future, other officers or myself would not get injured or killed. Like my time in Vietnam, the negative aspects I saw and experienced made me more determined to survive.

In 1979, then Gang Specialist Hillard was assigned to Mayor Jane Byrne's security detail, a position he held throughout her four years in office. Hillard made the rank of temporary sergeant while serving on the mayor's detail. Mayor Harold Washington was elected to succeed Byrne in 1983, and Hillard stayed on the mayor's detail for his first year in office. Hillard says that serving on the mayor's security detail helped him to gain a lot of experience and insight regarding the myriad political issues facing the city, as well as a better understanding of the community, how to handle crises, and how to work with the media. This work experience would benefit him as he continued to rise through the ranks and eventually become superintendent of police.

In 1984, Hillard was accepted into the FBI National Academy in Quantico, Virginia. The 11-week program is designed to train local and state law enforcement leaders in the most current management techniques and crime-fighting strategies, focusing on research, technology, and best practices. Upon graduating from the FBI Academy, Hillard was reassigned from the mayor's executive security detail to sergeant, in the 9th District. He was then quickly assigned to the Chicago Police Department Intelligence Section. Within a matter of months, there was an opening for a supervisor on the Chicago Terrorism Task Force (CTTF), and Hillard was assigned as a coordinator of one of the two units. Hillard would spend the next six years working terrorism cases.

The Chicago Terrorism Task Force was under the purview of the FBI and included federal agents, Chicago police, state police, and other law enforcement and prosecutorial agencies. All task force officers had federal authority as Deputy United States Marshals. The FBI paid for everything, including overtime pay, office space, cars, and other equipment. The task force operated incognito and with great independence. Hillard was assigned as supervisor of the task force surveillance team. The team was outfitted with the most technologically sophisticated equipment available and even had access to two airplanes. Surveillance details that might begin in Chicago could end up in New York, Los Angeles, Boston, New Orleans, or Houston. In several cases, the team traveled outside of the United States. Each of the task force members was given a code name and $1,500 cash. They were instructed to always keep $200 cash in their pocket and $1,300 in American Express traveler's checks. It was not unusual for task force members to unexpectedly have to trail a suspect for several days. In each vehicle, members carried extra clothing and even had hospital urinating bottles so that they could relieve themselves during lengthy surveillances. Once the surveillance began, the task force followed the suspects to their final destination.

Hillard says, "The Terrorism Task Force was an assignment made in heaven. It had the best and the brightest people assigned to it, and we had everything we needed to do the job right." Al Qaeda was not a known terrorist threat in the United States at the time, but the task force investigated cases involving middle-eastern terrorist groups and black, white, and Puerto Rican militant groups operating domestically.

During his time with the task force, Hillard developed many personal friendships with his partners and gained respect for the exceptional investigative skills and dedication that they brought to the job. Hillard says, "The Terrorism Task Force did not lose one major case during the time I worked with these guys – Task Force Supervisor William Dyson, Lt. Nate Gibson, Lt. Andy Greenlee, Lt. John Guarnieri, John Eshoo, Curt Blanc, Tommy Raines, Fred Wheat, Jerry Lewis, Mary Green, Al Dotson, Rick Hahn, and Chris Brennan. They were all 'top notch.'"

In 1991, Hillard was promoted to commander of the 6th (Gresham) District within the Patrol Division. Chicago is divided into 25 police districts, and the Gresham District has one of the highest crime rates in the city. Hillard served as district commander for two years and implemented a number of successful programs. He worked extensively with school, church, and community leaders to encourage young people to stay away from crime and lead productive lives. He also created the 6th District Community Network Task Force to address community concerns and problems. Hillard recognized the potential of community policing initiatives and worked diligently to develop close ties between the police and the residents of the 6th Police District.

In 1993, Hillard was promoted to Deputy Chief of Patrol in Area Two. The city has five police areas, and Area Two is comprised of five of the 25 districts located in the southernmost section of the city. The districts include Grand Crossing, South Chicago, Pullman, Gresham, and Morgan Park. While serving as deputy chief of patrol in Area Two from 1993 through 1995, Hillard helped set up the Enhanced Gang and Drug Enforcement Program, designed to saturate major drug-trafficking areas with enhanced police presence. The program was eventually adopted in all five areas. Hillard also established a special team to combat drug problems in the schools, initiated administrative procedures to reduce the backlog of criminal investigations, established a District Gang Graffiti Report, and set up a task force in conjunction with the FBI to combat increasing homicide rates.

In December of 1993, early in his tenure as deputy chief of patrol in Area Two, Hillard faced yet another life-threatening episode. This threat would be more subtle than those he faced in Vietnam and on the streets of Chicago, but in many ways, it was more dangerous. This time Hillard faced an internal threat: colorectal cancer.

Hillard first became concerned when, for a period of several weeks, he noticed blood in his stool. His doctor at first thought it was probably hemorrhoids. However, Hillard wanted to be sure, so the doctor performed a proctoscope. Hillard went home, took sitz-baths, and ate a lot of vegetables and roughage, but the bleeding continued. The doctor immediately scheduled an appointment for Hillard with gastrointestinal specialist Dr. Ernestine Hambrick.

On December 8, 1993, Dr. Hambrick performed a colonoscopy. The next day Hillard called the doctor for the results, but Dr. Hambrick would not consult with him over the phone. She told him, "No, I don't operate that way. I want to talk to both you and your wife. I want you to come in and talk to me." Hillard asked, "Is it good or bad?" The doctor said, "Terry, I want to talk to you and your wife together."

Hillard and his wife reported to Dr. Hambrick's office for the test results. The doctor told them that she had discovered a spot and that the results from the colonoscopy indicated that it was malignant. The doctor explained, "The good news is that the cancer is in its infancy stage." Hillard said that after hearing the news, he and Girl spent about another 30 minutes with the doctor, during which she explained her recommendation for surgery. Hillard said that after hearing the word *cancer*, Girl totally shut down. He didn't think she heard another word after the diagnosis was given.

Dr. Hambrick wanted to do the surgery right after the New Year, but Hillard insisted that it be performed right after Christmas. He wanted to spend Christmas with his family, but he was anxious to get the surgery done as soon as possible. The doctor agreed, and the surgery was performed on December 28, 1993. Dr. Hambrick removed three feet of his colon. After the surgery, the doctor explained that the cancer had not metastasized through the intestinal wall and that she was more than certain she had removed all of the cancer. As a result, Dr. Hambrick did not recommend chemotherapy or radiation treatment. She said that Hillard should stay in the hospital for an additional four or five days, and, if things went well, he could go home. He would stay off work and recuperate for another four to eight weeks.

About four days after the surgery, Hillard and Girl were sitting in his hospital room and noticed that his stomach was hard and distended. The next thing they knew, Terry was spewing green bile from his mouth. The valve that leads from the stomach to the small intestine had become paralyzed. Immediately, the resident doctor and intern on duty came into the room and started working on him. They quickly discovered that Hillard had contracted pneumonia as a complicating factor.

The next week was one of the most difficult of Hillard's life. He was fed intravenously with tubes running down his throat and nose, and a regimen of antibiotics and other medicines kept him bedridden. After about the seventh day, the doctors said that Hillard was starting to come around and that the antibiotics were working. Dr. Abraham Gimble, Hillard's primary care physician, told him that he would have to stay in the hospital for several more days until he was stronger. He remained on intravenous feeding the entire time. During his 18 days of hospitalization, Hillard lost more than 28 pounds. This amount of weight loss, on an already thin body, made him look emaciated and gaunt.

When Hillard was released from the hospital, his house was in the process of being completely renovated. The dust would not be conducive to his recovery, so the entire family went to live with Girl's mother (Mother Brown) for the next four months. Hillard was so weakened by the illness that Mother Brown had to care for him as he slowly gained enough strength to get out of bed and walk again. Hillard began the process by walking in the basement of her apartment building, first for short distances with her assistance, then on his own, increasing the walking distance day by day. Later, Hillard's children would walk with him at night when they got home from school. In April 1994, nearly four months after the surgery, Hillard felt that he had gained enough strength to return to work.

He was so thin that his suits didn't fit. He attended his daughter Terri's grammar school graduation at St. Dorothy's Church and commented that "it seemed like everyone was looking at me, out of the corner of their eyes. I knew what they were thinking, 'This doggone guy is ready to check out.'"

Hillard says that his bout with cancer at 52 years of age had a significant and sobering impact upon his life: "When you find yourself sitting there across the table from a doctor who is a cancer specialist and she tells you that you have 'the Big C,' malignancy, I don't care how brave you are, it sends chills down your spine and you stumble a bit." When Hillard left Dr. Hambrick's office that day, he thought to himself, "What the hell is going on?" He thought, "It was like being shot, but this time, being a lot older, and a lot more mature, and knowing what life is about, I started thinking, I better take this seriously because cancer is serious; cancer doesn't play around."

Hillard developed a close personal relationship with Dr. Hambrick during his illness. He later learned that her brother had died from colorectal cancer. Dr. Hambrick semiretired shortly after treating Hillard, but the two kept in touch by having the occasional lunch and working on a few projects together. Hillard says he had two important revelations as a result of surviving cancer. First, he learned that the black community does not like to talk about cancer. Second, Hillard found that police officers, because of their macho attitudes, think that they are immune to cancer and, therefore, often ignore the early warning signals. After his own experience, Hillard felt compelled to talk about surviving cancer in the hope that he could persuade others to be aware of the early warning signals and seek screening and treatment.

Working with Dr. Hambrick, Hillard offered programs in which he talked to black community groups and Chicago police officers about colorectal cancer. His objective was to provide education and awareness. Dr. Hambrick developed a questionnaire containing six questions about the symptoms and early signs of cancer. The questionnaire was sent to every member of the Chicago Police Department and said, "If you answer 'yes' to two or three of these questions, you need to see your doctor."

Following the initial survey, a tabulation of responses, and a longitudinal follow-up study, the Chicago Police Department developed a videotape that was shown to officers department-wide, again emphasizing the importance of monitoring signs of cancer. One officer named Gerald was featured on the tape. Gerald initially had some warning signs, but he did not seek medical attention. The film dramatically drove home its point by having his brother state, "Gerald did not follow up, and cancer took his life."

Following his stint as deputy chief of Area Two, Hillard was appointed as the first African American to hold the position of chief of detectives in Chicago. In this capacity, he supervised nearly 1,200 employees responsible for the investigation of crime. He is credited with establishing a Domestic Violence

Program to identify family members who are most at risk. He also began to assign the same detective to investigate repeat domestic violence reports from the same victim. In addition, he implemented a sex offender registration program and opened new lines of communication with the public as part of the Chicago Alternative Policing Strategy (CAPS) program. Under Hillard's leadership, the Detective Division, for the first time, sent letters to the families of homicide victims expressing condolences and explaining the investigative process.

In early 1997, while Hillard was chief of detectives, a 9-year-old girl was brutally attacked in the Cabrini Green Housing Complex. Referred to by police as Girl X (to protect her identity), she had been raped, poisoned, choked, cut, and left for dead. The investigation continued for several months, and although there were numerous leads, no arrests had been made. The story of Girl X was gaining national attention because of the brutal nature of the crime, the girl's age, and the fact that it happened about the same time as the Jon Benet Ramsey case in Boulder, Colorado. Hillard was impatient to get the case solved. He called upon his old friends from the Chicago Terrorism Task Force and told them "unofficially" to start working on the case. He said, "Whatever it takes, get this guy."

As chief of detectives, Hillard did not have oversight of the Terrorism Task Force, but he knew that his friends in that unit would be relentless in getting the crime solved. They went to work immediately, working as many hours as necessary to follow up on the available leads. Within a month, the unit got a confession, and an arrest was executed. Once the arrest was made, the Terrorism Task Force members turned everything over to the Detective Division and walked away. Hillard did not want them to take credit for solving the case; their identities had to be protected at all costs.

In his 29th year with the Chicago Police Department, Hillard had prepared himself through education, training, and experience to be an effective leader. His talents and contributions had already been recognized, but his potential was just beginning to reveal itself. Events that developed within the Chicago Police Department in the waning days of November 1997 would soon affect Hillard, his family, his career, and the entire city.

Superintendent Matt Rodriguez was appointed by Mayor Daley in April 1992 to head the Chicago Police Department. On December 1, 1997, Superintendent Rodriguez retired amid revelations that he regularly fraternized with a convicted felon by the name of Frank Milito. Milito and Rodriguez had been long-time friends. Rodriguez had vacationed with Milito and frequented the Italian restaurant, named Orso's, that Milito owned in Chicago's Old Town neighborhood. In 1986, Milito had plead guilty to two federal felony counts of mail fraud and spent nine months in prison. Shortly after the story linking Rodriguez and Milito broke, the mayor and the superintendent met, and Rodriguez decided to retire. Rule 47 of the Chicago Police Department Personnel Code forbids Chicago police officers from fraternization with a convicted felon. Complicating the situation was the fact that a number of high-profile police brutality and corruption cases had dominated Chicago news, and the Chicago Fraternal Order of Police had held a no-confidence vote on Rodriguez just a few weeks previously.

In a public statement announcing his intention to step down, Superintendent Rodriguez placed the department above his personal concern by stating,

> No one individual is more important than the work of the 17,000 men and women of the Chicago Police Department. If one event or the events associated with any one person begin to stand in the way of the progress of our department, then that individual needs to recognize that fact and move on. (Belluck, 1997)

Rodriguez had served for five and one-half years as superintendent and was widely respected for his steady hand and his commitment to community policing. Dr. Dick Ward, associate chancellor of the University of Illinois at Chicago and a member of the commission investigating police brutality and corruption, said he thought the superintendent "was one of the best the city has had" (Belluck, 1997). Nevertheless, the burden of the situation had convinced Superintendent Rodriguez to retire after 38 years of police service. Mayor Daley immediately began his search for a new superintendent of police.

Chapter 5

CHOOSING A SUPERINTENDENT

The search for a police superintendent, or "Top Cop," for any major city in the United States is a significant and complicated process, which must be given great thought and careful consideration. When one superintendent leaves and another is appointed, it is critical to understand and consider the historical, contextual, and political environment in which such change occurs.

In the case of Chicago in December of 1997, the announced retirement of Superintendent Matt Rodriguez occurred suddenly and without warning. Rodriguez, unlike most major city chiefs, had enjoyed a longer than normal tenure. As chief administrator of a major metropolitan police department with 17,000 employees, the superintendent is responsible for all that occurs on his watch. Rodriguez had weathered the storms of numerous controversies over a five-year period, but he did not do so without sustaining considerable criticism from several sectors, including rank-and-file police, the community, and the media. The last controversy to surface, Rodriguez's friendship with a convicted felon, was the straw that broke the camel's back.

By all accounts, at the time of this crisis, Mayor Richard M. Daley was a supportive and loyal boss who was not afraid to take personal and political heat in order to protect those who worked for him. Daley understood that incidents of police brutality and corruption, while always regrettable and unacceptable, are most often the single and isolated act of a few rogue cops; that such behavior is not usually systemic and widespread; and that the superintendent cannot be held responsible for every single action of 13,500 sworn police officers. The mayor clearly understood that Chicago is not unlike any other major city in this regard. The mayor also was sympathetic to the friction that often naturally develops between police management and working police officers, especially as it relates to labor issues affecting salary, benefits, and promotions and to disciplinary actions and proceedings. Rodriguez's troops' lack of confidence in him did not lead the mayor to replace his superintendent; however, it seems that the single and critical factor related to the events leading up to Rodriguez's departure had to do with the fact that the mayor was caught off-guard by the sudden revelation of the superintendent's friendship with a convicted felon. Just a month earlier, Daley's city council floor leader, Alderman Patrick Huels, was forced to resign after reports surfaced that he personally received a $1.25 million loan from a city trucking contractor who had previously received a $1.1 million subsidy from the city with Huels' help (Spielman & Casey, 1997b).

Rodriguez met with the mayor before the story of his and Milito's relationship broke and would later say, "I saw some concern and a little sadness in the mayor as we were in our discussion. I had never placed that look in the mayor's face in the past 5½ years, so I probably felt more badly than he did" (Belluck, 1997). The mayor needed to distance himself from the scandal quickly, and he needed to send a strong message to all who watched that a new direction was coming. The mayoral election was just over one year away, so political timing was especially relevant as well.

In discussing his decision to retire, Superintendent Rodriguez did not feel that his Rule 47 violation was the sole factor that ultimately led to his decision to step down. The decision was more complex than that and was finally reached because of a combination of factors. As Superintendent Rodriguez said, using an apropos analogy, "Sometimes it's like you're batting .385 or .400, but you strike out three times in one inning. That seems to be the period that we're running through now" (Carpenter & Spielman, 1997). As one sympathetic Chicago police officer said, "When you're at the top of the chain of command, you get criticism from all sides, from the people below you, from the politicians, and from the public. No one can win in this job" (Jimenez & Cone, 1997). Tom Kirkpatrick, president of the Chicago Crime Commission, added, "This is not the kind of job you spend 20 years in and have a peaceful time. There is built-in controversy on the first day anyone takes over" (Fornek, 1997). This analysis could apply to every police chief position in the nation. Sometimes it's not the event but the timing of the event, or the sequencing of numerous events, that will determine whether a chief ultimately survives or must move on. Rodriguez, upon his departure, emphasized the political nature of the top police job by stating, "The most important selection that a major urban mayor has today is chief of police. . . . In many instances, that selection can make or break a man" (Spielman & Casey, 1997a). No one knew that better than Mayor Daley.

Daley took quick and deliberate action to appoint First Deputy Superintendent John Townsend as the acting superintendent while the search for the new superintendent got underway. Townsend was a 66-year-old, 41-year veteran of the Chicago Police Department who had once served as a bodyguard for the mayor's father, Mayor Richard J. Daley. At this point in his career, Townsend was not interested in being considered for the superintendency; however, he was a knowledgeable and trusted friend of the mayor who would be a good steward of the department as the search for the superintendent moved forward.

The city of Chicago has an established police board comprised of civilians appointed by the mayor who are statutorily responsible for advertising and interviewing applicants for the position of superintendent of police. The police board usually conducts a nationwide search with the consultation of an executive recruiting firm, then chooses to interview the top eight to twelve prospects. Following its interview process, the police board submits the names of the three top candidates to the mayor for his consideration. The mayor then conducts his own interviews with the top three candidates and either makes his selection from among them or chooses to reinitiate the search process through the police board if he finds that none of the three candidates are acceptable.

Mayor Daley made it clear from the start that he wanted to find the best candidate from throughout the nation to serve as the city's next police superintendent. Even though the city of Chicago and Mayor Daley personally have a long tradition of hiring from within departments to fill top positions, the mayor insisted that he was open-minded and simply wanted to find "the best." It is rare for an outsider to become head of the Chicago Police Department. In the twentieth century, there had been only three Chicago police superintendents who came from outside the department, the last in 1960 when Mayor Richard J. Daley appointed academic Orlando W. Wilson. Wilson, dean of the University of California at Berkeley's School of Criminology, was brought in to eradicate corruption in the CPD and to modernize the force. In his seven-year tenure, Wilson made considerable progress and in the process became known nationally as the father of the professional policing movement.

It was widely believed, however, that although a nationwide search was being conducted, the final selection of the superintendent would come from within the department. The reasons seemed apparent. According to sources, Mayor Daley did not trust outsiders. He believed that they didn't understand the city, the department, the neighborhoods, the communities, and the political environment. Furthermore, Daley was a practical person, and it just made sense that with more than 13,000 sworn police officers in a police department with a plethora of qualified, proven leaders, there would be at least one person who was qualified to be superintendent. At his core, Mayor Daley was loyal to his personnel, and he expected loyalty in return. Bringing in an outsider would have sent the wrong message – that the mayor lacked the confidence, the faith, and the loyalty that was so critical for him to acknowledge in the hardworking members of the department.

The Chicago media, police unions, community groups, private citizens, and politicians all had their own ideas about the candidates best suited for the position of superintendent. Speculation regarding the mayor's eventual choice was an active topic of discussion by all concerned. A *Chicago Tribune* editorial explained that "Richard Daley has made a lot of appointments in his 8 years as mayor, and he will make a lot more. But the choice he is about to make – who best to replace Matt Rodriguez as superintendent of police – is easily the most important." The editorial emphasized,

Here's an organization with 18,000 employees, 13,000 of whom carry badges, guns, and the terrible responsibility that entails. Here's a polyglot city of 2.7 million saints and sinners, including more than a few drug dealers with fists of cash for buying corrupt cops . . . the job demands a special kind of person. . . . Our advice: get the best possible person for the job. ("Find the Best," 1997)

Many Chicago observers also speculated that the next superintendent chosen would be African-American. Superintendent Rodriguez had been from Hispanic and Polish descent, and several factors favored the appointment of an African-American this time around. First, the black community had increasingly become outraged over incidents of white police officers allegedly beating black citizens. In the most publicized case, white police officers were alleged to have brutally beaten an 18-year-old African-American youth named Jeremiah Mearday and then, as if to add insult to injury, arrested him for resisting arrest. There was a growing concern among the African-American community that the police were systematically singling out blacks for arrest and abuse. The Reverend Paul Jakes, Jr., spokesman for the Greater Chicago Committee Against Police Brutality, stated,

The coalition wants the new police superintendent, whether black or white, to be sensitive to the black community, have a proven commitment to public safety in all neighborhoods, have a plan to eliminate police brutality and misconduct, and improve training and screening of officers. (Metsch, 1997)

No one could argue with the merits of such demands. Given the fact that 36% of the population of Chicago was African-American, the voice of the black community did not go unnoticed. Appointing an African-American superintendent would have an immediate healing effect. The second factor that led people to believe that the next superintendent would be African-American had simply to do with the racial representation of management and leadership positions within city departments. Mayor Daley had earlier selected Edward Altman as the city fire commissioner. Altman was white. It simply would not have looked good for a white mayor to appoint another white person to such a highly visible administrative post. Finally, as it happened, a significant number of the top-ranking police officials in the City of Chicago Police Department – those most respected by the rank and file and the community – were African-American. The names of three highly-qualified African-American superintendent candidates were immediately mentioned; they were Charles Ramsey, deputy superintendent of the Bureau of Staff Services; James Whigham, deputy superintendent of the Bureau of Technical Services; and Terry Hillard, chief of detectives. No matter who was to be selected as the next superintendent, one thing was clear. The selection process would be thorough, deliberate, and time-consuming. The process, from beginning to end, would take nearly four months.

An editorial article that appeared in the *Chicago Sun-Times* on November 16, 1997, focused on the importance of the search process.

The new police chief must possess leadership skills strong enough to clean up the department's image while fostering changes to restore police morale. Any candidate tapped for the job must be willing to stand up for Chicago cops as well as stand up to them. . . . The Chicago Police Department is broken, and it will take a pair of deft hands to see that it gets fixed. ("Rodriguez's Legacy," 1997)

Shortly after the announcement of Superintendent Rodriguez's retirement, Hillard was in his police vehicle with one of Rodriguez's commanders on his way to a departmental event. While listening to the public news radio station WBBM, he heard his name mentioned as a possible contender for the superintendency. Minutes later his cell phone rang; it was Girl reacting to the radio announcement. She said, "What's this about? Where is this coming from? Being superintendent is extremely challenging, Hillard." He responded, "Girl, I don't know anything about this. It was on the radio. Remember we talked about the media. . . . It's probably someone down at city hall or the department dropping my name. I haven't talked to the media. No one has asked me if I want to be superintendent." Girl replied, "Oh, Hillard, you know, this is going to be a challenge and very demanding." He finally said, "Girl, let's just leave it alone for the time being; we will talk about it further when I get home."

Hillard said that once he got home, he and Girl spent several hours talking about whether he should apply for the superintendent's position. Girl had questions and concerns: "What does this job really involve and require? What is the process? Are you prepared to spend the required time for this job? You can't compromise your values and principles!"

Hillard explained to her that he had been around a number of former superintendents including Rodriguez, LeRoy Martin, and Fred Rice. He told Girl what he thought were the pros and cons of the job from what he had observed. He told her that under no circumstance would he change the things he believed in, his principles, or values in order to get the position. He told her he would sell himself "as is," for better or worse. After lengthy discussions, Girl totally supported Hillard's decision to go for the superintendency if that's what he wanted. She said, "Do what you think is best for you and the department. Whatever you do, we're going to support you. Go for it."

Hillard's two children were split on the decision; his son, Dana, was for it completely, in fact, excited; but his daughter, Terri Lee, was totally opposed. She believed that the job would place too much stress on him and the family, too many headaches. She said, "Hey, forget it! Let someone else take the heat."

Hillard next went to his mother for advice. She was very direct, saying, "Unless you're going to put 110% into it, don't do it. If you think you're going to go there and think you're going to put in 75%, 80%, or 100% . . . that's a very demanding job. If you're going to put 110% into it and you really want it, go for it. But, if you have doubts, don't do it." Terry had listened to his mother all of his life. The chores he had done as a child were reminders of what she would expect of him if he went for the job.

Rudy Nimocks had been a deputy superintendent of the Chicago Police Department under Mayors Harold Washington and Jane Byrne. In fact, Nimocks was once considered for the superintendent's job, but some internal politics got in the way. Nevertheless, Nimocks was one of Terry Hillard's mentors, and the two were close friends. At the time, Nimocks was 71 years old and was serving as chief of police for the University of Chicago Police Department. According to Hillard, "Rudy was one person who would tell it to me straight." Terry invited him to lunch. After lunch, the two took a walk, and Nimocks said,

> Let me tell you one thing. That's a hell of a job. If you really want it, if you know you really want it, then go for it. But don't take it just to be superintendent; take it because you are going to give the city and the department 100%. If you have doubts or don't think you can handle it, don't take it because it can come back on you and it can be a killer.

Hillard had always surrounded himself with bright, capable, and trustworthy staff. In Hillard's capacity as chief of detectives, Jim Molloy served as his lieutenant; Marjorie O'Dea was his sergeant (and one of his right-hand people); and Skip Dorn was an investigator whom Hillard had known and worked with in the Gangs Crime Unit on the South Side years ago. Then, there was Scott Keenan, a youth officer, and Hillard's personal secretary, Ellie Foster, who had been with him for years. This was Hillard's team, a team of people who had worked well together, trusted each other, and respected their boss.

Hillard sought their advice. All of them individually and collectively encouraged him to apply for the superintendency. They also offered to assist him as he prepared for the selection process. Hillard explains,

> You have to understand when an individual applies to become superintendent, they immediately consult with professional advisors – attorneys, academics, and others – to help them prepare for the police board application and interviews. I didn't have that, but I had my team. I had my lieutenant, my sergeant, a youth investigator, a detective, a patrolman, and my secretary.

Hillard's team immediately started preparing him for the selection process. In late December 1997, Sergeant O'Dea gathered the application materials, and the team developed potential interview questions that they would ask Hillard in a mock interview. The first question-and-answer session with his team took place on Christmas Eve 1997. It lasted two and a half hours, and the team was thorough and relentless. Hillard says,

> I'm sitting there thinking this is supposed to be my doggone staff – folks I believe in, folks I trust and have a lot of confidence in. They were treating me like shit. Playing the devil's advocate, you know. They told me, "The police board is not going to give you a bye, give you a pass. They are going to be very hard on you." They said, "Then you might have to get prepared for interviews with the mayor and probably his staff."

After the initial mock interview, Hillard and his team would meet after work for about three to four hours of questioning every night, seven days a week, up until the time that he went to the police board interviews. They even met on New Year's Day. Thanks to the team's hard work, Hillard felt that he was well-prepared for anything the board might ask.

The police board required applicants to submit lengthy and detailed responses regarding past work experiences, education, family, and financial information, as well as statements of management philosophy and goals. In addition, the board required each applicant to submit written essay responses to the following seven questions:

1. Discuss your management, budgetary, and administrative experience, which you believe qualifies you to serve as the superintendent of a police department of Chicago's size and complexity.
2. What steps would you take to further advance community policing?
3. Recent figures show the number of reported murders in 1997 was about the same in New York City as it was in Chicago, despite the fact that New York City has more than twice the population of Chicago. What do you think explains this discrepancy?
4. Do you think it is important in fighting serious crime to have a low tolerance for minor threats to public order, or is the Chicago Police Department better off devoting all of its resources to fighting serious crime and effectively ignoring minor offenses?
5. Discuss what you would do to reduce violent crime, narcotics trafficking, and drug-related activities in Chicago.
6. Discuss what you would do as a superintendent to keep morale high among police officers while maintaining sufficient discipline to avoid brutality, corruption, and other forms of police misconduct.
7. What should the criteria be for hiring and promotions within the Chicago Police Department? Discuss the role standardized tests, other objective tests, and performance-based reviews should have in making promotion decisions.

The questions posed were largely reflective of problems and issues that the department was currently facing: corruption, brutality, low police morale, minority advancement, an intractable murder rate, and the ever-present problems of gangs, guns, and drug trafficking.

The police board received 49 applications for the position of superintendent according to a *Chicago Tribune* story released on January 20, 1998. Thirty-three applications were from inside the department, and 16 were from outside the department. Chicago Police Board President Demetrius Carney stated that the board would review the list of applicants and their credentials and produce a short list of candidates to interview ("Forty-Nine Applicants," 1998). Approximately two weeks later, the *Chicago Tribune* reported that the police board had narrowed its list of applicants and would invite 11 finalists for formal interviews with the board. The finalists to be interviewed were all male and included six Caucasians, four African-Americans, and one Hispanic. The list included all three of the African-American Chicago Police Department candidates who were previously thought to be the front-runners for the position: Charles Ramsey, James Whigham, and Terry Hillard. Other Chicago police personnel on the list included Ronald Evans, an African-American commander; James Maurer, a white deputy chief of patrol; Harley Schinker, a white commander; Ray Risley, white and chief of organized crime; Charles Roberts, white and assistant deputy superintendent in charge of the police training academy; and Joseph DeLopez, an Hispanic commander (Martin & Mills, 1998b).

Two candidates on the list were from outside the department. They were Terrence Gainer, the then director of the Illinois State Police, an attorney, and a 20-year veteran of the Chicago Police Department; and John F. Timoney, the former number two administrator for the New York City Police Department. Both men were white. Gainer was a surprise candidate, but according to insiders and news reports, he did not stand much of a chance of being the mayor's choice. He had run unsuccessfully against Daley for Cook County State's Attorney in 1988. Timoney also was thought to have little chance of surviving the final selection process. New York and Chicago have always had a bit of rivalry, and according to sources, Mayor Daley would be reluctant to bring in a New Yorker to solve Chicago's problems.

Hillard was called for his interview with the police board. He said that although his staff had prepared him well, he wanted to reach out to one more person with whom he wanted to have a mock interview before he went to the police board. Hillard referred to this person as "the Mouthpiece," a nickname that had carried over from their days of working together on the Chicago Terrorism Task Force. That person was Jeremy Margolis, a former federal prosecutor, former director of the Illinois State Police, and a well-respected attorney in private practice. Margolis had advised politicians, including governors. Hillard says, "I wanted someone to interview me who I knew could be brutal, and that person was 'Mouthpiece.' He could do it." Hillard went to Margolis's law office and was drilled for about three and one-half hours. He says that when he left Margolis, he felt very confident that he was prepared for anything the police board might throw at him.

Hillard expected the police board interview to last two and a half to three hours. Instead, the interview lasted only a little over an hour. When Hillard was finished with the interview, the chairman of the police board simply thanked him. "No one told me I did very good, and no one told me I did bad," he says. "They just said, 'You'll be hearing from us one way or the other.'"

In early February 1998, the police board gave its final list of the top three candidates for superintendent to Mayor Daley. The three finalists were Charles Ramsey, Terry Hillard, and Raymond Risley. When the finalists were announced, it was widely believed by the press and by department and city hall insiders that Ramsey was the clear front-runner. Hillard was considered to be a distant second choice possibility, and Raymond Risely was considered a compromise choice made by the police board in order to exclude New Yorker John Timoney and to make all three finalists Chicago police officers.

Ramsey had gained Mayor Daley's favor as a lead person in implementing Chicago's Community Alternative Policing Strategy (CAPS) Program. This innovative program made developing positive relationships between the police and community a priority and was heralded nationally for its success. In a *Chicago Tribune* article published on January 18, 1998, it was reported, "The guy (Ramsey) is totally steeped in the philosophy that the mayor believes in (CAPS)." The article further stated, "Ramsey, who is 47, is widely viewed as a forward-thinking, media-savvy leader who stands apart from the other potential candidates to succeed Matt Rodriguez" (Martin & Mills, 1998a). The *Chicago Sun-Times* said, "Ramsey is known as a glib, smooth talker, able to speak to the press without having to agonize over each word he says" (Roberts & Spielman, 1997). The *Sun-Times* ran an article on February 8, 1998, with the headline, "Ramsey Favorite for Police Superintendent." The article quoted an anonymous confidant of the mayor who said, "Barring any unforeseen development in interviews that Daley is conducting with each of the candidates, Ramsey will be Chicago's next police superintendent . . . positively, absolutely, it's Ramsey." According to Spielman, "Other mayoral advisers said Ramsey's selection was 90% certain, but Daley still must establish a 'comfort level' with Ramsey face to face" (1998b).

Although Hillard was not viewed as the front-runner, those who knew him well praised his talents, abilities, strong personal characteristics, and skills. Hillard's personality and style contrasted with Ramsey's. Hillard was described as quiet and reserved, almost shy. The *Chicago Tribune* reported that "Hillard is especially popular with his subordinates and among residents in some South Side neighborhoods where he was once a district commander." The article quoted one high-ranking police source who described Hillard as, "a firm and fair manager. After he's told you you're wrong about something, that's it. You move on. . . . There's no finer gentleman" (Martin & Mills, 1998a). Michael Sneed, a columnist for the *Chicago Sun-Times*, said, "The guy is a gentleman, a cop beloved by his staff and revered by his peers" (Sneed, 1998). The Chicago Fraternal Order of Police indicated that either Hillard or Ramsey would be an excellent choice. Hillard, however, had the coveted reputation of being "a policeman's policeman." Former Superintendent LeRoy Martin said that Hillard "is quiet, but quiet doesn't mean he's timid. Don't mistake that. . . . When he gets his ire up, he can be a very stern, determined person" (Roberts & Spielman, 1997). Others described Hillard as a "squeaky clean" family man with solid principles and values.

In a *Chicago Sun-Times* article on December 12, 1997, the contrasting styles of Ramsey and Hillard were examined in terms of which might be the best fit for the mayor. The article stated, "There's a concern in some mayoral circles that Ramsey may be 'too' practiced and independent, and therefore harder for the mayor to control. Whereas Hillard may be more guarded – the kind of guy who's not going to go off and say stuff Daley doesn't want him to say" (Roberts

& Spielman, 1997). As the selection process proceeded through January and early February, Hillard was attracting more attention as a viable candidate. On February 13, 1998, the *Chicago Sun-Times* ran a story entitled "Hillard Gains Support in Competition for Top Cop." As reported in the story, "There was a time when Hillard, the 54-year-old chief of detectives, was a long shot to replace Matt Rodriguez. But that was before what mayoral aids called 'a quiet ground swell' of support for him that has thrown the competition up for grabs" (Spielman, 1998a).

Hillard knew that speculation was just that, speculation. In the end, it was the mayor's opinion that counted. When Hillard was asked by a reporter what would happen if he was not selected, he said, "If I'm not the person, I'll be here the next morning bright and early, giving 110–120% like I've tried to do for the last 29 years. . . . A lot of folks aren't going to want to hear that, but that's the way I feel" (Spielman, 1998a).

Sarah Pang, one of Mayor Daley's deputy chiefs of staff, called Hillard to schedule his personal interview with the mayor. The first interview, held on a Saturday, lasted three hours and 45 minutes and was just Hillard and the mayor, one on one, with no staff present. When Hillard came out of the mayor's office, Pang said, "Terry, I have worked for the mayor for a lot of years, and I have never seen him talk to anyone for nearly four hours." Then she asked, "What did you guys talk about?" Hillard vaguely replied, "You name it, we talked about it, not only the job and personal history, but what I had done in the Marine Corps, family, just a variety of other things we talked about." Hillard's second interview with the mayor lasted two hours and 50 minutes, and his third and final interview lasted two hours and 15 minutes. It was clear that the mayor wanted to make the right choice in selecting his next superintendent. In total, the mayor spent nearly nine hours in private interviews with Hillard.

At the end of the final interview, Daley made it clear that if Hillard got the job, the mayor would handle the politics, and Hillard would run the police department. The mayor told him,

> If I don't come to you and ask you to promote somebody, or to transfer someone, then I don't expect any other politician to come to you and ask you that. So if I don't do it, no one else should have the privilege of doing so. So you run the department. I'll be there if you have some things you want to run by me, but it's your department to run. Just make sure that of the people you select, that you have confidence in them, and that they are loyal to you, to the department, and that they are competent. If you get the position, that's what I expect of you.

Approximately two weeks later on a Wednesday morning, Hillard was in a meeting with detectives and department officials discussing a rash of violent bank robberies that had occurred on the North Side. One of his secretaries, Karen Huels, interrupted the meeting and told him that a lady named Rosemary was on the telephone and needed to talk to him. Huels did not know who Rosemary was; Hillard knew that she was the mayor's personal secretary.

He politely left the meeting, telling his staff to continue their discussions and that he would be right back. Hillard says that he knew this call meant one of two things: Rosemary was calling to say that the mayor wanted to talk to him because he either got the job or he didn't. The decision had been made.

Hillard closed his office door, answered the phone, and said, "Yes, Rosemary, what's up?" She said, "It's up to the mayor to tell you that. Hold on, I'm going to put the mayor on." When Daley came on the phone, Hillard said, "Good morning, Mr. Mayor." The mayor responded, "Good morning, Mr. Superintendent." Hillard said, "Pardon me?" Daley repeated, "Good morning, Mr. Superintendent." The mayor told him that he had had a sleepless night, but that he had made up his mind and that Hillard was his choice for superintendent. Daley said that he wanted to hold a press conference at city hall in about two hours but told Hillard to keep it quiet, as he did not want the press to know about the selection prior to the official announcement. The mayor then put Sarah Pang on the phone with Hillard to work out the details for getting him and his family down to city hall.

Hillard remembers that the mayor's instruction to keep the decision quiet was difficult because he was at police headquarters; everyone was watching in anticipation of the mayor's final selection. Sarah Pang told Hillard to get to city hall within an hour and a half to meet with the president of the police board, Demetrias Carney. Hillard was told to be in uniform, and after his meeting with Carney, the two would walk over to the mayor's office. Hillard told Pang he would call his wife to attend the press conference, but said the kids wouldn't be coming. He said, "My kids are in school, where they belong."

Hillard then went back into the meeting and tried to hide the fact of the exciting news he had just received from the mayor. He says, "When you have just received such dramatic life-changing information, you try to keep a straight face, and you want to go back into the meeting with the same facial expression you left with." When he reentered the meeting, he said, "Tell me more about this series of bank robberies." As his staff started to further update him, Hillard was feeling fidgety and unfocused and did not hear what was being said. Fearing that his trained detectives could sense his uneasiness, he said, "Okay, look here, Lieutenant Molloy and I have to make a real quick run, go to another meeting, you know. Get the game plan together, get back in touch with the deputy chief, and let me know exactly what is happening." Hillard noticed that Molloy was looking at him, so he said, "Let's go." Molloy followed Hillard into his office, and Hillard closed the door. Molloy asked, "What's up, Boss?" Hillard replied, "We've got to go to the mayor's office." When Molloy asked why, Hillard said, "There's something going on, but I can't tell you right now. We just have to get down to the mayor's office."

Hillard asked Molloy to sneak his uniform out of the office in his trench coat because it was raining outside at the time. He told him to get in his car, meet him a block away at Tenth and Wabash, and gave Molloy his uniform. Hillard puttered around in his office for another ten minutes or so, being careful not to draw attention, and then went to the elevator. When the elevator did not come, Hillard walked down the stairs to exit out of the back door of the building. When Hillard left the building, an observant police officer working building security took notice. It was an uncommon occurrence for the chief of detectives to exit through the back door. Hillard says, "From what I understand, when I walked out of the back door and the door closed, the officer on duty said, 'It's Hillard,' and the rumors started."

Molloy picked him up on Tenth Street and dropped off his boss at city hall to meet with one of the mayor's press people and Demetrias Carney. Ellie Foster went to pick up Girl at the principal's academy. At the mayor's press conference, Daley spoke first, followed by Carney and then Hillard. The press then wanted to hear from Girl, the new superintendent's wife. Hillard says that Girl handled the questions very well and referred to him as the "Top Cop." That moniker stuck with him throughout his superintendency.

After the press conference, there were a number of photo shoots in the mayor's office, after which Hillard went back to police headquarters. By this time, the word was out. Everyone knew that Terry Hillard was the new superintendent of police.

When he got back to the department, Hillard went to the O. W. Wilson Auditorium, which had a seating capacity for about 150 people. Hillard was overwhelmed to see that there were about 250 people already there to congratulate him. After he left the auditorium, he walked back to his office. There to greet him was his team, the people who had helped him through the entire selection process: Lieutenant Molloy, Sergeant O'Dea, Investigator Dorn, Officer Keenan, and Ellie. The team hugged and high-fived each other. The team had made a sign that said, "Not bad for a bunch of amateurs." That sign is now encased in Hillard's dining room cabinet. Later that day, Judge Abraham Lincoln Marovitz, a friend of Hillard's, swore him in as superintendent.

The newspapers were quick to provide laudatory commentary about the appointment. The *Chicago Tribune* put the selection of Hillard and his challenges in context:

> In the 1990s, a police superintendent in a big city must be able to juggle many responsibilities, not all of them directly related to fighting crime. The job often entails dealing with often conflicting constituencies, including minority communities, the police union, and city hall. All can cut into the superintendent's popularity. (Metsch, 1998)

A *Chicago Sun-Times* commentary, dated February 19, 1998, said,

> Mayor Daley picked a "policeman's policeman" who can provide stability and a sense of continuity to a much-troubled police department. He also has picked a low-profile commander who shuns the spotlight and likely will stay the course rather than shake up the police force with drastic change. And that combination might be just the right formula for repairing damage done to the department and the city by recent scandals and controversies.

Following Hillard's appointment, a *Chicago Tribune* editorial said,

> His quiet professionalism earned Hillard both the respect of his peers and the notice of his superiors, who advanced him methodically up the district, area, and headquarters' ladders. . . . Hillard possesses the hard-won credibility it takes to lead . . . and [now] Daley must give his appointee latitude to do just that – lead. ("Lead on," 1998)

Responses from individuals in positions of authority, including the mayor himself, were overwhelmingly positive. Deputy Superintendent Mike Malone, chief of the Bureau of Investigative Services and Hillard's boss when he was chief of detectives, stated, "Hillard displays absolute loyalty to those around him and gets it in return, because he is patient, approachable, and open-minded. . . . He's very dynamic in a quiet way. He goes out of his way to say he never wants to be surrounded by yes men" (Spielman & Roberts, 1998a). Those close to Mayor Daley said,

> When Hillard finally got a chance to sit down with the mayor, in his first of three long interviews, a "special connection" developed between the two men. It's hard not to like the guy. . . . Three minutes into the conversation, he's telling you about his kids. He focuses on gangs and narcotics like a laser beam. The mayor just had a comfort level with the guy. (Spielman & Roberts, 1998a)

Mayor Daley himself, in discussing his selection of Hillard, said,

> I trusted a gut feeling that Hillard was the best possible person. . . . Terry Hillard's overall understanding of the department from top to bottom is outstanding. . . . He has a vision for the police department, and he understands the issues. He will be a take-charge superintendent. (Mills & Martin, 1998)

Bill Nolan, speaking on behalf of the Fraternal Order of Police, commented, "We have somebody on our side – somebody who is going to stick up for us and not have a knee-jerk reaction to public outcry" (Johnson, 1998).

On February 18, 1998, Hillard was appointed by the mayor as his selection for superintendent of police. Hillard would serve as acting superintendent until such time that the Chicago City Council took official action to approve the mayor's choice. On March 11, 1998, Alderman William Beavers, chairman of the Chicago City Council Police and Fire Committee, gave his full endorsement of Hillard as the next superintendent of police. He said, "Hillard's credentials are impeccable."

Two early decisions Hillard made, one while serving as acting superintendent and the other shortly after becoming superintendent, gave further indication of Hillard's strength of character and humbleness. Before he was confirmed, several police department staff members told Hillard that he should immediately move into the superintendent's office. He refused. Hillard told them that he would be operating out of the chief of detectives' office until he officially became superintendent. He says,

> People would tell me, "You're superintendent," and I would tell them, "I'm not superintendent until I'm ratified by the city council." It was probably more than

likely, over 90% certain, that I was going to make it. But hell, I didn't want to be so arrogant as to think I was superintendent, until the whole body of the city council acted.

Daley's nomination of Hillard as superintendent of police was unanimously confirmed by the city council on March 11, 1998. Police Board President Carney stated, "Hillard has a reputation of being 'a policeman's policeman.' When the 11 semi-finalists were asked the question 'If not you, then who?' 90% of them chose Hillard" (Spielman, 1998a).

On the first or second day after the confirmation by the city council, a man from Building Management came into Hillard's office and said, "Superintendent, we're going to get you a new conference table." Hillard said, "Oh, is that right? What's wrong with the conference table I have?" The guy said, "It has a big scratch on it." Hillard then asked, "How much will this new conference table cost?" The reply was, "About 18–20 grand." Hillard politely said, "You won't be getting me a new conference table. I don't need heat like that. I haven't been superintendent a week, and you're talking $20,000 for a conference table? Not hardly. Let that son-of-a-bitch stay right where it is; let's put some polish on it."

After being confirmed, Hillard immediately started bringing in his crew from the chief of detectives' office to help him with his transition to superintendent. Hillard's team, who had been with him for a long time, was excited. Hillard says, "We all knew we were going to make a difference here."

Hillard's leadership as superintendent was yet to be demonstrated, but from his past, it was obvious that certain basic principles and beliefs would be ever-present in all decisions that he made. Three separate early responses gave a clear indication of Hillard's priorities and frame of reference. First, in responding to a question about police morale, Hillard said, "I've never forgotten that the backbone of this department are the men and women who patrol our streets and keep the city safe. As superintendent, I intend to keep those men and women uppermost in my mind" (Metsch, 1998). Second, when questioned about whether he would be his own person as opposed to the mayor's yes man, Hillard had said,

> I'm 54 years old, a former Marine. I've been through colon cancer. I've been shot. I've survived Vietnam. At this stage of my life, I figure I've earned the right to say what I want to say. I'm not a yes man. I speak my mind, and if I have something to say, I say it. (Mills, 1998)

Finally, and probably most telling, when Hillard was asked in an interview prior to being appointed superintendent, "What in your background has prepared you to get to this point?," he responded, "I come from a family of five boys and five girls. It was a very close-knit family. They believe in trust, loyalty, education; go to church; and do the right thing" (Spielman, 1998c). What a good answer – do the right thing – truly a solid foundation for a superintendent of police. Hillard's reign as superintendent of the Chicago Police Department had begun in earnest, but many difficult challenges lay ahead.

Chapter 6

TAKING CHARGE: THE CHALLENGE
OF THE SUPERINTENDENT

*The Chicago Police Department with 17,000 personnel, is
as large as a multi-national corporation, but more complicated to manage in almost every dimension.*

– American Police Beat

Imagine a fairy tale in which Terry Hillard awakens from a long sleep on the
morning of February 19, 1998, takes a look around, and says to those there
with him, "I've been asleep for a long, long time, what's new?" A man dressed
in a Chicago police uniform says, "Well, we've got some good news, and
we've got some bad news. The good news is that you've been selected as the
next superintendent of the Chicago Police Department." Hillard says, "That's
wonderful; now what is the bad news?" The officer responds by saying, "The
bad news is that you've been selected as the next superintendent of the
Chicago Police Department."

Being in charge can be a blessing or a curse. If things go well, you're a hero,
but if things spin out of control, you're the villain. A newly appointed superintendent of the Chicago Police Department should understandably be extremely proud of the confidence that all have placed in him; out of 13,500
sworn personnel in the Chicago Police Department and the potentially tens
of thousands of police managers from throughout the nation who might have
applied, the selection of one man to head the second largest police agency in
the nation is indeed significant. At the same time, it must be recognized that a
tremendous amount of responsibility rests squarely on the shoulders of that
one individual. The superintendent must be able to set forth direction and
policy that effectively reduce the incidence of crime throughout the city while
ensuring that police strategies and tactics do not negatively affect the guaranteed rights and freedoms of the citizenry. The superintendent must be able to
instill confidence and pride in those who work under his command while concurrently ensuring that swift and deliberate action is taken to discipline officers
for all types of departmental infractions. The superintendent must keep the

mayor happy by promoting the mayor's agenda, protecting the mayor from political scandal, and being careful not to step on the mayor's toes. Confidential information regarding the investigation of high-profile cases must remain secure, yet at the same time, the superintendent must appease the media and community's demands for information about those cases. The superintendent must operate within an arena where intractable social problems exist – poverty, unemployment, substandard housing, broken families, and inadequate educational opportunities – all of which contribute to the problem of crime but are beyond the scope of his power and the power of his department to remedy. And finally, the superintendent must carefully balance his professional life and personal life to ensure that he is not consumed or overtaken by the job and that the stresses of the job do not negatively affect his health, family, productivity, and perspective. Quite simply, a superintendent who is overwhelmed cannot be effective, and yet the nature of the job demands constant attention and effort.

Terry Hillard's superintendency must be placed in historical perspective. The Chicago Police Department was created in 1835, two years before Chicago had even been incorporated as a city. In previous years, Chicago residents were protected by county authorities and United States' soldiers stationed at Fort Dearborn. In the 1850s, the size of the police force greatly increased as the city grew. Additional police personnel continued to be added as Chicago's population exploded in the last half of the 19th century.

Early in the developmental history of the department, specialized police units were formed to address specific and emerging crime problems. The department was also quick to incorporate advancing technologies to further enhance its crime-fighting capabilities. In the beginning, policing was conducted exclusively by foot patrol or walking the beat. Police call boxes were installed at various intersections throughout the city in 1881. The Detective Division was created in 1861; the Traffic Division in 1882; the introduction of fingerprint identification in 1905; the first female Chicago Police officer was appointed in 1913; a centralized Chicago Police radio system was introduced in 1930; and in 1942, all Chicago Police squad cars were equipped with two-way radios. In 1952, walkie-talkies allowed for better and more direct police communication.

In its long history, the Chicago Police Department has undergone continuous reorganization brought on by population growth, technological advancement, changing crime problems, riots and protests, and numerous incidents of departmental scandal and corruption. One event that placed the Chicago Police Department in the national spotlight occurred in the summer of 1968 when the city of Chicago hosted the Democratic National Convention. The country was in the midst of turmoil, and over 100,000 people, mostly young, converged upon the city to protest the United States' involvement in the Vietnam War. Chicago Police, National Guardsmen, and Federal Troops were ordered to control the angry crowds. In the conflict, more that 600 protesters were arrested, and more than 200 police officers were injured. The national television networks reported on the clashes between the protesters and the police and often portrayed police as oppressive. The department has weathered numerous such incidents, as well as the administrations of numerous mayors and superintendents, some of whom were effective and some of whom were not.

At the time Hillard assumed the superintendency, the Chicago Police Department was the second largest in the nation with 17,000 personnel. He had a sworn force of 13,439 and served a population of just under three million people; operated on a budget approaching $1 billion; had a fleet of 3,735 vehicles; controlled 25 police districts covering more than 228 square miles; and received more than 4.5 million calls for police service annually, of which 3.5 million calls were for 9-1-1 emergency response. In his first year as superintendent, the department recruited, hired, and trained 821 rookie police officers (Chicago Police Department, 1998, pp. 31–35). Hillard also took over the superintendency at a time when society at large was experiencing a technological boom in the areas of computer and information management, communication instrumentation, and the emergence and use of such dynamic crime fighting tools as DNA testing. These and other scientific and technological advances would continue to have an impact on policing throughout Hillard's administration.

Hillard says that when he was first appointed superintendent, the immediate demands of the job, such as appointing his administrative team, establishing his administration's goals and objectives, and clearly communicating his priorities, took precedence above all else. He had little time to reflect upon his appointment. Hillard said that it was not until several months after his appointment, when he and his wife were flying back to Chicago from a police conference, that the magnitude of his position hit him. The return flight was late at night and took a landing path that brought the airplane directly over the city. As Hillard, Girl, and the other passengers looked down upon the expansive, never-ending glowing lights of the city and its maze of intersecting streets, a passenger who had recognized Hillard turned to him and said, "Just think, you're chief of all that." Hillard says that the flight was the first time he fully realized the scope and responsibility of his new position.

The primary responsibility of the Chicago Police Department is to respond to and investigate crime, and there is never a shortage of work in this regard, regardless of who happens to be serving as superintendent. In Hillard's first year as superintendent, he and his department faced 253,608 reported incidents of major crimes, including 703 murders; 2,387 criminal sexual assaults; 23,117 robberies; 36,740 aggravated assaults and batteries; 36,009 burglaries; 121,537 thefts; 31,826 motor vehicle thefts; and 1,289 arsons (Chicago Police Department, 1998, p. 9). On a weekly basis, the superintendent and the department faced the following workload: a total incidence of 4,877 major crimes, including 13 murders; 46 criminal sexual assaults; 445 robberies; 706

aggravated assaults and batteries; 692 burglaries; 2,337 thefts; 612 motor vehicle thefts; and 25 arsons. In addition, the department made 58,000 arrests
annually (1,115 weekly) for narcotics violations; 32,000 arrests (616 weekly)
for simple assault and battery; 2,929 arrests (56 weekly) for driving under the
influence; 37,500 arrests (721 per week) for disorderly conduct; 58,000 arrests
(1,115 weekly) for traffic violations; 4,800 arrests (92 weekly) for prostitution;
10,900 arrests (209 weekly) for vandalism; and 4,000 arrests (76 weekly) for
weapons violations (Chicago Police Department, 1998, pp. 25–26). This level
of crime, although fluctuating somewhat from week to week and year to year,
remains relatively constant. Fortunately, the national crime rate (as well as the
crime rate in Chicago) has been in steady decline since 1991, but the aggregate
crime statistics nevertheless remain staggering.

The primary contributing factors fueling Chicago's crime problem are
gangs, guns, and drugs. With the exception of Los Angeles, no other large
American city experiences the dangerously high levels of these three factors in
combination. Chicago murder rates are among the highest in the nation. As a
Chicago Tribune article put it, "Police have long recited the mantra that most
murders are the result of a deadly trinity that runs rampant in Chicago: street
gangs, guns, and drugs" (Huppke & Heinzmann, 2004, p. 10). In order to understand the complexity of the police department's response to crime, it is first
necessary to examine in detail the most telling and disturbing violent crime:
murder.

In the past 25 years, more than 19,000 homicides have been committed in
Chicago. The city averages 760 homicides per year, or two per day. From
1979 through 2003, the most homicides (925) were recorded in 1992. No
matter how the statistics are analyzed, both the total number of homicides and
the homicide rate in Chicago are unacceptable. If considered in the realm of
public health statistics, both numbers clearly constitute an epidemic (Joanes,
2000, p. 307). An editorial by the *Chicago Tribune* entitled "The Summer Killing
Season" puts the city's problem of homicide in perspective: "In Chicago, no
day dawns without assurance that, by midnight, not a single murder will occur.
But through the summer months, as more bullets fly down city streets that
double as shooting galleries, the likelihood of street slaughter only rises" (2004,
p. 12).

Imagine yourself as superintendent of police. The city streets that you are
responsible for protecting are full of guns and drugs. Your enemy is a massive
countercultural organization of gang members that is at least triple the size of
your police force, and it is better armed. Your enemy has embraced violence
as a way of life, as the acceptable method of dealing with conflict. If a member
of one gang disrespects a member of a rival gang, whether it be over territor-
ial boundaries, money, drug trade, or something as minor as the attention of
a girl, shooting and killing are likely responses. As one former gang member
remarked, "It's survival of the fittest. You can't trust nobody because the
person watching your back probably has a gun to your head, waiting to take

you out. What is worse is that many have come to view a violent, lethal response as justified" (Huppke & Heinzmann, 2004, p. 11). Furthermore, "These
homicides exact an immeasurable toll: young lives lost; a new generation of
Chicagoans scarred, doomed to grow up in an environment where life is regarded as shockingly cheap" (Huppke & Heinzmann, 2004, p. 10).

One of the pressures placed upon any new superintendent is that the news
media, citizens, politicians, and even academics attempt to explain crime
problems in oversimplified terms and in the process notoriously attempt to
compare crime statistics between cities. A *Chicago Tribune* article provides an
example, for its authors wrote,

> The bottom line is homicides in U.S. cities have been falling for a decade after
> the bloodbaths of the crack cocaine wars in the late 1980s and early 1990s. But
> Chicago has seen a slower decline in the number of murders compared to other
> large cities, especially New York. (Huppke & Heinzmann, 2004, p. 10)

It is always interesting to watch as the news media hurries to announce on an
annual basis which city will claim the distinction of becoming "The Murder
Capitol" of the United States. Chicago, New York, Detroit, Los Angeles, and
Washington, D.C., are always closely watched, and any fluctuation in either
the actual number or rate of murders in the respective cities is noted and analyzed. Here are the facts: in a 23-year (1976–1998) comparative examination
of the cities mentioned above, each city recorded a huge number of homicides. New York City had 37,013 murders during this time; Los Angeles had
18,453; Chicago had 18,222; Detroit had 12,685; and Washington, D.C., had
6,661. During this period, New York had an average population of approximately 7.3 million people; Los Angeles averaged approximately 3.3 million;
Chicago had approximately 2.9 million; Detroit had approximately 1.1 million; and Washington, D.C., had an average population of just over 600,000.
The murder rates (number of murders per 100,000 people) of these cities,
however, paint a very different picture. During the same time period, Detroit
recorded a murder rate of 50; Washington, D.C.'s rate was 48; Chicago's rate
was 27; Los Angeles' rate was 24; and New York City recorded 22 murders
per 100,000 people (Joanes, 2000, Tables 1, 2, 7, 8, and 10).

It is important to realize, too, that each major city is different, not only in
terms of population and number of police officers, but also in terms of the
social conditions and types of criminal activity that might be encountered
there. Crime is not easily explained, and year-to-year fluctuations in crime
rates are not attributable to any single factor. If we knew for certain what
caused people to murder more or to murder less, we would assuredly institute policies and tactics designed to ameliorate the problem. The fact is that
Chicago is different from Los Angeles, which is different from Detroit, Washington, D.C., and New York City. If one looks just at the numbers of homicides committed in these five metropolitan areas in the 23-year period
analyzed, it is staggering to realize that more than 93,000 people were killed

(nearly twice as many American lives as were lost in the Vietnam War), that tens of thousands of promising lives were extinguished, and that these victims will never be able to realize their dreams and enjoy their families. What is more troubling is that the killing continues.

The purpose of taking pains to provide an analysis of homicide rates in the respective cities is to emphasize the fact that the study of crime is complex and inexact. Furthermore, the policing profession, while always striving to employ new philosophies, strategies, and tactics designed to reduce crime, often is at a loss to explain changes in crime rates and patterns. In this sense, policing is a never-ending experiment. The social sciences simply cannot definitively document the effect that policing tactics have on crime and crime reduction.

One thing is certain: crime in the United States has been decreasing steadily and significantly for more than a decade. The reasons for this decline, however, are not clear. Some authorities point to "demographic change or the economic boom of the 1990s, others to the waning popularity of crack cocaine" (Skogan, Steiner, & the Chicago Community Policing Evaluation Consortium, 2004, p. 52). Still others believe that tougher laws and increased terms of imprisonment serve to keep offenders locked up longer, thereby preventing recidivist acts of crime.

Hillard took over as superintendent of the Chicago Police Department at a time when the crime rate in Chicago had been in steady decline for six years. From 1991 through 1997, major crimes in Chicago had decreased by more than 19.5%. This obviously was very good news, but, as detailed previously, the rate of decline must be placed within the context of the actual number of crimes still being committed annually – and that number was substantial when Hillard took over. Also, newly appointed Superintendent Hillard took leadership of a police department that was in its fifth year of implementing a comprehensive community-based policing program known as the Chicago Alternative Policing Strategy (CAPS). Mayor Richard M. Daley had fully endorsed the CAPS program from its inception in 1993. The goal of CAPS is to bring the police and the community together in the fight against crime. The department had come to realize in the early 1990s that a new philosophy of combating crime was needed; traditional policing with its reliance upon simply responding to calls for service was not working. The CAPS program started as an experiment in policing supported largely through federal grants, but it quickly gained national recognition as an innovative policing strategy. As an integral component of CAPS, the police department retrained all of its officers to work more closely with citizens. Their charge was to enlist the active involvement of city residents in "neighborhood beat meetings," to work in cooperation with other city agencies and community groups to identify crime problems, and to develop strategies to make neighborhoods and the community at large safer. Although Hillard inherited responsibility for the continued success of the CAPS program, he had already been well schooled in the CAPS

policing philosophy as a top-ranking member of Superintendent Matt Rodriguez's staff. He had witnessed the successes of CAPS firsthand, and he saw
much more potential for expanding and enhancing the city's adopted crime-
fighting philosophy well into the future.

The continued and steady decline in Chicago crime rates and the implementation of a relatively new citywide crime reduction strategy led Superintendent Hillard to the decision to stay the course, as opposed to abruptly
changing policing philosophy, strategy, and tactics in midstream. This decision
is critical to understanding the leadership and personal characteristics of Hillard.
In some cases, new leaders change organizations for the sake of change, as a
way of announcing their arrival or exerting their authority. Such radical change
is often counterproductive and places the egocentric concerns of the leader
above the good of the organization. Newly appointed leaders also may feel that
change is expected of them and that one way to justify their new appointment
is to show that they are doing things differently. In taking over as superintendent, Hillard used a "look and see" approach; his management style required
evaluation of things as they were, consideration of alternatives for improvement, and implementation of change in a methodical, well-thought-out manner.

One of Hillard's first priorities was to reconnect the superintendent's office
with the officers who worked the streets. In the first several months of his superintendency, Hillard went to the 25 police district stations and met with officers on their own turf, speaking to them at roll call, at the training academy,
and on the street. He assured them that he had their best interests and the interest of the department in mind, and he generally and genuinely listened to
their concerns. Hillard says, "I wanted officers to know their leaders stand with
them as they perform the difficult job we have entrusted them to perform. It
is these officers, not the individuals at the top, who are responsible for the success of the department." Hillard remembers that before he took office, there
was a tendency for police superintendents to communicate by memorandum.
This simply was not Hillard's style. Police morale had suffered considerably in
years past, so Hillard was intent on showing the men and women of the
Chicago Police Department that he was there to support them and that he
cared about them. Hillard says that as superintendent, it was his challenge –
and his commitment – to ensure that the substantial talent of Chicago police
officers was properly developed, nurtured, and effectively utilized.

The same style of personal engagement and communicative openness that
Hillard demonstrated toward those who worked for him would later be extended to the entire Chicago community. Superintendent Hillard launched a
major initiative to open up dialogue between the police and their community
partners. Hillard recognized the need for engaging the community:

> The department needed to balance effective crime control strategies with equal
> appreciation of how citizens are treated. . . . Reducing crime cannot be accom-
> plished at the expense of losing the trust and active involvement of any of our
> community partners. (Chicago Police Department, 2000, p. 5)

Hillard had studied and embraced the CAPS program and determined that in its short developmental history of five years, the program was only beginning to reach its true potential. Terry Hillard would eventually take police-community relations to a much higher level, primarily because of his determination and willingness to open himself and the department up to the community. It would soon become clear that Terry Hillard was not only the superintendent of police but also a goodwill ambassador to the community. (Superintendent Hillard's effectiveness in working with the community through the CAPS program is discussed at greater length later in this book.)

As Hillard began his superintendency in Chicago, New York City was receiving national and international acclaim for a dramatic decrease in reported crime, particularly homicide. New York City homicides had peaked in 1990, and by 1997, they had plummeted from 2,262 to 767, a drop of 66% (Bowling, 1999, p. 531). Chicago homicides had peaked in 1992 with 939 murders and had decreased to 757 murders by 1997, a drop of 19%. Although Chicago homicides were being reduced significantly, and at a far greater rate than the national average, they were not declining at the same level as in New York City. Inevitably, New York City became the model by which all other cities would be evaluated. Local and national media began inquiring about what was happening in New York City. They wanted to know what the NYPD was doing to effectuate such a dramatic decrease in homicides and other violent crimes. People in Chicago and virtually every other city across the nation wanted to know why their respective cities couldn't follow the lead of New York City and reduce crime in a comparative fashion. For the newly appointed superintendent in Chicago, these would become persistent questions requiring careful consideration and response.

Many factors likely played a role in New York's dramatic fall in crime rates. In 1994, William Bratton was appointed as commissioner of the New York City Police Department by newly elected Mayor Rudolph Giuliani. Giuliani was a long-time federal prosecutor who characterized himself as a conservative and as a tough crime fighter. Giuliani ran for mayor on a platform of cleaning up the city and restoring community safety. Bratton had previously been head of the New York City Transit Police and had instituted an aggressive policing strategy based on strict law enforcement and zero tolerance. He advocated an enforcement policy wherein arrests on the subways were made for all offenses, no matter how minor. The homeless, beggars, hawkers, and rowdy youth — all were put on notice that the subway system was under strict police control. Vandalism, disruptive behavior, and fare beating would result in arrest. Bratton's theory was that tolerance of disorderly behavior (e.g., smoking, loud and boisterous actions, graffiti, drunkenness, loitering, and other minor infractions) would lead to a "general acceptability" of an environment of disorder; that such disorder, if left unchallenged, would invite further disorder; and that the commission of more serious crimes would eventually result. Following the implementation of this newly developed policing strategy, there was a dramatic

reduction in subway robberies between 1990 and 1995. When Mayor Giuliani appointed Bratton as Commissioner of the NYPD, it was clear that this
seemingly effective style of policing would soon be extended citywide.

Giuliani and Bratton's approach to fighting crime in New York City was
called the Quality of Life Initiative. The objective of the strategy was to restore public order throughout the city by aggressively enforcing laws against
public drunkenness, loitering, vandalism, littering, public urination, panhan-
dling, prostitution, and other minor misdemeanors and "public order" infractions. This crime-fighting strategy was based largely upon the "Broken
Windows Theory" originally conceptualized by George Kelling and James Q.
Wilson in the early 1980s. The theory asserts that if community norms and
values are allowed to gradually decline, if windows are broken and not fixed,
if weeds are allowed to grow, and if public drunkenness, loitering, and other
public order infractions are tolerated, then the message is sent that the neighborhood is in disorder, thereby inviting further neighborhood decline, further
social disorder, and flourishing criminal activity. The Broken Windows Theory
advocates police involvement not only in law enforcement, but also in the
maintenance of order, in the belief that by eliminating minor disorder, major
crime will also inevitably be deterred.

There is no doubt that New York City experienced a dramatic decline in
the rate of violent crime beginning in the 1990s. The question is whether
this decline was spurred by the introduction of the new Quality of Life Initiative or by some other combination of factors. At the same time that New
York City initiated its new Quality of Life strategy, it also initiated a component enforcement strategy directing police to engage in aggressive "stop-
and-frisk" actions. The stop-and-frisk strategy was designed to get guns off
the street and make arrests for minor offenses as well as warrant and parole
violations. Concurrently, the department was actively deploying its highly
touted street crimes unit to identified high-crime areas. Finally, it must be
noted that in 1991, prior to Giuliani's administration, New York Mayor
David Dinkins had added 7,000 new police officers to the sworn force. This
additional deployment of cops on the beat, no doubt, had some impact on
crime reduction.

An article of considerable interest recently appeared in the *British Journal
of Criminology*, entitled "The Rise and Fall of New York Murder: Zero Tolerance or Crack's Decline?" The authors examined New York City homicide
rates between 1985 and 1990 and noted that there was a 63% increase during
this time, from 1,384 in 1985 to 2,245 in 1990. The authors suggest that the
dramatic rise of New York City's murder rate from 1985 through 1990 had to
do with the sudden emergence of the crack cocaine markets beginning in
1985. Their research shows that as crack cocaine addiction reached epidemic
stages in the last half of the 1980s, the murder rate in New York City skyrock-
eted. Then, as crack cocaine fell off as the drug of choice in the 1990s, the
New York murder rate concurrently fell into decline. The authors conclude

that the falling murder rate more likely was related to patterns of crack cocaine use than to aggressive policing:

> When crime rises, no one wants to take the blame, but when it falls, everyone wants the credit. In New York, only a circumstantial case has been made for the link between aggressive policing and falling crime, and yet the media and politicians have already reached a verdict, ignoring other credible suspects. Among the most convincing explanations for the rise and fall of New York murder in the last decade of the [twentieth] century is the simultaneous rise and fall of crack cocaine. (Bowling, 1999, p. 12)

Another recently published academic study compared New York City homicide rates and their decline with homicide rates in several other major U.S. cities including San Francisco; San Jose; Cleveland; San Diego; Washington, D.C.; and Detroit. That study's conclusions "refute the claim that the recent decrease in New York's homicide rate is more dramatic than that of any other U.S. city" (Joanes, 2000, pp. 299–300). The author concludes, "The fact the other cities employing different policing strategies experience greater declines in their crime rates calls into question the claim that NYPD's tactics have produced an unrivaled decrease in crime" (Joanes, p. 300).

Despite emerging evidence to the contrary, the philosophy of aggressive New York-style policing with its proclaimed crime reduction successes continues to receive accolades as a national model; however, as we all know, to every action there is a reaction. On February 4, 1999, unarmed Amadou Diallo was shot and killed by New York City police as he crouched in the foyer of an apartment building. When the shooting was over, 41 police bullets had been fired. This single incident led critics to take a closer look at New York City policing. After receiving numerous citizen complaints, the Office of the Attorney General for the state of New York initiated a study of the NYPD stop-and-frisk strategy. While the stop-and-frisk tactic is legal, allowing police to temporarily detain, question, and, at times, search civilians on the street, it has the potential for abuse if not conducted properly. New York Attorney General Eliot Spitzer, in his initial findings and after meeting with several New York City citizens' groups, concluded that "road blocks, car stops, stop-and-frisk street encounters, and order maintenance law enforcement techniques all were consistently cited as major sources of tension between NYPD and minority New Yorkers" (New York Attorney General's Office, 1999, p. 4). In fact, just days following the police beating and sodomization of Haitian immigrant Abner Louima with a toilet plunger inside a bathroom at Brooklyn's 70th Police Precinct, Mayor Giuliani created a task force on police-community relations. The goal of the mayor's task force was to foster better communication and understanding among members of the police department and residents of New York City. In policing, a proper balance must always be maintained between dutiful enforcement of the law and protection of the guaranteed rights of the citizenry.

New York City is New York City; its cyclical crime trends, like those in any other city, are probably best understood through an assessment of myriad contributing factors, not by the introduction of a single police initiative. As one researcher notes, "Some strong claims have been made by police chiefs about the 'success' of their strategies and tactics, but the fact is that we still do not really know which strategies are most effective and why" (Bowling, 1999, p. 10).

In the city of New York in the 1990s, two very strong personalities wished to take credit for the significant decrease in crime rates – Mayor Giuliani and Police Commissioner Bratton. Conservative commentator George Will recently reported, "In New York City, between 1993 and 2001, thanks largely to the measures instituted while Bratton was Mayor Rudy Giuliani's Police Commissioner between 1994 and 1996, crime was reduced 64% – including a 75% decrease in gun homicides" (Will, 2003). Will's commentary , however, does not make sense. Forget the fact that the murder and crime rates in New York City began to fall in 1991, several years before Bratton became commissioner, and that Will gives credit to Bratton for reducing crime rates in New York for five years after Bratton departed; the fact is, there is no mortal human being, regardless of his or her intelligence, hindsight, and foresight, who could oversee a police department for two years and legitimately take credit for a decline in crime that spanned eight years. In Bratton's case, he seemed to accept the praise graciously and, in fact, was later hired to perform the same magic in Los Angeles. If he can do a repeat performance, he will be regarded as the best police chief in the nation.

In policing, as in any other professional endeavor, humility is the best thing one can ever hope for. At times, police officials must accept the realization that certain factors are beyond their control and, in fact, are beyond the ability of developed practice and science to explain. Outside factors largely control the wax and wane of crime trends, not the police and their tactics. This is not to say that police administrators must surrender their efforts to seek improved crime-fighting methods but rather that they must be careful not to overstate incremental successes. It is interesting to reflect back upon the comments of former New York City Police Commissioner Robert J. McGuire, who, in the 1970s, was asked to explain to reporters what he and his department had done to produce a drop in the city's homicide rates from one year to another. An observer present at the news conference noted,

> Although he [McGuire] admitted that he had been tempted to take credit for the murder decrease, [he] told reporters that he doubted that the police department had in any way affected the homicide rate. "Murders," the Commissioner said, "seem to have a life of their own, and to be relatively immune from police intervention." (White, Fyfe, Campbell, & Goldkamp, 2003, p. 194)

Conventional wisdom has not changed in the intervening years. Current thinking among both criminal justice practitioners and scholars is that, in general, homicide rates are manifestations of social and economic variables over which police have little control (White, Fyfe, Campbell, & Goldkamp, 2003, p. 195).

Chicago and New York were two very different cities at the time Hillard became Chicago's superintendent. To be sure, the crime strategies of each department stood in sharp contract to one another. Hillard had a responsibility to be concerned with Chicago, not New York. His strategy was to fight crime by forging a partnership with the community. As Chicago Congressman Danny Davis stated,

> I'm always intrigued by the notion that police are going to stop violence. . . . It's the most ludicrous thing I've ever heard. The mere presence of additional law enforcement personnel can help, but we need people to be mentors, big brothers, scout leaders; we need to foster the evolution and development of certain morale values. (Huppke & Heinzmann, 2004, p. 10)

A *Chicago Tribune* editorial entitled "Attacking Murder in Chicago" stated, "Law enforcement can only do so much. The best weapon against homicide and other violent crimes is the determination of neighborhood residents to no longer tolerate shooting galleries in their midst" ("Attacking," 2003). Perhaps a citizen, who participated in a neighborhood meeting with Chicago police, said it best: "This is a people issue. People know they need the police, and police know they need the people. We just can't pit ourselves against each other" (Chicago Police Department, 2000, p. 6). If this was indeed a "people issue," Mayor Daley had chosen the right man to be superintendent of police. Terry Hillard's "people skills" were unparalleled.

Hillard felt comfortable with the direction he and the Chicago Police Department were headed as he assumed the superintendency, and the community would assuredly become partners with the police in their fight against crime. The adoption of a policing philosophy geared toward community policing should not be confused with a "soft on crime" approach. Quite to the contrary, the strategy was to marshal all available resources – including nearly three million citizens – in a concerted effort to reduce violence and crime. Terry Hillard spent most of his career as a gangs specialist, and he would go after gangs, guns, and drugs with a vengeance.

Chapter 7

POLICING CHICAGO STREETS: GANGS, GUNS, AND DRUGS

Thousands of young businessmen are recruited and put to work in the tough economic environment of Chicago every year. In the heart of this urban mecca of commerce, they learn their trade and how to interact and deal with the competition, most of whom are equally well skilled. If they're aggressive, the payoff is good. It is not unusual for a young salesperson to sell $10,000 worth of product in a week. On a commission of roughly 20%, a successful salesperson can easily earn more than $100,000 per year to buy a new vehicle, take care of his or her family, and have extra cash for personal enjoyment. The educational requirements for this position are not restrictive; applicants need not have an MBA from a prestigious business school. Most, in fact, are African-American and Hispanic youths from the streets of Chicago. The product for sale is illicit drugs, and they work for street gangs.

The *Chicago Tribune* recently documented the story of 17-year-old Andre Colvin, who by the age of 15 was making $2,000 per week, had three cars including a Ford Explorer, and carried a gun. He wasn't even old enough to have a driver's license under Illinois law. Fortunately, Colvin was smarter than most, for he had realized that retirement from this job was highly improbable. He was making an effort to get out of the business, get an education, and get on with his life. Although the money was alluring, he had learned, as the statistics show, that most youths in his situation eventually end up in prison or dead (Huppke, 2004, p. 14).

The economic reality of impoverished minorities in and of itself is a powerful incentive to join a gang and traffic drugs. As one high-ranking gang leader operating in the Robert Taylor Homes said in discussing gang intervention strategies:

> What are they going to give me? Teach me how to work a minimum wage job? Shit, I got a family; I got investments. At least we take care of the people in our Nation [gang]. Shit, even in all our buildings, if people support us then we make sure they ain't starvin, you know? They got food to eat and clothes for their kids. You got something better than that? Bring it on! But, don't bring that "go to school" shit when education don't guarantee you a good job. (Huff, 1996, p. 248)

As the *Tribune* article so accurately states,

> While downtown bankers and business people wrestle with multi-million dollar transactions, this economic engine (the sales of illicit drugs) outside the loop is efficiently generating untold millions every year – and costing hundreds of people their lives. (Huppke, 2004, p. 1)

In the June 13, 2004, Sunday edition of the *Chicago Tribune*, an article ran entitled "Gangs Built on Corporate Mentality." What was different about this article was its placement. The story was published headlining the newspaper's business section. The article reported that

> The Black Gangster Disciples ran a business that was the envy of Chicago's underground economy. The South Side gang's distribution network for heroin and crack cocaine brought in as much as $300,000 a day. . . . The Gangster Disciples and the Black Gangster Disciples adopted a pyramid-type organization led by a CEO-type leader. Each had its own Board of Directors that held regular meetings. . . . They owned a long list of business enterprises, including clothing stores, grocery stores, jewelry stores, restaurants, and air-brush shops. (Chandler, 2004, p. 9)

To understand the scope of the gang problem in Chicago, one need only consider the number of gang-related homicides. In a survey conducted by the U.S. Department of Justice, it was found that more than half of all homicides in Los Angeles and Chicago were reported to be gang-related in 2001 (59% and 53%, respectively). The total number of gang-related homicides (698) in these two cities alone was greater than the total number of gang-related homicides (637) reported by 130 other cities with gang problems with a population of 100,000 or more. The same study indicated that Cook County, Illinois, led the nation among the largest number of cities reporting gang activity – 118 in total (U.S. Department of Justice, Office of Juvenile Justice and Delinquency, 2003, p. 1). The United States Attorney for the Northern District of Illinois has estimated that Chicago has some 125 street gangs with more than 100,000 members. At least 20,000, and possibly as many as 30,000, are hardcore gang members. The Chicago Police Department has identified 130 individual gangs (Chicago Police Department, 2003, p. 8). These statistics alone indicate that Chicago is unique, rivaled only by Los Angeles, in the scope and magnitude of entrenched gangs and the problems such gangs create within the community and for police.

The history of Chicago gangs dates back more than a century, but the street gangs of today are very different from those in years past. They are much more violent, primarily because of their involvement in drug trafficking and their propensity to use weapons to protect their turfs and their share of the lucrative drug market. It is interesting to note that prior to the 1970s, Chicago gangs were not involved in drug trafficking to any large extent; however, "by the late 1970s, older African-American adult gang members in Chicago were reported to be significantly involved in drug dealing" (Howell & Decker, 1999).

The Chicago street gangs in operation today had their genesis in the 1960s with the emergence of the Black Peace Stone (P-Stone)Rangers. At that time, gang leader Jeff Fort organized some 50 individual street gangs, which were previously operating independently, into a single organization named the Black P-Stone Nation. The organization was controlled by a commission of 21 members called the "Main 21." The group promoted itself as a civic-minded community organization designed to improve conditions of the urban poor. Using this guise, the group made application for and received a federal grant totaling $1.4 million for specified antipoverty initiatives. In reality, the grant money was used to fund and promote the gang's criminal endeavors. The ruse was discovered through a federal grand jury investigation, and Fort was eventually sent to federal prison for mismanagement of federal monies.

A few years after the formation of the Black P-Stone Rangers, the Black Disciples, led by David Barksdale, and the Gangster Disciples, led by Larry Hoover, unified to form the Black Gangster Disciple Nation. Throughout the 1970s, the Black P-Stone Nation and the Black Gangster Disciple Nation controlled Chicago's gang drug trade and other illegal gang enterprises, and they became bitter rivals, expressing their anger by initiating the bloodiest gang wars in Chicago history (Chicago Crime Commission, 1995; Chicago Police Department, 2003).

Gangster Disciple leader Larry Hoover was convicted of murdering a rival gang member in 1974 and sent to state prison for 200 years. Operating from his prison cell, Hoover exerted great authority and power. It is said that Hoover is the architect of the current macro structure of Chicago gangs. He also made use of his prison time to organize Chicago gangs within the walls of the Illinois Department of Corrections. In the 1980s, Hoover orchestrated a gang coalition whereby two distinct alliances were formed: the "People" Nation and the "Folk" Nation. The gangs, or "sets," originally aligned with the Black P-Stone Nation aligned themselves with the People Nation; the sets originally aligned with the Black Gangster Disciple Nation aligned themselves with the Folk Nation (Chicago Crime Commission, 1995, p. 11; Chicago Police Department, 2003).

The five largest street gangs in Chicago are the Black Gangster Disciple Nation and the Maniac Nation Disciples, who are Folks, and the Vice Lords, the Latin Kings, and the Black Peace Stone Nation, who are People. The Black Gangster Disciples alone have from 18,000 to 25,000 members and control approximately two-thirds of the lucrative drug trafficking in low-income public housing complexes in Chicago. Although the most widespread and profitable criminal activity of today's gangs is drug trafficking, other illicit endeavors include murder for hire, extortion, vehicle theft/chop shops, burglary, robbery, prostitution, and other crimes committed for financial gain.

Although the People Nation gangs and the Folk Nation gangs still maintain allegiance in some form to their nations, such allegiances have weakened substantially in recent years, and interalliance feuds often occur. There have been gang wars, for instance, between the Gangster Disciples and the Black Disciples even though they are both Folks, and there have been similar brawls and shootings between the Vice Lords and the Black Peace Stone Rangers even though both gangs are People. Such feuding has caused many gangs to adopt an "every man for himself" mentality. Known as "renegades," many of these gang-bangers have just one allegiance: money.

The early to mid-1980s saw rapid growth in the use of cocaine as crack became the drug of choice in the inner cities (Howell & Decker, 1999). Cocaine is a highly addictive drug. Smoking crack cocaine allows extremely high doses of cocaine to reach the brain very quickly. Freebasing, or smoking crack cocaine, brings an intense and immediate high and can produce particularly aggressive paranoid behavior in users.

Like many businesses, there is always a competitive market for a commodity that is in high demand. The trafficking of illicit drugs is no different. Market control for profit is contingent upon several factors, including the control of territory, customer base, and the recruitment of salesmen who are aggressive and loyal to the "company." This control for market share leads to turf battles between competitive gangs, and turf battles become serious business – intimidation, violence, and death result.

The *Chicago Tribune*, in a story examining the economic impact of gang drug trade, revealed, "The drug dealers [whom they] talked to estimate that one active building in the Dearborn low-income house development complex can generate $20,000 to $30,000 a day in sales" (Huppke, 2004, p. 14). There are 16 buildings in that single complex. The sales and profit margin for illicit drugs are staggering. In 1999 alone, Chicago police seized 6,000 pounds of cocaine, 10,000 pounds of marijuana, 72,000 ecstasy pills, and various other narcotics worth an estimated street value of $350 million.

In attempts to explain why gangs are thriving in Chicago and other jurisdictions, two factors are most often cited. First and foremost, it is the economy. Gang leaders, who possess little education and extensive criminal records, are virtually unemployable. Even the service industries, paying minimum wage, are reluctant to hire ex-convicts and felons. Where else can individuals in such a predicament earn up to $150,000 per year? The second factor has to do with a decline in the social structures of inner city neighborhoods. Chicago, like many cities, has seen a massive exodus of its white middle class, who fled the inner cities for the suburbs, seeking job opportunities and upward mobility. The thriving steel mills and industrial businesses that once offered a good living wage to blue-collar workers who possessed limited education and work skills began to rapidly disappear. Dan Swinney, executive director of the Center for Labor and Community Research, told the *Chicago Tribune* that "the bottom dropped out in the 1980s, when companies like U.S. Steel, Wisconsin Steel, and Sunbeam shut down." During that decade, 150,000 high-paying, blue-collar manufacturing jobs were lost. An additional 50,000 manufacturing jobs left Chicago in the 1990s, leaving only service-oriented jobs that paid about one-third of a factory worker's salary (Huppke, 2004, p. 14).

In a study commissioned by the U.S. Department of Justice, Howell and Decker (1999) point out:

> The decline of manufacturing jobs in the 1970s and the development of technological and service industries led to economic restructuring in many cities. New jobs were created, but they were in the suburbs, leaving unqualified minorities in the inner cities. Dramatic increases in unemployment resulted, especially among minority males, and high employment rates were mainly concentrated in specific geographic areas. Drug markets provided "work" for displaced workers, and the growing popularity of crack cocaine opened new opportunities to make money. (p. 3)

Chicago youths are actively recruited by gangs to perform various tasks, including carrying drugs or guns, serving as "lookouts" for rival gangs and police, or serving as sex slaves for older gang members. The vast majority of gang members are male, are either African American or Hispanic, have deprived backgrounds, and come from dysfunctional families or disrupted social environments. The benefits of joining a gang include personal and family protection, recognition, fellowship, and brotherhood. The gang offers structure, organization, and discipline to insecure and wayward youths possessing limited resources. Gang membership brings with it identification and prestige, as well as alliances and loyalties to be shared with young people in similar situations and with older, dominant male role models. In a very real sense, the gangs become the family these youths have never known. Once they become gang members, young people see older members driving expensive cars, wearing gold jewelry, and carrying wads of cash. Such impressive displays of success send a clear message that crime pays.

Gangs are entrenched in symbolism. The clothing they wear, the hand signs they throw, the graffiti they paint, and the tattoos they display are all identifiers indicative of allegiance to a specific gang. These are impoverished youths who, by virtue of joining a gang, have a chance to be somebody. Gang membership also charts out "turfs" within Chicago where young people know they will be protected and taken care of, distinguished from other areas controlled by rival gangs where they know they will be in danger.

Professional sports team athletic wear, logos, and colors serve to identify and symbolize membership in individual Chicago gangs. The Vice Lords and Black P-Stones, for instance, wear Chicago Bulls athletic wear, while the Black Gangster Disciples wear Boston Celtics logos, clothing, and colors. Other gangs wear Atlanta Falcons, Boston Red Sox, Dallas Cowboys, Charlotte Hornets, Chicago Black Hawks, or Colorado Rockies colors. This clothing is worn in two different ways. The Folk Nation gangs wear clothing and accessories such as hats, belts, and earrings to the right side of their bodies. The People Nation gangs wear clothing and accessories to the left. If innocent inner city youths are not clued in on the symbolism of gangs, they can inadvertently show disrespect, which could lead to gang-initiated retribution in the form of a beating or even death. Or, as has happened on far too many occasions, innocent young people are shot down on the streets by gunfire exchanged between rival gangs because of mistaken identity. As the *Chicago Tribune* reports, "Many of the young men who kill or are killed grow up on the streets divided by constantly disputed gang boundaries, where the distance between safety and mortal danger can be two lanes of asphalt and a crumbling sidewalk" (Huppke & Heinzmann, 2004, p. 10). Such was the case with 25-year-old Joseph Budakovic, who was shot and killed by gang members who mistakenly took him for a member of a rival gang. Budakovic did not belong to a gang. He was merely at the wrong place at the wrong time and paid for it with his life.

The lack of training and work opportunities for minority youths, combined with the emergence of a highly profitable enterprise in drug trafficking and their need to meaningfully define their identity, has allowed Chicago gangs to thrive. For the protection of their share of real estate (or turf) and their marketing base for the distribution of drugs, violence has become a necessary means to an end. The tools of their trade are firearms, and the result is open warfare on the streets, which is primarily responsible for the extraordinary number of murders recorded year after year in Chicago.

Environmental design and architecture of living places have contributed to the problem. The Chicago Housing Authority (CHA) provides housing for 139,000 residents in family developments, Section 8 rent subsidies, and senior living. The Authority administers 20 housing developments, including the renowned Cabrini Green Homes, Robert Taylor Homes, ABLA Homes (ABLA is an acronym for four housing developments constituted on one large site and includes the Jane Adams Homes, the Brooks Homes, Loomis Courts, and the Abbott Apartments), and Dearborn Homes. These and other complexes are notorious for gang activity and have been cited nationally as examples of failed public housing policy. According to the CHA,

> What began in the 1930s as a noble and well-intentioned effort to provide transitional housing for low-income families expanded dramatically in the 1950s and 1960s and eventually evolved into the isolated islands of poverty and crime widely associated with public housing. (Chicago Housing Authority, 2004)

The Robert Taylor Homes were built in 1962 on the city's South Side and were composed of 28, 16-story high-rise buildings. When they were built, they were the largest public housing complex in America. At one time, more than 4,300 individual housing units were available for occupancy. The Robert Taylor Homes isolated urban poor minorities in one massive housing development and were once dubbed "the biggest concentration of poverty in America." The homes are currently undergoing extensive demolition and reconstruction. Most of the original buildings have been razed; only five remain, housing 1,800 residents. The Authority has plans to rebuild 2,388 new units, which will be a combination of mixed rental and privately owned units.

The Cabrini Green Homes were built in 1942 and are just blocks from Michigan Avenue. Originally, Cabrini Green was home to about 15,000 residents, but it currently houses only 4,700. The units are run down and dirty and present many public health problems for residents. The Dearborn Homes, built in 1950, house 800 residents in 16, 6- and 9-story buildings; the ALBA Homes, built in 1938, have 1,467 individual units.

The Chicago Housing Authority has a long history of mismanagement and lawlessness, which finally prompted 1995 Federal Housing Authority Secretary Henry Cisneros to step in and take over management of the Authority. Since that date, the CHA, with the assistance of the U.S. Department of Housing and Urban Development, has developed a ten-year plan to rebuild and rehabilitate 25,000 housing units by 2009. The plan calls for the demolition of a number of high rises and the creation of new mixed-income communities with contemporary town homes and low-rise buildings – a process known as gentrification (Chicago Housing Authority, 2004).

Minority children are constantly exposed to the violence and danger that permeate the poverty-stricken Chicago public housing environment. They are not there by choice, but, in fact, many are babies of teenagers, forced to grow up in rat-infested, gang-controlled drug houses. Furthermore, their parents are helpless in offering protection. The gangs are in control, and they do not understand the concept of nurturing and care. Parents are unable to protect their children, and there is a plethora of tragic incidents of brutality, mayhem, and murder that demonstrate the plight of these youths.

Eric Morse was a 5-year-old resident of the Ida B. Wells Housing Development Complex on the South Side of Chicago. In October 1994, Eric was tortured and thrown from the 14th floor of the high rise. The assailants were two young boys, one ten and the other 11 years old.

Dantrell Davis was a 7-year-old boy walking to school, accompanied by his mother. A shot fired from the 10th floor of Cabrini Green Public Housing building hit Dantrell in the face, and he died instantly.

Robert "Yummy" Sandrifer was a gang member with the Black Disciples. He was only 11 years old. He had recently shot three other Chicago youths, aged 14, 16, and 17 years, in a gang-related shooting. He was silenced by his fellow Black Disciples in order to keep him from talking to police. Yummy's body was found dumped under a viaduct with a bullet through the head.

Girl X (her name was not released by police for purposes of protection) was a 4'8", 64-pound girl living in the Cabrini Green Housing Complex. In February 1997, this 9-year-old girl was found unconscious in the stairwell of her apartment building. She had been raped, choked, poisoned, and marked with gang graffiti scribbled on her body. She survived but is maimed and crippled for life.

The Chicago Housing Authority's ten-year plan to rehabilitate, rebuild, and redistribute living spaces for poverty-stricken residents is an experiment in action. Some argue that gentrification will promote racial, economic, and social integration, resulting in improved lives for the citizens. Critics contend that moving the impoverished to new living spaces does not address the fact that they are still poor. Yes, the walls will be painted and the carpets will be clean in the new housing structures, but the inhabitants' day-to-day lives – educational, employment, and economic opportunities – will be unaltered.

It is also unclear how the redistribution of living spaces within Chicago will affect street gang activity. Some believe that by tearing down the troubled housing-complex high rises and moving people to more dispersed locations, gang activity will naturally subside. Others believe that no matter how people are dispersed and housed, gangs, the "economic engine" of drug trafficking, will survive. In fact, there is one theory that claims that as the CHA ten-year plan is implemented, gang wars and deaths will increase because gang territories and "turfs" will be disrupted. Bloody and bitter battles between rival gangs to establish or re-establish dominant territory for the control of criminal activity may be the result. A black Chicago police officer who has worked in the Chicago housing complexes for years and grew up there himself is doubtful about gentrification:

> The people who are being relocated are going to take what they do wherever they go. I think it is more than rehabbing buildings and landscapes. These people need help. They are undereducated and chronically unemployed. I go into 200 of their homes a week. I see one computer and, more amazingly, I don't see any books. These kids have no role models except the drug dealers. Like all of us, they want nice things, and the only means they see as being available to get nice things is to follow their role models – the drug dealers. Many of the kids have a lot of promise but just give up because they live in hopeless situations. So, changing that area? The area will change. But where these seeds are put the same weeds are going to grow without other changes.

Small handguns carried by criminals and gang members are the tools of their trade. Their purpose is to intimidate, injure, and kill crime victims, rival criminals, and police officers. Handguns are cheap, easy to conceal, and easily disposable. With one pull of a trigger, the gun powder explodes and sends a projectile of lead speeding at a velocity of 1,000–1,500 feet per second into the body of the human target. Most gun-related homicides occur at a distance of less than seven yards between the shooter and the victim. If the bullet strikes the brain or the central nervous system, incapacitation and death are immediate; if the bullet strikes a major organ or artery, the victim will bleed to death in a short time; and if the bullet strikes a bone, fragmentation occurs and splinters of bone and lead are scattered throughout the body, thereby inflicting multiple internal injuries. Stories of the Wild West seem mild when compared with the urban warfare that occurs daily on the streets of American cities. Easy access to handguns and a disrespect for human life have turned city streets into shooting galleries.

Annual reports from the Chicago Police Department indicate that more than 10,000 firearms are recovered each year on the city streets. It is not surprising that firearms are the weapon of choice in nearly 80% of all Chicago murders and that young minority males are most often the victims and the offenders in cases involving murder. An analysis by the *Chicago Tribune* indicates some startling statistics in regard to the age, gender, and minority status of both the victims and perpetrators of homicides in Chicago:

> Sixty-four percent of the 598 homicide victims in 2003 were between 17 and 30 years of age; 72.6% of those murdered were black, while 17% were Hispanic. The suspected killers were similar in comparison to the victims: 73% of the suspected killers had prior arrests; 74% of the suspected killers were black, and 20% were Hispanic. In all 87% of those killed and 90% of those believed to be the killers were male. A startling 92% of murder victims were black or Hispanic; while 94% of the suspected murderers were black or Hispanic. (Huppke & Heinzmann, 2004, p. 11)

Chicago has one of the most restrictive ordinances in the country when it comes to gun ownership, yet more than 140,000 firearms have been confiscated by Chicago police since 1995. This is indisputably only a small fraction of the firearms actually on the streets. Gangs, guns, and drugs are a dangerous triad of factors creating a community of violence in Chicago. There is little surprise that Chicago battles murder as an intractable and persistent social phenomenon. Since 1995, more than 6,700 people have been murdered in Chicago, and of those, 80% of the victims died as the result of an incident involving a firearm.

Firearms are a necessary tool in drug trafficking, and Chicago has become a predominant national distribution center for drugs. Chicago police seize more than 10,000 weapons per year, whereas gun recoveries in Los Angeles and New York are considerably lower – 6,985 and 3,981 respectively in 2003 (Heinzmann, 2004, p. 5). A recent study by the *Chicago Tribune* revealed,

> As Chicago toughened local restrictions on owning and selling firearms, gangs began turning to the homeland of their grandparents for firepower. Across the south, gun laws are much more lenient than in the north. Anyone with a Mississippi ID can walk into a dealer's shop and get as many guns as desired. (Heinzmann, 2004, p. 5)

There has been a pipeline of guns and drugs being transported to and from Mississippi and other states where gun purchasing laws are more lenient. The gangs recruit "straw buyers" who have no previous criminal record and are able to purchase caches of cheap weapons that gangs refer to as "throw aways." In many cases, the serial numbers on the guns are scratched out so that they cannot be traced. The beauty of this system is that gangs do not have to steal weapons; they can use weapons that have been purchased legally and simply dispose of them once they have been used in the commission of a crime. These weapons are difficult to trace back to the gang or its members.

The *Chicago Tribune* documented the story of a straw buyer named Charles Westbrooks from Jonestown, Mississippi. Westbrooks was described as a good kid, who was recruited by a cousin from Chicago to buy guns for the Mickey Cobra Chicago Street Gang. The business plan was simple: "Guns would come up to Chicago; marijuana would go back to the Delta for Westbrooks to peddle"

(Heinzmann, 2004, p. 1). The business plan worked for a while until federal Alcohol, Tobacco, and Firearms agents moved in and arrested Westbrooks. He was sentenced to 33 months in federal prison for gun trafficking. In 2001 alone, Westbrooks bought at least 95 guns that were destined for the hands of the Mickey Cobras in Chicago (Heinzmann, 2004, p. 5).

The Chicago Police Department and the Federal Bureau of Alcohol, Tobacco, and Firearms (BATF) have been working cooperatively over the past few years to aggressively trace crime guns taken off of Chicago streets. Data collected through this process clearly demonstrates that there is a lucrative black market established for the sole purpose of providing Chicago gangs with weapons to be used for criminal purposes. Nearly 90% of crime guns confiscated by Chicago police officers are guns that had been purchased legally and then sold to gang members.

In 2002, the BATF traced 8,570 crime guns taken from the streets of Chicago. Only 4,583 (53%) of the guns traced could be linked to the purchaser, and only 3,054 (35.6%) could be linked to both the purchaser and processor seller. The study found that 2,298 (57%) of the traceable weapons were purchased from federally licensed gun dealers in nearby suburban communities or downstate Illinois; 478 (10%) were purchased from federally licensed gun dealers in Indiana; 445 (9.7%) were purchased legally in the state of Mississippi; and 738 (16%) were legally purchased in other states, including Wisconsin, Kentucky, Georgia, Tennessee, Texas, and Arkansas. The primary weapon of choice is the handgun, comprising 86% of those confiscated and traced. Fifty-one percent were semiautomatic pistols, and 34% were revolvers. Fourteen percent were long guns, meaning rifles or shotguns (U.S. Department of the Treasury, 2002).

The disparity in laws from state to state pertaining to firearms ownership and purchasing makes gun running a thriving business. If Chicago firearms laws are restrictive, it is not much of an inconvenience to go to the suburbs, Indiana, or Mississippi. Nearly 41% of crime guns recovered in Chicago were first purchased from legal gun dealers 250 miles or more from Chicago. It is also telling that 41% of traced crime guns were purchased from 12 identified federally licensed gun dealers (U.S. Department of the Treasury, 2002, p. 6). In other words, straw dealers go to gun shops where the owners are cooperative and don't ask a lot of questions. There is little doubt that these federally licensed dealers know that the guns are being purchased for illegal activity, but they do not see that reality as being their problem. In one conversation between a federally licensed gun dealer and an undercover police officer posing as a gang straw buyer, the dealer recommended hollow-point bullets as ideal for street shootings since they would be less likely to hit bystanders. In another case, the undercover officer told the dealer that someone had come around and started a little trouble and that he needed a little more firepower. The gun dealer showed him several Lorcin handguns, as well as a military style AR-15 rifle with a price tag of $1,400 (Carpenter, 1999).

The *Chicago Sun-Times* documented the story of 3-year-old Angel Thomas of East 102nd Avenue in Chicago. On November 12, 2003, Angel was shot at point-blank range in the chest with a .38 caliber revolver while she lay asleep in her bed. The alleged killer and his two accomplices had been living with the victim's mother before she threw them out for not paying rent and for keeping guns around her children. They also were said to be upset because they didn't like the spaghetti she had cooked for them. They returned intent on killing the entire family but took their rage out on 3-year-old Angel and fled. All three implicated in the murder were alleged members of the Gangster Disciples. The three weapons confiscated were traced back to Mississippi and Indiana (Main & Sweeney, 2004).

Chicago police know the tragedy of imported guns firsthand. In the summer of 1998 and in the winter of 1999, two top-rate police officers were shot and killed in separate incidents by gang members possessing weapons purchased by straw buyers. Officer Michael Ceriale was killed by a .357 caliber revolver fired by a 16-year-old member of the Gangster Disciples. The weapon was purchased by straw buyer Ezra Evans at Chuck's Gun Shop in the Chicago suburb of Riverdale just months earlier. According to police, Evans was found to have purchased 13 handguns over the course of 11 months in 1997 and 1998, all of which were turned over to two members of the Gangster Disciples street gang (Carpenter, 1999).

John Knight was an experienced tactical officer who pulled over a gang member named John C. Scott for suspicion of crack cocaine possession. Scott exited his vehicle and began to flee on foot. As Officer Knight started to jump out of his unmarked squad car to give chase, a tiny orange dot illuminated his forehead. Scott emptied his gun, killing Knight and wounding his partner. The Ruger 9-mm pistol equipped with laser sight used in the shooting was purchased by a straw buyer in downstate Springfield, Illinois (Carpenter, 1999).

The organization Americans for Gun Safety conducted a study of guns sold by federally licensed gun dealers between 1996 and 2000 who were linked to crimes or considered suspicious. The top two gun dealers on the list were Chuck's Guns in Riverdale, Illinois, with 2,370 such guns sold, and Don's Guns and Galleries in Indianapolis, Indiana, with 2,294 guns sold. The gun that killed Officer Ceriale was purchased at Chuck's Guns, and two of the three weapons recovered in the shooting incident that killed Angel Thomas were purchased at Don's Guns (Main & Sweeney, 2004).

The most prevalent illicit drugs available on the streets of Chicago are crack cocaine, powdered cocaine, marijuana, and heroin. Chicago is one of only two American cities that serve as a primary national market for all of these illicit drugs (the other being New York City). National drug experts estimate that several tons of cocaine are transported to Chicago annually. The Office of National Drug Control Policy reported that Chicago recorded 54,205 drug-related arrests in 2002, of which 26,582 were for possession of a controlled substance; 16,227 Chicagoans were admitted to emergency treatment facilities for cocaine abuse and 12,982 for heroin abuse that same year (Office of National Drug Control Policy, 2004, pp. 4, 9).

According to a study by the National Institute of Justice, Chicago drug users have little problem buying their drugs of choice. On a scale from one to ten, with one being "not difficult at all" and ten being "extremely difficult," drug users in Chicago rated the difficulty level for purchasing cocaine, crack, heroin, and marijuana as "one" (Office of National Drug Control Policy, p. 83). The drugs are not only available, but also moderately priced. One rock of crack cocaine can be purchased for $5 to $20; a gram of crack cocaine goes for $50 to $150; and a gram of powdered cocaine costs $125. Heroin is similarly priced, going for $125 per gram or $20 for one hit. Marijuana costs about $10 for a loose bag, or $80 to $200 per ounce. Most drug purchases occur in open air drug markets, public housing developments, private residences, and other gang-controlled sites (Office of National Drug Control Policy, p. 90).

The connection between crime and drug use is astonishingly apparent when one considers that 85% of adult male arrestees in Chicago in 2002 tested positive for some type of drug, either cocaine, opiates, marijuana, methamphetamine, PCP, or some combination thereof. Forty-eight percent of those arrested tested positive for cocaine; 26% tested positive for opiates (heroin); and 49% of the Chicago arrestees tested positive for marijuana (Office of National Drug Control Policy, p. 5). Violence and collateral criminal activity also often are associated with the distribution and use of cocaine, crack cocaine, opiates, and marijuana:

> Law enforcement reports that rivalries between distribution groups, especially gangs, account for most cocaine-related violence, much of which involves increases in homicides, armed robberies, and assaults when distributors of crack cocaine move into new market areas. (U.S. Department of Justice, 2003, p. 2)

Although more violent criminal behavior is exhibited by crack cocaine users than by users of marijuana or heroin, collateral criminal activity is associated with all categories of drug usage. The overwhelming need for users to support their drug habits also often leads them into nonviolent criminal activity including prostitution, burglary, theft, and drug distribution.

Chicago has been identified as a primary illicit drug wholesale distribution center in the United States for all three drugs – cocaine, heroin, and marijuana. Chicago's drug trade is not limited to inner-city users. Chicago drug markets supply users representing all socioeconomic, ethnic, and racial categories. White upper- and middle-class Chicagoans and suburbanites, as well as the inner-city impoverished, turn to Chicago gangs for the purchase of illegal drugs. A rock of cocaine, a dose of heroin, or a marijuana joint that is purchased on a street corner in Chicago has traveled thousands of miles by any combination of transport, including boat, air, rail, commercial trucking, or private vehicle. The majority of illicit drugs in Chicago are transported from South America or Mexico through the Mexico-Central America Corridor. It is estimated that 72% of all cocaine and a large percentage of the heroin and marijuana imported to the United States follows the Mexico-Central America transportation route, while 26% of cocaine, heroin, and marijuana enters the United States through the Caribbean Corridor. An estimated 90% of all cocaine on the streets of Chicago comes from Columbia. A small percentage of the heroin available in Chicago is transported from southeastern or southwestern Asia (U.S. Department of Justice, 2004, p. 7).

South American countries are the largest producers of cocaine and heroin destined for the United States and Chicago. Columbia, Peru, and Bolivia produce cocaine, while Columbia alone produces the majority of opiate (heroin) product. Mexico is the chief supplier of marijuana and black tar heroin. A smaller percentage of marijuana is imported from Jamaica and Canada or is domestically grown in the United States. In 2001, for example, the National Drug Intelligence Center detected 521 metric tons of cocaine departing South America and moving toward the United States (U.S. Department of Justice, 2004, p. 5). These drugs are transported by boat to rendezvous points off the coasts of Southern Mexico in the Pacific Ocean to the west or by way of the Caribbean Sea to the east, where Mexican drug traffickers load the goods. Mexican drug trafficking organizations then transport the drugs on land, by vehicle, or by small aircraft through Mexico to the southwestern U.S. border. Nearly 80% of the cocaine seized at ports of entry along the U.S./Mexican border in 2001 was seized in border towns in California, Arizona, and Texas (U.S. Department of Justice, 2003, p. 6). Marijuana is produced primarily in Mexico and follows the same transportation route into the United States. Texas, Arizona, California, and New Mexico continue to account for the vast majority of marijuana seized.

Heroin is often transported in a manner somewhat different than cocaine and marijuana. The primary market areas for heroin are Chicago, New York City, and Los Angeles. It is estimated that 13 to 18 metric tons of heroin enter the United States each year, primarily through these venues. Heroin is typically smuggled into the country carried by couriers on commercial flights. The most likely route for Chicago-bound heroin is from Columbia (South America) to Miami International Airport or JFK International Airport in New York City and then to Chicago. Couriers conceal heroin internally (in body cavities or by swallowing latex-protected quantities), in checked and carry-on luggage, or within items packed in luggage. Heroin, unlike cocaine and marijuana, is not imported in large quantities and can be more easily concealed on a person (U.S. Department of Justice, 2003).

Many of these drugs end up in Chicago. Mexican distributors are largely in control of the Chicago drug trade. The Mexican criminal organizations warehouse the drugs, transport them to Chicago, and then sell them wholesale to African-American and Hispanic gangs in the city. Chicago street gangs, such as the Gangster Disciples, Latin Kings, and Vice Lords, control most retail distribution of cocaine, heroin, and marijuana in the city. Wholesale drugs not sold for distribution in Chicago are sold to retail drug dealers in smaller cities throughout the Midwest, including Des Moines (IA), Fort Wayne (IN), Grand Rapids and Detroit (MI), Cleveland and Columbus (OH), St. Paul (MN), and Milwaukee (WI). The Chicago High Density Drug Trafficking Area reports that several tons of cocaine are transported to Chicago annually both for local consumption and for further distribution throughout the midwest (U.S. Department of Justice, 2003, p. 8). The same is true for marijuana. Nearly 50% of marijuana transported to Chicago is bound for smaller markets.

The following case involving the federal prosecution of a crack cocaine distribution network, operated by Chicago street gangs, illustrates the magnitude of criminal conspiracy and sales involved in Chicago drug trafficking:

> On November 12, 2003, two high-ranking members of the Gangster Disciples street gang were convicted in a federal jury on charges of conspiring to distribute crack cocaine. The convictions followed a 3-week trial held in the U.S. District Court for the Northern District of Illinois. Prosecutors alleged that the defendants managed a retail-level drug distribution operation that sold several kilograms of crack cocaine per week in public housing complexes on the West Side of Chicago. The defendants were indicted in September 2002, along with 34 other Gangster Disciples members, on charges including conspiracy to distribute powder cocaine, crack cocaine, and heroin. The indictment alleged that the gang members earned as much as $10,000 a day from selling drugs at Chicago's Rockwell Gardens Public Housing and St. Stephen's Terrace Apartment complexes and allocated earnings from the first and fourth days of each month to attorney's fees, bonds, court costs, and member expenses. The September 2002 indictment and arrests culminated a 31-month federal investigation by the DEA, U.S. Department of Housing and Urban Development (HUD) Office of Inspector General, and Chicago Police Department. (U.S. Department of Justice, 2004, p. 11)

This operation alone had generated approximately $350 million in annual sales before being disrupted. It implicated only 36 individual distributors. Even though the bust has been recognized as effective police work by all accounts, it represents only a fraction of the drug trafficking that occurs day after day on Chicago streets.

The deadly triad of gangs, guns, and drugs creates an environment that threatens the health, safety, and welfare of all Chicagoans. While federal, state, and local governments in the United States justifiably spend hundreds of millions of dollars annually to combat the potential catastrophic threat of international and domestic terrorism, on a daily basis neighborhood terrorism inflicted upon city residents by organized street gangs is exceedingly more lethal and far more disruptive to public safety maintenance. Chicago police officers are on the frontline in this battle. Their job is to protect citizens by interrupting criminal activity presented by this explosive triad of factors. To say the least, the challenge to Chicago police is formidable.

Chapter 8

THE FOUNDATION OF
CHICAGO-STYLE POLICING:
COMMUNITY, INFORMATION, AND
ACCOUNTABILITY

Superintendent Terry Hillard brought significant change to the Chicago Police Department and built a framework of organizational strength centered on openness, inclusiveness, teamwork, and innovation. Hillard's management team has said that he always wanted to hear everyone's opinion, was open to new ideas, and would take the necessary time to listen to each staff person's thoughts during a meeting. Hillard would require everyone in the meeting to speak and to share their thoughts – he believed that it was important for them to not just be at the meeting but to actively participate. His staff said that Superintendent Hillard did not like "yes men" or "yes women." As one deputy chief said, "The superintendent could tell when a staff person was just saying what they thought the boss wanted to hear, and he didn't like it. The superintendent knew that the final decision would be his alone, and he wanted to be sure that he had considered all possible views." After thoroughly discussing the issue at hand, Hillard's staff said that he would act decisively and remain resolute and committed to the course of action he had taken.

According to Hillard's staff, he also had an ability to recognize talent and to match people with positions in order to best utilize their skills for the good of the department. They said, "Like a champion chess player, Hillard would strategically move staff to facilitate management effectiveness and to achieve organizational goals." And everything, according to Hillard's staff, was based on teamwork. Hillard believed in the ability, talent, and skill of the people who worked for him, and he routinely gave them the latitude, support, and confidence to move forward on projects. Once a goal was set, it was the team's job to get the goal accomplished. When the job was successfully completed, it was the team, and not the superintendent, who received the credit.

The Chicago Police Department's management team, under the direction of Superintendent Hillard, set out on a course of action that would drastically change the way police work was done. It established resolute priorities designed to facilitate citizen safety by treating every law-abiding citizen as both a partner and a customer. Chicago-style policing would be built upon a solid foundation emphasizing community involvement, information exchange, and management accountability on the part of police.

The Police and the Community

In April 1993, Chicago launched a major crime fighting initiative, which called upon the police and the community to work in partnership to develop strategies for reducing crime and ensuring community safety. Called "Chicago Alternative Policing Strategy" (CAPS), the program began as an experiment in five police districts and, based upon its initial success, was expanded citywide in 1995. A core tenet of the community policing philosophy as it emerged nationwide in the last two decades was that police alone cannot, and should not, be responsible for addressing the myriad factors contributing to problems of crime and social disorder. Furthermore, the community and its citizens, working together as partners with police, could significantly impact crime and improve the "quality of life" in their respective neighborhoods.

The following definition of community policing is offered by a leading scholar:

> Community policing is a new philosophy of policing, based on the concept that police officers and citizens working together in creative ways can help solve contemporary community problems related to crime, fear of crime, social and physical disorder, and neighborhood decay. The philosophy is predicated upon the belief that achieving these goals requires that police departments develop new relationships with law abiding people in the community, allowing them a greater voice in setting local police priorities and involving them in efforts to improve the overall quality of life in their neighborhoods. It shifts the focus of police work from handling random calls to solving community problems. (Trojanowicz & Bucqueroux, 1990, p. 5)

The community-oriented policing paradigm broadens the traditional police mandate to include order maintenance, conflict resolution, and problem solving, and it refocuses service delivery to address a broad range of community needs (Rosenbaum & Lurigio, 1994). The following explanation of CAPS was prepared by the Chicago Police Department and placed in promotional materials distributed to citizens:

> While traditional policing relied almost exclusively on police to fight crime, CAPS creates a partnership of police, residents, government agencies, and other members of the community. The community shares responsibility with the police for setting crime-fighting priorities in their neighborhoods and for designing and implementing problem-solving strategies. (Skogan, Steiner, & the Chicago Community Policing Evaluation Consortium, 2004, p. 88)

The crime theory of "broken windows" suggests that community disorganization, left unchecked, leads to a decay of the neighborhood and sends a clear signal that nobody cares – not the police, not the citizens, not the community. New opportunities for crime then emerge, attracting more criminals and further social disorganization: "Gambling and drinking lead to robberies and fights; prostitution and drug sales attract those who prey on the customers. Social disorder thus begets an even broader range of problems and can, in short order, inundate an area with serious and victimizing crime" (Skogan et al., 2004, p. 76). The Chicago Police Department describes the broken windows' philosophy of CAPS as follows:

> CAPS recognizes that graffiti, abandoned vehicles and buildings, malfunctioning street lights, and other signs of neighborhood disorder do have an adverse effect on both crime and the public's fear of crime. By addressing these relatively minor problems early on, police and other government agencies can prevent them from becoming more serious and widespread problems. (Skogan et al., 2004, p. 76)

Chicago's CAPS strategy of combating crime stands in stark contrast to New York's policing style. Even though both New York and Chicago embrace the broken windows' theory of crime, their strategic response is operationalized in very different styles. Professor Wesley G. Skogan of Northwestern University made the following observation:

> An important feature of Chicago's approach to solving (crime) problems is that it does not just involve arresting people. Unlike New York's "zero tolerance" approach to addressing community problems by making tens of thousands of arrests for minor offenses, Chicago's solution for broken windows is to fix the windows. (Skogan et al., 2004, p. 76)

Chicago's strategy enlists both the community and the police in identifying and correcting neighborhood problems that allow crime to occur and recur. In this sense, the strategy is preventive, and solutions are designed to be sustainable. New York's strategy, on the other hand, reacts aggressively to crime when it occurs by effectuating arrests for even minor violations such as loitering, public intoxication, and public disobedience. New York invokes a strong police response with minimal public involvement, whereas Chicago calls upon community members to take responsibility for their neighborhoods through partnership and involvement with the police.

The Chicago Community Policing Evaluation Consortium recently published a ten-year evaluation study of the CAPS program. The results of the study are promising and will be reviewed in more detail later in this chapter. It should be noted, however, that national and international politicians, scholars, practitioners, and citizens alike recognize that the police and the community must work cooperatively to fight crime and restore public order. This is true particularly in the inner city of major metropolitan areas. As one police researcher stated, "Community policing offers the best approach to the delivery of citizen safety and can be thought of as the next step in the evolution of police practice" (Pearl & Campbell, 2004).

At the time that Terry Hillard was appointed superintendent of police, Chicago's CAPS program had already been expanded citywide and was operating in all 25 police districts. Superintendent Hillard fully understood the importance of the CAPS program, not only to the police department and citizens but to the city at large. Mayor Richard M. Daley made sure that the CAPS program was not merely a police program but was indeed a city government initiative. The mayor committed the necessary resources of all city departments to the CAPS program and to the concept of improving the quality of life for all Chicago citizens through interdepartmental cooperation and enhanced service delivery. All quality-of-life issues were to be addressed: run-down buildings, abandoned cars, graffiti, litter, trash, and illegal dumping. Every city department – from Streets and Sanitation, to Buildings, to Transportation, to Legal – was brought into the fight. As Mayor Daley stated,

> In a city as diverse as Chicago, we know there will always be differences among people. But what's special about Chicago today is that we are moving beyond those differences to pursue our common interests. The fact is no matter who you are or where you live, you want the same things: safer streets, better schools for our children, decent jobs, and a good quality of life. And we know that we work best when we work together to achieve these things. (Chicago Police Department, 2000, p. 8)

It is important to understand that while CAPS had been implemented citywide in 1995, it was still evolving and experiencing growing pains in 1998 when Hillard became superintendent. Program implementation as comprehensive and multidimensional as CAPS requires massive reorganization and the building of cooperation and trust between city departments, the police, community groups, and citizens. What is required is a change in organizational culture, and that is developed over time. Although early success of CAPS had been realized during Superintendent Matt Rodriguez's term, there was more to be done on Superintendent Hillard's watch.

In speculations about Mayor Daley's choice of Terry Hillard as superintendent of police, there is little doubt that the mayor saw a close fit between Hillard's well-developed people skills and the expressed goals of CAPS. Hillard is personally unassuming and polite. He can enter a room of 200 people and spend time talking one-on-one to a person without giving the impression that he is pressed for time even though there are usually dozens of people waiting in the wings to talk to him. He is concerned yet unpretentious and has an easy smile. He will ask people how things are going or about their children and listen carefully to their responses. People might assume that a superintendent of police would become self-important and aloof, especially when interacting with the average citizen on the street. This is not Terry Hillard. He treats everyone as important and affords them the respect and attention that they deserve.

Although quiet, soft-spoken, and loving in his approach to people, Hillard is also disarmingly charismatic. He has a special charm that draws people toward him. He has a personal manner and style that engenders trust, loyalty, and respect. His personal qualities contributed significantly to his effective leadership style and served to make him the perfect advocate, in fact, the perfect salesperson, for community policing.

Terry Hillard was made for community policing, and community policing was made for Hillard. Other police superintendents with more rigid and reserved management styles would not do as well in promoting community involvement with the police. Hillard not only became a champion of community policing, he indeed became an ambassador to the people of Chicago. He has an ability to bring people together, to energize and unite them in fighting for the good of the community. By the end of his superintendency, Hillard had become one of the most beloved public figures in Chicago – attaining rock-star-like celebrity status.

Early in his administration, Superintendent Hillard took a huge risk. He recognized that tensions existed between the Chicago Police Department and the minority community, particularly African Americans. Several high-profile cases of alleged police brutality against members of the black community had dominated the news prior to his appointment as superintendent. Hillard made the decision to go right to the source – to the leaders of the city's minority communities – for a clear reading on the nature and extent of the problem. What Superintendent Hillard called for was an interactive community forum on race relations between members of the Chicago Police Department and leaders of Chicago's minority communities.

There is one theory of thought in government that if things are quiet, one should not create a stir. In other words, react when you need to react, and don't invite criticism. Hillard knew that if tensions existed between police and the minority community, it was best to deal with them head on. Such a willingness to discuss racial tensions was not an acknowledgment on Hillard's part that the police were at fault. Superintendent Hillard fit into two categories – he was a police officer, and he was a member of the black community. What he sought was a common understanding and shared appreciation of both perspectives with the hope of forging a partnership to curb the tide of cynicism and distrust between the minority population and the police. If the police needed to change, police practices and policies would be altered in order to enhance race relations; but if minority communities needed to take stock of their positions with respect to police, that was expected as well.

The Forum was entitled "Strengthening Relations Between Police and Minority Communities: Ensuring Accountability for Effective Policing in Chicago's Diverse Neighborhoods." Hillard invited his top-level command staff and other members representing all departmental ranks, and he personally invited an equal number of community minority leaders who he believed would "tell it like it is" – those who previously voiced their criticism of the department when it was deserved but who were also willing to be supportive of the department's efforts when it was warranted (Chicago Police Department Special Report,

2000). The forum was facilitated by Dr. Chuck Wexler, executive director of the Police Executive Research Forum (PERF). The forum's agenda was pre-determined to allow for ample input and discussion from both the community representatives and the police. It lasted one full day.

Prior to forum, each participant was sent a survey of questions designed to solicit thought and opinion focused on the following tasks:

- To identify the nature and extent of the problem of police-minority relations
- To document best practices for solving identified police-minority problems
- To solicit ideas and opinions about what the police superintendent could do to improve police-minority relations
- To solicit ideas about what the community could do to improve police-minority relations
- To determine how terminology, semantics, and communication affects police-minority relations (Chicago Police Department Special Report, 2000)

The forum was conducted at the city's historic Cultural Center and included representatives from such organizations as the Chicago Urban League; the Gay and Lesbian Task Force; the Nation of Islam; the Chinese Mutual Aid Association; the Coalition for the Remembrance of the Honorable Elijah Muhammad; and a number of other religious, educational, and community organizations representing minority interests. The forum's agenda was designed so that members representing the minority community were asked to express their thoughts and opinions in the morning session. Police representatives at the forum were not allowed to respond or even speak during this time; they were instructed to listen and take notes only. Throughout the morning session, Dr. Wexler, serving as facilitator, asked the community representatives questions, clarified points, challenged positions, and stimulated discussion; however, the morning session belonged to the community. Following the morning session, all participants engaged in casual conversation and informal discussion over a box lunch.

In the afternoon, it was time for the police to speak and for the community members to listen. The police representatives reacted to what they had heard in the morning and offered their own perspectives, ideas, and opinions. Again, Dr. Wexler facilitated the police session in order to bring clarity and focus to the discussion. Finally, the late afternoon session was an open discussion among all forum participants and was designed to summarize the problems, ideas, and opinions that had been discussed during the course of the day. The concluding session was entitled "Reaching Consensus."

Approximately one week following the forum, Hillard called a press conference with forum participants standing by his side. Hillard acknowledged that "police-race relations" in America is a serious and real problem and that, in Chicago, there is an expressed willingness on the part of the police and community leaders alike to confront the issue assertively, both on a citywide level and in each neighborhood. Hillard summarized five consensus points that had emerged from forum discussions, and he vowed to actively involve both the police and the community in seeking viable solutions to improve police-community and race relations.

- *Communication* – A lack of effective communication was identified by both community participants and police as a major source of tension. It was noted that language and cultural differences, especially among immigrant and refugee communities, too often stood in the way of the development of effective relationships.
- *Respect* – There was a perception on the part of the community that there was a lack of respect by police for people as human beings, especially within the minority communities. Police also expressed concern that citizens made generalizations about all officers based on a particular negative experience they may have had with one officer.
- *Accountability* – Community participants expressed concern about a police disciplinary system that appeared to be unwieldy and unresponsive. It often seemed to the community that police protect their own.
- *Freedom of fear* – It was expressed that many members of the minority community, especially young males, feared encounters with the police. Community participants said there was a perception of "us vs. them." Police also acknowledged that they often had apprehension about how they would be judged if they made an honest mistake involving a member of the minority community.
- *Trust* – Community participants expressed concern that some police officers did not have an understanding of their communities and cultures, nor a commitment to working in partnership with them. (Chicago Police Department, 2000)

Immediately following the forum, Superintendent Hillard convened 92 of his top managers in a weekend retreat to discuss the forum issues and to charge them with putting together concrete steps of action to address each consensus point. Hillard said,

> I told them to critically examine everything we do and to make recommendations to me about how we can strengthen what we do – everything from recruitment . . . to selection and promotion . . . to training . . . to how we engage and disengage the public in our encounters . . . to informing the public on how we investigate and discipline our own officers.

The forum effectively provided minority community input for establishing short- and long-range departmental goals designed to improve "customer service." Many of the innovative programs that would be initiated during Hillard's superintendency emanated from the forum and the departmental retreat and planning process that followed.

By calling the community forum early in his tenure, Superintendent Hillard sent a strong message that the police were meant to serve the community, that the police and the community must understand each other in order to work together for citizen safety, and that he personally intended to be open to community concerns. In the process of opening up dialogue with the community, Hillard developed and nurtured personal and professional relationships with minority leaders that developed into mutual respect and trust. As one minority leader at the forum said, "This is the first time I have been asked to come to the table about such an important issue when the city was not in the aftermath of some overwhelming crisis." Another participant said of the forum, "What the Superintendent has embarked upon is a beginning and not an end – an intelligent discussion about the performance of the police department as it relates to the community" (Chicago Police Department, 2000). Indeed, Hillard had established a major theme for his administration: that the police and the community were equal partners. Superintendent Hillard's commitment to effective follow-through and change would be judged accordingly.

The Chicago CAPS program was operational when Hillard became superintendent, but he implemented many improvements to further enhance and strengthen the program in the neighborhoods. To understand CAPS, it is necessary to understand the basic organizational structure of police service in the city from the bottom to the top (patrol beats to headquarters). Chicago is organized into 281 police beats at the neighborhood level. The police beats are then accordingly organized into 25 police districts, and the police districts are organized into five police areas. All report to headquarters. Each police district is headed by a commander. The CAPS program within each district is overseen by one lieutenant and a CAPS sergeant. A basic tenet of community policing in Chicago is that the police beats and the police districts are primarily responsible for identifying and solving their own unique neighborhood problems. Chicago has diverse neighborhoods, each varying in racial composition and other distinctive demographic characteristics including crime rates. In one respect, Chicago's police districts might be viewed as 25 individual police agencies, each serving the needs of its respective citizenry.

The racial composition of citizens in the 25 police districts shows that Chicago is still a segregated city, with many neighborhoods being predominately African-American or Hispanic or white. For example, the 18th District is 80% white and 20% minority; seven of the police districts have a combined citizen population of 589,168, with 520,534 of them being African-American. That represents a nearly 99% black population in those districts. In five police districts, the Hispanic population is more than 50%. The unique demographic and cultural differences in each district and the corresponding problems and needs of their citizens must be well understood if community policing is to work.

Chicago beat officers are trained in the CAPS model to work with the community as a primary mission of their assignment. In fact, Chicago has developed and deployed "rapid patrol response units" in each district to answer certain low-priority calls for service so that uniform beat officers can spend more time working within the community.

Central to the work of the CAPS beat officer is problem solving. All officers are trained in a five-step problem-solving model: (1) problem identification and prioritization, (2) problem analysis, (3) design of response strategies, (4) implementation of the plan, and (5) assessment and evaluation of outcomes. Citizens are also provided training on problem solving. "Beat meetings" are the cornerstone of CAPS. Conducted monthly, beat meetings are attended by both police officers and neighborhood residents and are designed to identify problems and develop solutions. A recent study of the CAPS program found that

> Beat meetings are one of the most unique aspects of Chicago's community policing program. The meetings have several purposes: they provide a forum at which police and residents can exchange information and prioritize local concerns. As they have evolved, beat community meetings have become venues for regular reports by the police to the public on what they have done since the last meeting in response to problems that were discussed. (Skogan et al., 2004, p. 6)

Obviously, a necessary component of an effective and successful beat meeting is community participation. Recognizing this, Chicago launched a major initiative to market and advertise the CAPS program to the public. The advertised campaign slogan was "Get with the Beat." Through television, brochures, flyers, newsletters, posters, and radio, the department initiated a citywide marketing blitz. Informational materials were distributed at public libraries, businesses, schools, churches, and community meetings. In one year alone, more than $950,000 was spent just on CAPS television advertisements. This investment spoke to the priority and commitment of the city in implementing CAPS, and the investment paid off. Skogan found that in 1996, 53% of Chicago citizens were aware of the CAPS program, but by 2003, 80% of residents were aware of CAPS. Citizens' attendance at beat meetings rose from 58,600 in 1996 to a sustained average of 66,000 over the next several years. In 2002 (the last year in which complete information is available), 67,300 people attended a total of 2,916 beat meetings. Interestingly, citizens who attended the beat meetings in greater numbers were those who lived in high-crime, troubled areas. As noted,

> Attendance is especially high in poor areas with bad housing, in predominately African-American beats, and in areas where schools and health programs are not effectively meeting residents' needs. Meeting attendance is highest in high-crime areas because attendance is driven by a concern about crime. (Skogan et al., 2004, p. 12)

Police officers attending the monthly beat meetings are required to file departmental reports documenting expressed citizen concerns. Officers also complete numerous City Service Request Forms, which specify problems that need to be fixed – from abandoned buildings and vehicles, to graffiti, to gang and drug activity. The purpose of the reports is to notify respective city departments of existing neighborhood problems. Consistent with the broken windows' theory of crime, citizens often complain about social disorder issues including loitering, public drinking, disruptions around schools, street prostitution, gambling, teenage misconduct, and vagrancy. These are all visible indicators that a neighborhood is in social disorganization – that law-abiding citizens are losing control of their neighborhoods to less than desirable elements of society. A description of public drinking, as recorded by an observer in an inner city neighborhood, provides a vivid example of the problem of social disorder:

> In one South Side area, groups of men (and a few women) regularly congregated near liquor stores – usually in vacant lots – or they sat on milk crates and curbs in alleys and on street corners, never straying far from carry-out liquor outlets. There they sat, passing around bottles wrapped in brown paper, surrounded by overgrown weeds, empty snack food bags, cans, and broken bottles. When the police ask them to move, they never went far, scuffling around the corner to the other side of the street. Just to give the illusion of movement. (Skogan et al., 2004, p. 101)

A second factor that combines with social disorder as a broken windows' issue is physical decay in the neighborhood, a problem often discussed at beat meetings. Signs of physical decay include graffiti, which sends a clear message that gangs have moved into the neighborhood; abandoned and dilapidated buildings; litter, trash, and junk, including appliances and furniture dumped on the curbs and street; and abandoned cars, which have been stripped and left to rust. Using the example of abandoned buildings, one observer provides a clear illustration of broken windows' theory:

> The ravages of time, weather, and decades of neglect have left many buildings in poor neighborhoods with crumbling mortar, peeled paint, rotten framing, broken windows, and leaky roofs. If left empty for long, scavengers pick them clean of items of value, including stained glass, light fixtures, elaborate wooden molding, copper electrical wiring, and bathroom fixtures. Even aluminum siding will be stripped overnight and exchanged for cash at recycling centers. Squatters may move in, and drug dealers find it easy to set up shop. (Skogan et al., 2004, pp. 96–97)

In addition to concerns regarding issues of social disorder and neighborhood decay, drug dealing on the streets remains the number one concern voiced by Chicago residents, followed by gang violence. As one observer noted, "Outbursts of gang violence . . . are frequently tied to conflict over control of street drug markets and illegal arms sales. Turf battles easily escalate into shootouts with semi-automatic weapons that put everyone in the neighborhood at risk" (Skogan et al., 2004, p. 63). At the street level and in the neighborhoods, residents are very much concerned about open drug markets where drug dealers sell in plain view on street corners, seemingly unconcerned about detection by the general public or the police. This display of confidence and arrogance on the part of drug dealers sends a message of control, that the gangs are in charge of the streets and that they will do as they damn well please. As one observer wrote,

> In one beat we have studied intensely, drug dealing takes place everywhere: along the major arterial and shopping streets, in front of liquor stores, in front

yards of houses and apartment buildings, along side streets, and on many street corners. Scores of men and teens loiter in the vicinity, some yelling, "Rock!" and "Blow!" at passing cars to advertise their wares. Buyers pull over, exchange a few words and a handshake, and then move on. As police approach, cries of "Five-O" warn everyone to lie low, and they slowly scatter. (Skogan et al., 2004, p. 62)

Identifying problems related to crime, social disorder, and neighborhood decay and proposing viable solutions through action planning are the heart and soul of beat meetings. The meetings are composed of the police and the citizenry who work together – worrying, struggling, hoping, planning, venting, dreaming – to make the neighborhood a safer place to live and to raise a family. Through this process, police gain a better understanding of the community and the community of the police. Trust, confidence, and friendships begin to break down barriers on both sides of the "us vs. them" mentality. The conflict is not between the police and the community; rather it is the police and law-abiding citizens versus the criminal elements of society. One telling sign of this new partnership against crime is the number of community events that have been organized at the beat level. Marches, rallies, block parties, vigils, and walking citizen patrols have all been organized in order to send a strong message that citizens care about their neighborhoods and do not intend to tolerate crime and disorder.

Each of the 25 police districts has formed a District Advisory Committee (DAC), which is composed of residents, community leaders, business owners, clergy members, school officials, and other organizational representatives. The city provides each DAC with funding for crime prevention and safety programs. The advisory committees meet regularly to assist district commanders in the establishment of district priorities and are charged with identifying and securing the necessary commitments and resources to bring about solutions to neighborhood crime problems.

Indeed, Chicago's CAPS program is designed not only to take complaints but to find solutions, to follow through with action planning, and to evaluate successes. To reiterate, it is clear that the city supports the CAPS program. The city has put in place a CAPS Implementation Office, which is staffed with civilian community outreach workers. The charge of this office is to promote the CAPS program, to work with the police department and other city departments to coordinate city services, and to work directly with the police districts on coordinating action plans. In addition, Chicago has assigned corporate attorneys to work out of the five police areas to assist police districts in going after gang and drug houses, abandoned buildings, and absentee or negligent landlords. This unit, called the Drug and Gang House Enforcement Section, uses all available means including negotiating with landlords, strict ordinance enforcement, civil litigation, and criminal prosecution to clean up problem properties or shut them down altogether.

Another team of city code enforcement inspectors from the city departments of Buildings, Fire, Police (and sometimes Revenue and Health) work together to target problem buildings. They look for building code violations and signs of drugs, gangs, and other illegal activity. In one year, the Strategic Inspection Task Force (SITF), working with city attorneys, inspected and corrected problems at 6,000 properties throughout the city. A study of SITF found that "crime decreased where SITF and city attorneys operated, not only in targeted buildings but in a half-block area around each building" (Skogan et al., 2004, p. 78).

In attacking graffiti, the city formed a team of "Graffiti Blasters" who are armed with 19 high-pressure sprayers. At the request of any property owner, the team arrives to "Give Graffiti a Blast," as their logo implies. The city considers these property owners to be victims of crimes, having sustained property damage, and the cleanup is at the city's expense – to the tune of $4 million annually. The city also sponsors neighborhood cleanups.

The most poignant example of the citywide commitment to the CAPS program is Operation CLEAN (City Services Law Enforcement and Neighborhoods). Coordinated by the CAPS Implementation Office, the goal of CLEAN is "to deliver, in a coordinated manner, a massive amount of city services to high-crime areas in an attempt to improve the quality of life for residents." The city recognizes that these quality-of-life issues affect public and officer safety and rank high among underlying causes of crime and social disorder problems in target areas. These "service blitzes" are described in a recent study of the CAPS program:

> These service blitzes, held about 30 times per year, include aggressively towing seemingly abandoned cars, graffiti removal . . . , tree trimming, rat poisoning, sewer cleanup, clearing and mowing vacant lots, repairing streets and sidewalks, installing new street signs and lamp posts, and painting fire hydrants and other public structures. (Skogan et al., 2004, p. 87)

In addition to the cleanup, the Strategic Inspection Task Force and the Drug and Gang House Enforcement Section come armed to go after buildings with gang and drug problems. Operation CLEAN is clearly a coordinated city crackdown on neighborhoods experiencing crime and quality-of-life problems. A service coordinator working out of the CAPS Implementation Office reported keying in 669 individual service requests as he got organized for one day's Operation CLEAN (Skogan et al., 2004, pp. 87–88).

A recently released study of CAPS provides evidence that crime in Chicago is on the decline, that Chicagoans are less fearful of crime than in years past, and that the quality of life in the neighborhoods has improved considerably. As the authors of the study state, "Wherever big city policing is heading, Chicago is at the forefront" (Skogan et al., 2004, p. ix).

Information Technology and Management

The effectiveness of the police in solving crime has always been dependent on their ability to obtain reliable information. In the case of an unsolved murder, police often question dozens of possible witnesses, interview family, friends, and associates of the victim, and go door to door in the hope that someone saw or heard something. Police lean heavily upon their "informants" and try to "squeeze" prostitutes, drunks, gang members, and others who operate illegally in the neighborhood for information that they may be reluctant to share with the police. Every police officer also has his or her own read on a given neighborhood, based upon information and knowledge garnered by working there for an extended period of time. Officers know the citizens, both the law-abiding and the criminal, and they know the neighborhood culture and the subtle behavior patterns of those who reside there. Such familiarity helps police intuitively know when something is out of order or suspicious in that neighborhood. When police say they have a hunch or a gut feeling, they are drawing upon a wealth of information and personal knowledge that they have organized and stored away regarding their beat and the people they encounter.

The collection and exchange of information regarding crime and criminal activity in years past has been informal and unsystematic. Part of the problem had to do with the sheer volume of crime data and the cumbersome process of filing detailed handwritten reports and case information. The other problem had to do with the organization and retrieval of information. Even if police agencies had collected detailed information related to crime and criminal activity, that information was not immediately retrievable in a format useful to officers on the street. Over the past two decades, there has been an industrial and societal revolution in information technology, management, and application. Information is now retrievable with the stroke of a few computer keys. All segments of society are now fully involved in the information revolution, including the police. The Chicago Police Department was well aware of the value of information and information management in combating crime. In preparing for 21st-century policing, the Chicago Police Department sought to implement a state-of-the-art, intelligence-driven information technology network equipped with data warehousing capacity. The department felt that all police intelligence should be accessible in one spot, with all tools leveraging and feeding the information repository.

Superintendent Hillard made it clear that restructuring the department's crime data information system was a top priority of his administration. Necessary personnel and financial resources would be made available in pursuing a state-of-the-art information technology system. After looking at numerous information system applications in use at other law enforcement agencies, Chicago officials decided to start from scratch and build their own system from the bottom up.

The Chicago Police Department forged a public/private partnership with database giant Oracle wherein Oracle invested millions of dollars in consulting and training services, and Chicago, in turn, put up $12 million in cash. Oracle retained shared ownership of intellectual property rights and was given the freedom to charge other clients for customized application and consultation. The system became known as CLEAR (Citizen Law Enforcement Analysis and Reporting) and was developed at a total cost of $40 million.

A young police officer named Ron Huberman became involved early on in the development of the CLEAR system and worked to ensure that street-level cops were consulted on system design and implementation. Huberman recognized that unless the system was useful to the cop on the street, it would not be accepted and used as intended. Huberman said, "I've worked the street and understand what officers need to solve crimes" (Pastore, 2004, p. 6). Huberman enlisted for his team 18 Chicago police officers who had an interest in information technology. Deputy Superintendent Barbara McDonald, who is credited with envisioning CLEAR, said, "All our technology tools have been developed by members for members. . . . It isn't some vendor coming in and saying, 'This is what you need'" (Pastore, p. 6).

The CLEAR database contains readily accessible information gleaned from arrest reports; provides information on warrants, wanted persons, and court orders; provides criminal activity reports by district, beat, street, and address; includes criminal rap sheets with aliases, nicknames, and distinguishing physical marks; displays mug shots and fingerprints; provides records of seized property and evidence tracking; provides information from forensic reports; and gives current information on open cases. In addition, CLEAR contains protected management information on police personnel activity including the number of arrests by each officer, citizen complaints, and many other performance indicators. To date, more than 2,000 police vehicles have been equipped with touch-screen notebooks providing officers access to more than 8.5 million police and crime reports. The CLEAR system is dynamic, as well, for police officers on the beat routinely enter new information via "contact cards" that feed the system and cross-reference, integrate, and update existing police files.

The use of information technology and the efficient collection and sharing of crime data are changing policing in Chicago in dramatic ways. In years past, police officers worked many hours developing and following up leads. If a witness to a crime said that the assailant had a distinguishing tattoo or that during the commission of a crime the perpetrator was referred to by a nickname, that information might be useful only if the officers working the neighborhood could match the nickname or tattoo to someone they knew. Now, through CLEAR, the investigating officer can initiate a query based on one specific detail such as a "nickname" or "tattoo," and a citywide or regionalized search can pull up all data files that match. All individuals entered in the system matching the search parameters will be identified by name, arrest record, known accomplices, gang affiliation, hangouts, mug shots, and closeup pictures of their tattoos or distinguishing marks.

In addition, district commanders and police officers receive continuing updates regarding crime patterns and criminal activity occurring in their areas through CLEAR. Crime-mapping capabilities provide a visual display of crime on a street-specific basis. Police managers are able to deploy officers to hot spots or problem areas more efficiently. Police now know not only where gang shootings are occurring but are able to predict with some degree of accuracy where shootings are likely to occur in the near future. As Deputy Superintendent McDonald said, "They're using CLEAR data to anticipate where crime may occur so we can have the resources there before it happens" (Pastore, 2004, p. 4). The crime information provided by CLEAR is not simply accessible; it is also almost instantaneously accessible. The Chicago Police Department documented the following workflow improvements enabled by CLEAR:

- Accessing mug shots – from up to 4 days before CLEAR to 4 seconds with CLEAR
- Pulling up a rap sheet – from 4 hours previously to seconds with CLEAR
- Logging in seized property and evidence – from 3 hours previously to one hour with CLEAR
- Checking offenders' prison status and release dates – from 30 minutes previously down to one minute with CLEAR (Pastore, p. 6)

Finally, CLEAR serves to complement and enhance the department's community policing program. District commanders and their management teams are able to access CLEAR to get a better read on crime patterns in specific neighborhoods. This information is then incorporated into their strategic crime-fighting plans. Although certain data are accessible only by police, data on incidents of neighborhood crime and crime patterns are made available to the public and are distributed to citizens attending beat meetings. As Superintendent Hillard stated, "In our partnership with the community, we feel it is imperative that the citizens are provided with current information regarding crime in their neighborhood. Parents want to protect their families, and they are better able to do this with current and accurate information about crime."

In a speech to police recruits on July 23, 2002, Superintendent Hillard spoke of the CLEAR system and described how CLEAR was revolutionizing the way Chicago police officers do business:

> For these graduates, there is no better time to become a Chicago police officer. Yesterday, we introduced a new way of doing things at the Chicago Police Department. CLEAR is going to redefine how police officers fight crime. CLEAR is a new way we are using technology to gather and analyze information. CLEAR will help us solve crimes that were difficult to solve before. It guides police to where crime is taking place so we can stop it in its tracks. When it comes down to fighting crime, the days of being reactionary are long past. We are problem solvers. In order to solve problems, our members and our residents need reliable information. The better the information and the sooner it's analyzed, the better equipped everyone is to work together to solve problems. CLEAR is changing the way we think, the way we strategize, and the way we fight crime.

Indeed, the concept of visualizing a police officer with a star and a gun needs to be updated to include a star, a gun, and a computer. CLEAR has been so successful in Chicago that Illinois Governor Rod Blagojevich recently provided funding to implement the system statewide. Soon all of the state's 1,200 law enforcement agencies and 38,000 police officers will be able to store and retrieve crime data contained in one integrated system. Other large metropolitan police agencies throughout the country and, in fact, throughout the world, are looking at what Chicago has done with CLEAR. In this new era post 9-11, the sharing of information among and between police agencies is critical to combating threats to homeland security. Terrorists don't operate within defined police jurisdictional boundaries, and neither do most other criminals. The national integration of crime information and data is an essential element in defending America's homeland, and CLEAR may be a model that deserves further examination at the federal level.

Chicago's CLEAR system recently received national recognition from *CIO (Chief Information Officer)* magazine by being chosen as the sole winner of the 2004 Grand CIO Enterprise Value Award. The magazine noted,

> Enterprise Value in its highest form is the opportunity for IT (information technology) to transform a business, to bring a whole new model into existence. . . . The Chicago Police Department totally changed the game. . . . CLEAR is an enterprise vision of how anytime, anywhere access to centralized, rational data can empower intelligence-driven crime-fighting. While other police departments are struggling to integrate legacy data and applications, Chicago decided in the 1990s that to have maximum impact, all policing intelligence should be accessible in one spot, with all tools leveraging and feeding the repository. (Pastore, 2004, pp. 2–3)

CIO officials were impressed not only with CLEAR's efficiency as a crime fighting tool, but also with the labor savings and productivity improvements realized from a management perspective. The Chicago Police Department estimated a labor savings of $88 million over a two-year period following its implementation. As a result of efficiencies in information management, 345 clerical positions were no longer needed, and 90 once-deskbound police officers were redeployed to the streets (Pastore, p. 5).

In receiving the prestigious CIO award, the Chicago Police Department beat out such renowned private companies as Ace Hardware, Continental Airlines, Dell, Pfizer, and Proctor and Gamble. Imagination and ingenuity in the government sector is seldom seen to be on a par with private enterprise. Superintendent Hillard, Deputy Superintendent McDonald, Officer Ron Huberman, and the Chicago Police Department proved that efficiency in serving customers' needs in the public sector is as important as it is in the private sector. In recognition of exemplary work, Superintendent Hillard promoted 32-year-old Ron Huberman, a patrol officer with five years' experience, to assistant deputy superintendent overseeing Information Services and Records. This rapid promotion of exceptional talent, essentially by-passing the command structure, is unheard of in traditional law enforcement organizations. Hillard demonstrated that in his administration, promotions were based on what the candidate knows rather than who the candidate knows.

A commitment to community policing combined with the effective use of time-accurate information and crime data provides an organizational atmosphere that is open and fluid, capable of adapting to changing patterns of crime and disorder within the community. For such a police strategy to work, however, an additional component must be present: accountability on the part of the police.

Police Accountability

In February 2000, Superintendent Hillard created the Office of Management Accountability (OMA). OMA is headed by a deputy superintendent and was established to provide the necessary authority and appropriate organizational purview to bring overall improvement in the management and operation of the Chicago Police Department. OMA has a small staff of sworn officers and civilians, many of whom are trained as management analysts and crime analysts. The office's primary charge is to assess and evaluate the overall effectiveness of the department in meeting its established goals and objectives. Police managers at all levels are held accountable for achieving what they set out to achieve. Assessments focus on how well managers meet expectations related to four core departmental functions:

1. Reducing chronic crime and disorder identified at the beat and district levels
2. Identifying and containing or eliminating crime trends and patterns
3. Organizing community involvement and responding appropriately to community priority concerns
4. Managing the efficient use of police personnel and other resources

Chicago's 25 police districts can be viewed as 25 separate police agencies. As such, accountability for reducing chronic crime and disorder must logically start at the district and beat level:

> The 25 police districts are responsible for identifying local priorities, planning strategies to address them, and then executing their plans effectively. The role of OMA is to oversee this process, holding district commanders accountable for carrying it out. (Skogan, Steiner, & the Chicago Community Policing Evaluation Consortium, 2004, p. 64)

At the district level, management teams are composed of the district commander, three watch commanders, a tactical lieutenant, a CAPS management team leader, and a community policing sergeant. Representatives from the District Advisory Committee, the CAPS Implementation Office, or other special units may also participate as members of the district management team. Each district is responsible for developing a Strategic Operational Plan (SOP). The team is required to assess current and emerging crime problems and to develop specific strategies, means, and resources for addressing the problems. The district management teams meet monthly to assess and reassess problems, priorities, strategies, and successes. This process is dynamic in that it is influenced predominantly by changing crime problems, expressed community concerns, and emerging management issues. The district management teams know that they are going to be held accountable by OMA for achieving the priorities established in their District SOP.

Strategic operational meetings are also held on a quarterly basis in the five established police areas. These strategic planning sessions are usually conducted by the area deputy chief and are designed to assess how the individual police districts within the police area are doing in identifying and solving priority problems. The area meetings also provide an opportunity to plan police responses and initiatives affecting the police area as a whole. Since the department's special units operate out of Area Headquarters, deployment of Area Saturation Teams to specific high-crime areas within a district often is coordinated at the area meeting. Commanders from Detectives, Special Operations, Public Housing, and School Patrol and Vice, among other units, regularly attend and participate in area meetings. Chicago Police areas are large, and it is important for each district to share its strategic operational plans so that coordinated area responses and area resources can support district priorities. It is interesting to note that the largest police area in Chicago, Area 5, is the same size as San Francisco; Area 1 is larger than Milwaukee; and Area 4, the smallest police area, is slightly smaller than Minneapolis (Skogan et al., 2004, p. 80). In 2003, the Chicago Police Department, through OMA, also initiated weekly area meetings that focused specifically on district homicides, aggravated battery with firearms, and other forms of public violence involving firearms (Skogan et al., 2004, p. 142). These meetings, called VISE (Violence Initiative Strategy and Evaluation), are designed to combat Chicago homicides. Homicide patterns are assessed; intelligence information is reviewed; and deployment and investigative strategies are put in motion for an intensive coordinated response.

Strategic operational meetings at the district and area levels are largely designed to prepare the district management teams for accountability sessions held at police headquarters. These meetings are very formal and are held with the department's top brass in attendance. The superintendent; five or six of the department's most senior deputy superintendents; the chiefs of detectives, patrol, and organized crime; heads of other special units; the area deputy chief; and other city officials are all present (Skogan et al., 2004, p. 72). Only one police district is called to headquarters on a given day, when its district management team is to be put on the "hot seat" – to be held accountable for crime and police response within its district. As one researcher noted, "The accountability sessions represent a dramatic departure from business as usual at the Chicago Police Department, for in the past, districts and units usually enjoyed freedom from close scrutiny" (Skogan et al., 2003, p. 72). The headquarters' accountability meetings are where the district commanders' feet are held to the fire when the top brass want to see results.

The director or deputy superintendent of OMA starts the headquarters' sessions with an overview of the department's core functions. He and his staff then present a *PowerPoint* presentation of the district's crime trends, noting both increases and decreases in crime rates over time and identifying emerging neighborhood problems. OMA does its homework by preparing for weeks and by thoroughly analyzing district crime data. The district's SOP is then evaluated thoroughly to determine how well the district management team did in executing its plan and how effective it was in resolving prioritized problems. OMA also collects information regarding community needs as expressed by citizens at beat meetings and asks the district management team to explain how community needs are being addressed. OMA routinely deploys inspectors from Auditing and Internal Control to assess the extent to which districtwide operations are correlated to problems listed in beat plans. Finally, OMA addresses district management issues. Such issues range from officer deployment and arrest rates to evaluations of police sick leave, police vehicle crashes, and the number of complaints filed by citizens against police. OMA wants to know what the district is doing to correct district management problems. As one district lieutenant said of the headquarter meetings, "It's like studying for the Bar exam" (Skogan et al., 2003, p. 72).

OMA's supervision of the Chicago Police clearly imposes oversight and requires systematic problem analysis, strategic planning, and evaluation at all levels of the organization, but particularly at the district levels where the fight against crime must be won. OMA expects answers to the following questions: Are districts doing what they said they would do through their establishment of strategic operational plans? Are districts conducting their enforcement efforts in the right places? Are districts alert to new trends in crime? Are districts effectively using the resources at their disposal? What strategies are working or not working in the district? Are important management issues being addressed? (Skogan et al., 2003, pp. 137–139).

An important feature of the headquarters' accountability meetings is that districts are given short notice as to when they will be called to appear. As such, they are required to be prepared and accountable at all times. OMA's establishment forced district commanders to understand that accountability matters. In order to be successful, district commanders must know their district, assemble an effective management team, manage efficiently, stay focused, and honor their commitments to do what they set out to do. As one district commander said, "It keeps everyone on their toes and is a much tougher, but better, way to do business. I can't imagine going back [to the old way]. Accountability will be one of the superintendent's lasting accomplishments" (Skogan et al., 2003, p. 89).

Preparing for Excellence

True leaders inspire people to do their best. Creating vision for organizational excellence requires much more than inheriting a title and telling others what to do. Superintendent Hillard created an atmosphere for organizational change within the Chicago Police Department that challenged and inspired new thinking based on openness, inclusion, and the application of advanced technologies and proven management principles.

All organizations tend to become comfortable with the status quo. Police organizations in particular are more structured and less responsive to change because of their adherence to paramilitary bureaucratic structure. Simply introducing a new operational philosophy or program does not guarantee that the initiative will be accepted into the existing organizational culture. Organizational change must be managed effectively. The process by which new programs and initiatives are introduced and implemented within the organization is as important as the final goal. In the end, if the process breaks down, the goal will never be successfully achieved.

Superintendent Hillard introduced the change process by clarifying the mission of the Chicago Police Department. That mission was to "ensure community safety and to promote the quality of life for all citizens." The mission was based upon the four core operational goals of (1) reducing chronic crime and disorder, (2) responding to emerging crime trends and patterns, (3) addressing citizen concerns, and (4) managing effectively. As such, the foundational cornerstones of Chicago-style policing in the 21st century would become community involvement, information management and exchange, and police accountability.

Superintendent Terry Hillard at the 9/11 memorial held at Daley Plaza.

Terry Hillard (standing) with his family members in South Fulton, Tennessee. Terry's twin, Jerry, is on the left.

Terry Drew (Hillard), Wendell Phillips High School Class of 1961 senior photo.

Terry Hillard, Marine Corps graduation, October 29, 1963.

Left: Terry and Dorothy Hillard on their wedding day, May 9, 1970.

Below, L to R: Terry's mother-in-law, Mrs. Brown; Dorothy Hillard (Girl); Terry's step-father, Alfonso Drew; Terry's mother, Leila Drew; and Terry, at the Commander's Promotional Luncheon in 1991.

Right: Terry Hillard receives the Chicago Police Department's highest award, the Police Medal, following his February 14, 1975 shooting. Then Superintendent James Rochford is making the presentation.

Below: Terry Hillard is sworn in as superintendent by Judge Abraham Lincoln Marovitz at the former Chicago Police Department Headquarters on February 18, 1998.

President Clinton listens to Chicago Superintendent of Police Terry Hillard as he delivers remarks to police officials in the Rose Garden of the White House on Friday, May 29, 1998. Clinton announced a program to provide 700 additional police officers to target crime in specific neighborhoods in eighteen American cities.

Racial profiling campaign photograph for the Chicago Police Department. The campaign was entitled *Racial Profiling: Not in This City.*

Community leaders participating in the Cultural Diversity Forums.

Right: Terry Hillard and Arab-American spokesperson, Kareem Irfan, at a Cultural Diversity Forum.

Left: Superintendent Hillard and his command staff signing pledges to prohibit any form of racial profiling.

Superintendent Hillard receiving the Citizens Award of Appreciation from Mayor Daley and Glenn Carr, commissioner of personnel.

Superintendent Terry Hillard at the dedication of Gold Star Park, a public space honoring fallen Chicago police officers.

The honor guard bearing the casket of fallen Chicago Police Department member, Sgt. Alane Stoffregen.

Superintendent Terry Hillard presenting the American flag to Sgt. Stoffregen's mother.

Right: Superintendent Hillard holding a press conference outside the mayor's office following the E2 nightclub fire.

Four past superintendents and the present superintendent attend the annual Christmas luncheon in 2003. *L to R:* Terry Hillard, Fred Rice, Superintendent Phil Cline, Matt Rodriguez, and Leroy Martin.

Superintendent Terry Hillard and his granddaughter, Danae, in the superintendent's office.

Terry Hillard's granddaughter, Danae Hillard.

Terry Hillard's partner and good friend, First Deputy
Superintendent John Thomas.

Terry and Dorothy at his August 2003 retirement party.

Terry, Terri Lee, and Dana at Terry's August 2003 retirement party.

Terry's extended family at his August 2003 retirement party.

Superintendent Hillard in his office at the Chicago Police Department headquarters.

Superintendent Hillard being honored by his staff as he is driven away on his last day in office.

Chapter 9

THE MEDIA, THE POLICE,
AND MAJOR CASES

The Chicago Police Department, like any major metropolitan police agency, faces a never-ending barrage of tragic crime that takes an exacting toll on thousands of innocent victims. No sooner is one crime solved than several new cases are opened. Other crimes are never solved and linger in "open investigation" or "cold case" status for years, or even decades, until new leads develop. Annual clearance rates for murder cases in Chicago are less than 50%; for criminal sexual assault, 40%; robbery, 16%; and aggravated assault and battery, 46%. For property crimes such as burglary, theft, and arson, the annual clearance rates are just over 16%. Overall in 2002, the Chicago Police Department cleared only 20% of reported crimes (Chicago Police Department, 2002). This means that the majority of reported crimes go unsolved, not because of police incompetency but because of several factors, not the least of which is the volume of criminal activity and the lack of available manpower to properly investigate all leads and all crimes. Day in and day out, Chicago police officers work tirelessly to deploy necessary manpower and resources to stem the tide of crime. Despite their considerable effort, the workload simply outpaces the department's capacity. Adding hundreds or even thousands of new police officers to the force might ease the workload somewhat, but even such a drastic influx of additional officers would be insufficient to truly keep up with the pace of crime in the city.

It is obvious that with so much crime, Chicago police must prioritize cases and deploy manpower and resources accordingly. Murder cases clearly take precedence over burglary, robbery, and theft. Sprees of open gang warfare, driveby shootings, and the blatant operation of open drug markets require that the department immediately redeploy officers to the troubled areas. This continuous shifting of manpower necessarily means that while some police actions are intensified, others receive less attention. This process of prioritizing crime and police response is not a reflection of the department's unwillingness to investigate lesser crimes; it's simply a matter of focusing on the most dangerous crimes in order to best protect the citizens of Chicago with the resources available at any given time.

Murder is the most tragic crime. The sudden, senseless, and irreversible loss of a person's life at the hands of another human being and the rippling emotional devastation on family and loved ones last forever. It should not matter whether the murder victim is a white, middle class female shot to death while walking down Michigan Avenue in the middle of the afternoon or a 16-year-old African-American gang member killed in a retaliation murder at midnight outside a Chicago housing project. A life is a life. Both people are dead; both were killed by another human being; and both cases involve murder. In one sense, all crimes are major crimes, but in reality, "major crime" is defined by the unique nature of a particular crime (or series of crimes), the public response to the crime, and, most notably, the media's interest in and reporting of the criminal event. Police have little control over these factors.

The national television network has experienced radical change over the past decade. The days of waiting for evening news broadcasts are over. CNN, the Fox News Network, and MSNBC run continuous news stories 24 hours a day. Politics and crime are at the forefront of these 24-hour broadcast news programs. Television soap operas now compete for viewing time with real-life crime dramas. Cases such as the O. J. Simpson murder trial; JonBenet Ramsey; Chandra Levy; the Washington, DC, Beltway Sniper; Laci Peterson; Lori Hacking; and the recent shooting deaths of the husband and mother of U.S. District Court Judge Joan Humphrey-Lefkow in Chicago, Fulton County Superior Court Judge Rowland Barnes, and three other victims in Atlanta are reported obsessively by the national media. If you wake up at 2:00 AM and turn on Fox, you can see Greta Van Susteren interviewing a panel of four prominent prosecutors and defense attorneys and another panel of renowned forensic pathologists giving their expert opinion on the most recent national crime story. The Internet also provides continuous updates regarding the status of ongoing national crime stories, 24 hours a day, seven days a week.

How do the national media select a crime story that is worthy of extensive coverage? The answer, of course, is that they select stories that will sell. The murder of Nicole Simpson, the pretty ex-wife of national sports hero O. J. Simpson; the murder of JonBenet Ramsey, the child beauty queen daughter of a wealthy entrepreneur; the murder of Chandra Levy and her association with a prominent congressman from California; and the murder of Laci Peterson, a young pregnant wife who was thought to have the perfect marriage all had national news interest, in part, because all of the murder victims were white and attractive and in some cases involved prominent public figures and/or wealth. A search of the Internet reveals the enormous number of news stories reported on each of these cases: Nicole Simpson shows 1.9 million Internet entries; JonBenet Ramsey, 49,500; Chandra Levy, 118,255; and Laci Peterson, 636,000. The recent national crime story of the murder of young and attractive Lori Hacking in Salt Lake City, at the hands of her husband, generated 82,954 entries in just six months.

It is revealing to contrast the reporting on these stories with the more than 14,000 murders that were committed nationally in 2002 or the 600 to 700 murders committed annually in Chicago. Who has ever heard of a 3-year-old black child named Angela Thomas who was murdered while sleeping in her bed? Or 12-year-old Rene Guillen, or 16-year-old Juan Washington, or 20-year-old Frank Aseves, or 20-year-old Namoi Quashie, or 28-year-old Edgar Juarez, or 32-year-old Ricardo Mora? The list goes on – they were all victims of murder in Chicago in 2003. Their cases did not receive national news coverage. In fact, most of them received no media coverage at all. These victims simply became lost statistics, their deaths recorded only for purposes of public record.

Although cases such as Nicole Simpson, JonBenet Ramsey, Chandra Levy, Laci Peterson, and Lori Hacking reached notoriety, the stories of thousands of other victims go untold. It is astonishing that the media at times can be so blatantly biased in their reporting and yet never be called to task. They are quick to question the integrity of others but are never willing to reflect upon their own integrity and the obvious biases in their own reporting. The case of Andre Crawford serves as an example.

On January 30, 2000, Chicago police charged 37-year-old Andre Crawford in connection with the rape and murder of ten women on the South Side of Chicago. This string of murders took place from 1993 through 1999. According to news reports, the victims were presumed to be drug addicts and/or prostitutes working and living in predominantly African-American neighborhoods. The Crawford case clearly fits the definition of a serial killing spree, yet the case generated virtually no coverage. Most residents of Chicago are not even familiar with the case. One would think that the sexual assault and killing of ten women would become national news; however, the slain women were not white, wealthy, or connected to power – they were alleged drug addicts and prostitutes, and their deaths went largely unnoticed.

Shortly after Hillard was appointed superintendent, he became increasingly frustrated about the negative manner in which the Chicago news media reported on certain criminal cases and what he perceived as their unfair criticism of the Chicago Police Department. Superintendent Hillard was out of the city attending an FBI national conference and struck up a conversation with Department Chief Joe Dunne of the New York City Police Department. Hillard was sharing his frustration concerning the media when Chief Dunne asked Hillard two questions: "How many personnel does Chicago have assigned to work with the media? What are the working hours for the department's Office of News Affairs?" Hillard proudly said that he had five personnel assigned to the office and that the office was open from 8:00 AM to 4:30 PM, Monday through Friday. The New York official asked, "What happens when you have a shooting at 2:00 in the morning?" Hillard replied, "We handle it when we come in the next morning." As he answered these questions, the problem Chicago was facing with the news media became immediately obvious to Hillard.

The news media operates 24 hours a day, seven days a week, and developing stories that occur at 2:00 AM will most definitely be reported in the morning news. If a shooting occurs and the department does not have a spokesperson to respond, the media will put their own spin on the story. By 8:00 AM the next morning, the story will have already broken, and the police department will have essentially forfeited its opportunity to get on top of the story. Hillard immediately telephoned his first deputy superintendent, John Townsend, told him about the conversation with the NYPD official, and asked him to start working on the transfer of eight or nine additional staff to the Office of News Affairs. Hillard said he wanted the office open 24 hours a day, seven days a week.

According to Hillard, he learned that "you have to feed the press, or they will feed themselves." If the police are not available to respond to press inquiries regarding a police-citizen shooting at 2:00 AM, the press will go to the gang-bangers and local activists to get the story. There will be a story in the morning news with or without the police. Hillard gave instruction to his News Affairs staff to learn the deadlines for the city's many television, radio, and newspaper reporters. By taking reporters' schedules into account, the Chicago Police Department scheduled its press conferences to accommodate reporting deadlines. In this manner, CPD could better control their message and keep their message consistent.

Following up on Superintendent Hillard's orders, the Department conducted a search of police personnel who had previous experience in journalism and offered those best qualified positions in the Office of News Affairs. Additional training in "police media relations" was provided to the upper ranks of the department, including captains and lieutenants, and new protocols were established to clarify the handling of media inquiries on a 24-hours-a-day, seven-days-a-week basis. Finally, Hillard recruited Pat Camden as assistant press secretary and designated him as the CPD spokesperson on major crimes. Camden was an experienced police officer who worked in media relations under four different superintendents. Camden was articulate, photogenic, straightforward, and tough when it came to television interviews. If a major crime occurred in Chicago, it was Camden's face that citizens would see on the television news networks representing the Chicago police and the superintendent. Hillard himself would speak at organized department press conferences, while Camden was most often "at the scene" to respond immediately to developing crime stories and other major department incidents.

The following six cases brought considerable attention to the Chicago Police Department during the tenure of Superintendent Hillard. Each incident generated extensive news coverage and negative community and political response. While the details of each story are unique, the types of cases they represent are commonly problematic for all major city police departments.

Managing Difficult Murder Investigations

In the first year following Superintendent Hillard's appointment, Chicago recorded 703 murders. Occurring at a rate of nearly two per day, some of the murders received local news coverage; most did not. The story of a gang-banger getting shot and killed is not news in Chicago – of 703 murders, 180 (approximately 25%) were verified as being gang-related. Other causative factors leading to murder included street altercations, narcotics, robbery, burglary, domestic violence, and sexual offenses. In 1998, the Chicago Police Department "was unable to determine the reason for 198 (28%) of the city's 703 homicides. Combining verified gang-related murders with other and undetermined causative factors, it is likely that the actual percentage of gang-related murders in Chicago is more than 50%, conservatively.

Police are in the business of solving crimes. Certain cases are more difficult to solve than others, and the management of the investigative process is often critically assessed by the media and the community. Two cases involving murder investigations illustrate the importance of effective management of investigations: the case of Andre Crawford and the case of Ryan Harris.

The Andre Crawford Case

In a ten-month period, beginning in June 1998 through April 1999, there were six women murdered on the South Side of Chicago in the Englewood and New City communities. All of the murder victims were black, in their 30s and 40s, and known to have lived risky lifestyles, allegedly working as prostitutes and taking drugs. The victims were either strangled or beaten on the head with a blunt object, sexually assaulted, and left hidden in abandoned buildings. All six bodies were found within a three-block area along 51st Street.

In the spring of 1998, police were frustrated because all six murders were unsolved and the community was up in arms, accusing the police of not working the cases because the women were black, drug users, and prostitutes. The media were beginning to ask questions, and city hall was getting nervous. In April of 2003, the Chicago police caught a break. The Illinois State Police had linked DNA samples taken from the scenes of three of the murders to one individual, indicating that there may have been one person responsible for all of the killings – a serial killer. Police later linked DNA samples taken from four other murders to the same person. Superintendent Hillard immediately formed a task force and deployed 30 Chicago police officers and detectives to work with the state police and the FBI. Sergeant Albert Wolf was assigned as the task force coordinator.

Although law enforcers knew that the DNA of one person was found at the scene of three murders, they did not know to whom the DNA belonged. And because the women were prostitutes, it was possible (although improbable) that each of the women had sex with the same person prior to being murdered but that this person was not the murderer.

The task force developed an investigative strategy that employed good old-fashioned detective work – knocking on doors, following up on leads, interviewing people in the neighborhood, staking out locations, and searching abandoned buildings. The first series of tasks was to review all unsolved homicides in the area and to reinterview all suspects and ask them to voluntarily submit DNA samples. The samples were taken not only in the hope of identifying the killer but also to eliminate innocent persons of interest. More than 400 DNA samples were submitted and tested.

The investigations found that several of the murder victims knew each other, had common friends, hung out at the same locations to socialize, had sex with some of the same partners, used drugs, and ate at the same soup kitchen. Based upon this information, the task force created a profile of the offender. It was determined that the murderer was most likely a black male in his 30s or 40s; that he knew the victims and was familiar with the neighborhood; that he probably used drugs, most commonly cocaine, and drank heavily; that he was probably unemployed and homeless and frequented soup kitchens and shelters; that he probably had previous arrests including sex offenses; and that he had no vehicle and lived in the area of the murders.

Police identified 305 suspects fitting the profile and ordered a search of police records for each one of them. In addition, police checked all incarceration records of the suspects to determine how many of them were locked up in the Cook County Jail or the Illinois Department of Corrections when each of the murders was committed. If a person was in jail for any significant time during the killing spree, he was eliminated as a suspect. Finally, police interviewed the remaining suspects, asked them to give DNA samples, and checked to see whether their names were on the state register for convicted sex offenders.

By August 1999, the task force had developed an "A" list of likely suspects and had intensified its investigation of these men. On January 30, 2000, police arrested Andre Crawford based upon several leads and a positive link to the DNA sample obtained from his mother. Police charged him with ten counts of first-degree murder and 11 counts of aggravated criminal sexual assault. Later, an additional murder charge was filed against Crawford, making the total count 11. Police later learned that Crawford had relocated to the West Side of Chicago because he knew the heat was on. His move had made the investigation more difficult.

Andre, known as "Dre" on the street, confessed to the murders in a videotaped confession to police. DNA evidence linked him to seven murders, and he admitted to the other four. The criminal profile created by the police was quite accurate. Crawford was a 37-year-old black man, unemployed and homeless, who lived in the neighborhood, knew his victims, and was a drug addict. He would lure female acquaintances into abandoned buildings and promise to trade drugs and money for sex. He then either strangled or beat them with a blunt object until they were dead. After killing the women, Crawford would perform a variety of sexual acts on them, including vaginal, anal, and oral penetration. He concealed the bodies in abandoned buildings and would often return the next day to indulge in sexual acts with them once again.

When Crawford was arrested, he congratulated the police on their work in finding him, but said, "You have to admit, though, I was pretty good, too. I killed for eight years." Crawford had even attended community CAPS meetings convened to solicit the public's help in identifying the killer. He told police that he was insulted by the nominal reward offered by the Chicago Police Department for tips leading to his arrest. The FBI had offered a $20,000 reward, and Crawford told police that that amount was more appropriate to the crimes.

As with most serial killers, Crawford's propensity to kill increased over time until he was killing a woman every two months. This increased activity probably led to his capture. Although Crawford's killing spree began in September 1993 and ended with his arrest in January 2000, police had not identified any unusual pattern to link the multiple murders. If Crawford had committed the murders in a smaller community, the evidence of his killing pattern would have been immediately obvious, but in Chicago's 9th District, there were 291 homicides committed between September 1993 and June 1999. Crawford's murderous activity represented less than 4% of total murders committed during this period and, as such, did not set off alarm bells with the police. The facts that all of the victims were women and that the murders were occurring on a more frequent basis finally made neighborhood residents fearful and led them to work more closely with police.

Sergeant Wolf and his task force did an exceptional job of solving this case in nine months. Although DNA played a major role in solving the crimes, it was just good, old-fashioned police work that got Crawford off the streets. As Superintendent Hillard said, "Crawford's arrest was the result of tenacious police work. . . . These men and women worked night and day tracking leads, knocking on doors, and searching abandoned buildings" (Chicago AP, 2000, p. 31).

At any time in Chicago, there are most likely two to three serial killers on the loose. Some serial killers are caught by chance, and some are left to murder for years, undetected in a city that records hundreds of murders per year. While the names Richard Speck and John Wayne Gacy will be remembered; the name Andre Crawford will almost certainly be forgotten – a sign that murder is now commonplace and not all that alarming. In the end, however, Crawford is believed to have murdered and sexually assaulted at least 11 women – Patricia Dunn, Rhonda King, Angel Shatten, Sanguanta Langely, Sonji Brandon, Nicole Townsend, Evander Harris, Cheryl Cross, Tommie Dennis, Sheryl Johnson, and Constance Baily – each a victim who mattered to someone.

The Ryan Harris Case

The murder of an innocent child is almost always a top news story. The murder of Ryan Harris occurred just over five months after Hillard was appointed superintendent. It generated considerable news coverage, not only because of the tragic and grizzly facts surrounding her murder but also because of the police investigation that followed.

The following poem was written in tribute to Ryan Harris for purposes of putting a face and personality with just one of the thousands of victims who were slain in Chicago over the past several years. The poem also provides an introduction to the case:

Ryan's Eyes

It just took one look and then you would realize
The promise and hope in Ryan's eyes
Full of fun, laughter and cheer
A precious young child with nothing to fear
Cartoons, ice cream, jump rope and pretend
The sweet kisses and hugs she would receive and send
Innocent and loving in this cruel world, time and place
Ryan did not deserve the dishonor she would face
Taken so quickly, her smile and energy would fade
A senseless act would retract this perfect child God had made
And those of us who know and suffer the loss
Struggle to understand why good and evil must cross
You see, it just took one look and then you would realize
The promise and hope in Ryan's eyes.

– Thomas J. Jurkanin

Her beautiful brown eyes and angelic face made hearts melt. She was sweet, innocent, and petite–a child of African-American descent. Ryan Harris was only 11 years old when she was taken from this world by a cruel sexual predator and degenerate murderer. On July 28, 1998, Ryan's body was discovered:

> Ryan Harris' life was stolen from her – but not before she was bludgeoned to death with a brick, sexually assaulted with a foreign object, raped, and finally, suffocated with her own underwear. Her lifeless, rag-doll body was left – like garbage, half-naked – in the tall weeds and overgrowth behind a run-down brick building in the 6600 block of Parnell Avenue on Chicago's South Side. (Juvenile Justice, 1998)

When a young child is murdered, police respond in force. Although citizens may casually read a newspaper article recounting the brutal murder of a child, it is the police officer who sees the blood; it is the police officer who lifts the lifeless body; it is the police officer who witnesses firsthand the cruelty and mutilation that one human being is capable of inflicting upon another. Police are affected emotionally by the murder of a child – how could they not be – and they ask themselves, "What if this were my child, or my nephew, or my niece, or my grandchild?"

In the case of Ryan Harris, police investigated the case aggressively, and on August 9, 1998, just eleven days after her body was found, the Cook County

State's Attorney's Office filed murder charges in juvenile court against two young neighborhood boys. The Ryan Harris story, which received only nominal news coverage during the eleven days before the arrest, immediately received national attention because the two boys charged with the murder of Ryan Harris were just seven and eight years old – two of the youngest children ever to be charged with murder in the United States. According to Chicago police reports, the two boys had confessed to killing Ryan Harris. The boys allegedly wanted Ryan's Blue Warrior bicycle, so the seven-year-old boy threw a rock at her, hitting her in the head and knocking her off the bike. The boys, who had known and occasionally played with the girl, then allegedly molested her, dragged her unconscious body into the weeds, stuffed her underwear in her mouth, and put leaves and grass up her nose. In bringing charges against the two boys, a Chicago police spokesperson said that "their (the boys) confessions contained detailed information that could have only been known by individuals who committed the crime, or by the detectives who investigated it." According to the Chicago Police Department, "The boys' statements indicate that they are the perpetrators, and we have some physical evidence to corroborate their statements of involvement."

On September 4, 1998, nearly four weeks after the arrest of the two young boys, the Cook County State's Attorney's Office abruptly announced that all charges against the boys were being dropped based on crime lab reports. An attorney, speaking on behalf of the Cook County State's Attorney, stated,

> Yesterday afternoon we received a telephone call from the crime lab advising us that semen was present on the panties of the victim Ryan Harris. After we received the information, we were informed by medical experts that the possibility of semen coming from 7- and 8-year olds is highly remote. (Cook County State's Attorney's Office, 1998, p. 1)

Also on September 4, after being notified of the crime lab reports, Superintendent Hillard held a press conference to discuss the Ryan Harris case and the decision of the State's Attorney's Office to drop charges against the two boys. Hillard said,

> This case has been extraordinary from its inception. It remains a tragedy within a tragedy. The facts presented by the detectives in Area #1 and the State's Attorney's Office to the Juvenile Court were enough to establish probable cause. In hindsight, it is easy to question the investigation of this case. It is important to remember that at the time these two witnesses were being interviewed, they related facts that only could have been known to someone intimately involved in Ryan Harris's death. . . . The Chicago Police Department continued its investigation in the case and followed up on any and all leads. . . . Allegations of misconduct on the part of the detectives have been made. There has been no – I repeat – no misconduct on the part of any member of the Chicago Police Department. . . . The police must be concerned with facts. The detectives confronted with this tragedy behaved in a professional manner, complying with the spirit of the law. . . . We continue to pursue any and all information concerning the death of Ryan Harris. (Chicago Police Department, 1998)

In the weeks following the September 4 announcements, the Illinois State Police Crime Lab ran DNA tests on the semen taken from the panties of Ryan Harris against a DNA database of known convicted sex offenders. The results showed a close match to the DNA of Eddie Durr, a convicted sex offender who was in jail at the time of the murder. The State Police then checked the DNA sample against relatives of Eddie Durr and found a direct match with the DNA of Eddie's brother, Floyd. Floyd Durr had been living in the Englewood neighborhood where Harris's body was found and fit the physical description of a man who had been seen with her on the evening of her murder. Durr's physical description was also consistent with that given by the boys of a man who had bought several gifts for them in the days following the murder but prior to their arrest. At the time that the DNA evidence from the Harris case was found to be linked to Floyd Durr, he was already incarcerated in the Cook County jail facing charges of sexually assaulting three other young girls, all the approximate age of Ryan Harris. Upon questioning by Chicago Police officers, Durr said that he inadvertently discovered the dead body of Ryan Harris in the weeds where he saw two young boys whom he could not identify. He claimed he did not kill Harris, but that he did masturbate over the girl's dead body.

On April 22, 1999, Floyd Durr, age 30, was formally charged with the murder of Ryan Harris. Just weeks later, on May 11, 1999, Durr was found guilty of committing predatory sexual assault on another ten-year-old girl and was sentenced to serve from 24 to 120 years in the Illinois Department of Corrections. The disposition of charges against Durr in the Ryan Harris case and the two other cases involving sexual assault against underaged females are pending; however, the good news is that Floyd Durr is currently off the streets and will be locked up for a long, long time.

The Ryan Harris murder case is indeed tragic; however, what made the story particularly interesting to the media was the arrest of two boys, only seven and eight years of age. The drama that then developed was not about the cruel murder, but about the apparent misdirection of the investigation and the emergence of additional crime scene evidence that called into question the culpability of the boys. Although police eventually arrested Floyd Durr for the murder of Ryan Harris, many believed that the police had erred. The families of the two young boys filed a federal civil rights violation lawsuit against the Chicago Police Department.

Police Corruption – The Joseph Miedzianowski Case

Police officers face continuous observation, critique, and criticism from the media and the public at large, even if they consistently perform their duties in a competent and noble manner. As frontline representatives of government power and authority, police are expected to conform to the highest principles of discipline, reasoned discretion, and moral and ethical behavior. As in any profession, most officers of the law are trustworthy and honest and abide by a personal and professional moral code that brings honor to themselves, their law enforcement agency, and their community. However, as with those in other professions, including clergymen, accountants, lawyers, physicians, politicians, and teachers, a small percentage of those who are given the public's trust regrettably choose to violate it. Rogue acts of police corruption, brutality, and abuse of power committed by a few bad cops unfortunately tarnish the stars and badges of all good law enforcers.

As a career Chicago police officer, Terry Hillard always placed personal integrity at the top of his list of characteristics necessary to be a good public servant. One simply does not serve for 30 years in the Chicago Police Department without being confronted with temptation, which may come in many forms, such as offers of bribes and special favors, the temptation to engage in overly aggressive and prohibited police tactics, or the opportunity to look the other way to protect fellow officers who choose to engage in unethical police actions. Police officers take a pledge to uphold public trust, but the decision to uphold or violate that pledge is a solitary, individual one. Hillard is a compassionate, caring man who loves his fellow officers, but he has zero tolerance for those who violate public trust and dishonor their profession.

Hillard made it clear that as superintendent, he would be the strongest advocate for good cops and the worst enemy of bad cops. Ten months after Hillard's appointment as superintendent, Chicago police officer Joseph Miedzianowski was indicted by the U.S. Attorney's Office and arrested by officers of the Chicago Police Department's Internal Affairs Division as he reported for work at a West Side police facility. The indictment claimed that Miedzianowski ran a $2 million drug operation between Chicago and Miami. Miedzianowski was a member of Chicago's Gang Crimes Unit when charged with multiple federal offenses, including shaking down drug dealers, taking money to protect drug dealers, planting drugs on suspects, torturing citizens, arming gang members with guns and ammunition, alerting drug dealers to undercover drug investigations conducted by fellow officers, fixing cases, obtaining search warrants based on faulty information, and, in the end, running a large drug organization that transported cocaine and money between Chicago and Miami. In announcing the indictment on December 16, 1998, U.S. Attorney Scott Lazar called Miedzianowski the most corrupt police officer who has ever been indicted by his office. "Officer Miedzianowski is accused of committing the very crimes that he took an oath to protect the citizens of Chicago against. . . . Instead of protecting and serving the public, he is charged with protecting his drug-dealing associates and serving only himself" (U.S. Attorney's Office, 1998). Twenty-two coconspirators, including Miedzianowski's partner, Chicago police officer John Galligan, and Miedzianowski's mistress, Alina Lis, were also indicted and later convicted in Miedzianowski's drug ring operation. Superintendent Hillard stood with the U.S. Attorney at the press conference and said, "The Chicago Police Department will not tolerate corruption. . . . The community/police department partnership is based on mutual trust. When that trust is breached, corrective measures must be swift, direct, and have impact." Herbert Collins, Jr., special agent in charge of the Chicago Field Division of the FBI, said,

> The Chicago Police Department deserves to be commended for being on the offensive against corruption. The citizens of Chicago and many other communities have a right to honest police service, and this case is an excellent example of how federal and local law enforcement, working together, can achieve that goal. (U.S. Attorney's Office, 1998, p. 5)

Miedzianowski, a 22-year veteran of the Chicago Police Department, had received many department commendations for his work as a gang crimes specialist. He, in fact, obviously understood the gang culture too well, for he eventually became a convert to the criminal culture. It is estimated that the drug conspiracy headed by Miedzianowski distributed approximately 350 kilograms (770 pounds) of cocaine in the 1990s. "Multiple kilos of powdered cocaine were cooked into potent crack cocaine and distributed in North Side neighborhoods controlled by the Latin Lovers, Spanish Cobras, Maniac Latin Disciples, and Imperial Gangsters" (Lighty, 2003). Miedzianowski, whose police salary was $55,000 per year, was receiving at least an additional $250,000 per year in illegal money from dealing drugs and protecting drug kingpins and dealers. Although married, Miedzianowski had a girlfriend, Alina Lis, a 38-year-old Polish immigrant who served as a drug courier transporting drugs and money between Chicago and Miami. Lis was so devoted to Miedzianowski that she turned down a deal by federal authorities to testify against him at trial in exchange for receiving no prison time. When she turned down the deal, federal prosecutors sought and received a conviction against Lis that sent her to prison for 30 years.

The evidence presented against Miedzianowski by federal prosecutors was overwhelming, including more than 250 hours of telephone conversations between Miedzianowski, drug dealers, and gang members secretly recorded from his home telephone lines. In addition, every one of the 22 coconspirators in the case, with the exception of Lis, testified against him at trial in exchange for leniency in sentencing. Miedzianowski and the 22 codefendants eventually pleaded guilty or were convicted at trial. In one final bizarre revelation, it was discovered that Miedzianowski had conspired to have the lead U.S. Attorney, Brian Netols, assassinated and that he had devised a plan to escape from federal prison once sentenced.

At the sentencing hearing before U.S. District Judge Blanche Manning, U.S. Attorney Netols stated the following:

> When Mr. Miedzianowski carried his [star], #60015, for him it was not a [star] of honor, it was not a [star] of dedication to principles. It was simply and plainly one thing, Judge. It was camouflage. It was something to disguise the fact that he previously should have been a protector and had become a predator. It was the star that allowed him to commit the crimes he committed year after year after year. This was his security. This was his safe passage. This was his authority over

other people in the drug organization. When you look at what kind of police officer Joseph Miedzianowski was, he was someone who was nothing more than a traitor in the war on crime. . . . I think you need to send a message to the honest police officers, to those that are true heroes. . . . I think you need to send a message to them that the prosecution of Joseph Miedzianowski was done in great part to vindicate their names. (Lighty & O'Connor, 2003)

On January 24, 2003, U.S. Judge Blanche Manning sentenced Miedzianowski to life in prison, telling him that he

. . . betrayed society by dealing drugs and arming the street gang members who were part of his conspiracy to distribute crack cocaine on the streets he swore to protect. . . . There comes a time in every person's life to embrace what he or she has become, to check the compass of his heart, to remember paths traveled. I'm afraid to discover, Mr. Miedzianowski, what you are now, sir. You used your powers to infect a trusting society. (Lighty & O'Connor, 2003)

The Chicago Police Department and every major law enforcement agency in the United States faces corruption. In the early 1990s, CPD had seven officers – known as the Austin Seven – convicted in federal court for robbing drug dealers in the Austin Police District. Although the Chicago Police Department's selection and training procedures are stringent, including comprehensive background and character checks, psychological examinations, and training on ethical and moral behavior, it is an unfortunate fact that out of 13,500 cops, there are going to be some bad apples. The CPD's Gang Specialist Unit, comprised of about 120 officers, had been given tremendous freedom to pursue cases with minimal supervision. Partly due to the Miedzianowski case, Superintendent Hillard disbanded the Gangs Crime Unit (a unit which he loved and served in for many years) and reassigned its officers to the Detective and Narcotics Divisions where their actions could be more closely monitored and supervised.

There is a popular adage that if you give some people enough rope, they will eventually hang themselves. In the case of Miedzianowski, the temptation to become corrupt was much too strong, and his ethical and moral constitution was clearly too weak. The most effective way to dissuade police officers from becoming involved in corruption is to closely supervise their actions and to take immediate steps to prosecute them as the criminals they are if they choose to dishonor their police star. This was Terry Hillard's philosophy. Following the conviction of Miedzianowski, Superintendent Hillard said,

The Chicago Police Department congratulates the U.S. Attorney's Office on the successful conviction of Joseph Miedzianowski. We are pleased that justice has been served. . . . It is disheartening to see that a Chicago police officer chose to become involved in criminal activity. By doing so, he violated his oath to serve and protect the residents of Chicago. His criminal actions are a disservice to the people of this city and the 13,500 hard-working police officers who perform their jobs so admirably on a daily basis. . . . I have said all along that police officers who act like criminals will be treated as criminals. Today's verdict reaffirms that notion. (Chicago Police Department, 2001)

Police Pursuits – The Story of Qing Chang

Qing Chang, a 25-year-old Chicago resident, began the new year of 2003 with brilliance and promise – the same way she had lived her entire life. She was a remarkable young lady who entered Peking University in Beijing, China, at age 15 and graduated at 19 with a bachelor's degree in chemistry. In 1997, Chang moved to the United States to be with the man she loved, Yong Huang, who was pursuing a doctorate degree in organic chemistry at the University of Chicago. After relocating to Chicago, Chang enrolled at the University of Chicago, where in just a few short years she earned a master's degree in physical chemistry and a second master's degree in mathematics with an emphasis in computer science. Chang and Huang were married in Chicago in a private ceremony attended by only a few close friends. The couple's dream was to have a more elaborate, traditional Chinese wedding when they could afford to make a trip to their small hometown in China – a wedding that all of their family could attend.

Chang was employed by Thoughtworks as a computer software developer for almost three years and was just days from relocating to London to take on a new assignment. The offices of Thoughtworks are in downtown Chicago at 651 West Washington Boulevard. She lived nearby at the Presidential Suites at 575 West Madison and would walk to and from work every day.

On January 2, 2003, at about 6:15 PM, Chang was on her way home from work. She stopped at the intersection at Madison and Des plaines and waited for the traffic signal to change.

Just minutes prior to Chang's arrival at the corner of Madison and Des plaines, another scenario was developing in a nearby location. At approximately 6:09 PM, an African-American male and female entered the Redfish Restaurant at 400 North State Street and stole a wallet from the purse of a patron seated at a table. A bartender observed the crime but could only watch as the criminals hopped into a getaway vehicle where a driver was waiting.

The bartender immediately flagged down a Chicago police sergeant, explained the crime, and pointed out the offenders and the getaway vehicle. The sergeant activated his siren and Mars lights in an attempt to stop the vehicle, but the offenders refused to pull over. The sergeant immediately called the police pursuit in to the communications center. He later recontacted the police dispatcher to convey that, during the pursuit, the offenders had thrown the stolen wallet out of the vehicle and onto the roadway and that he had stopped to pick it up. During the chase, the pursuing sergeant was advised by the police dispatcher that another sergeant listening to the pursuit had advised him to call off the chase; however, since the pursuing officer was a sergeant, he was under no requirement to obey the order of another sergeant, and he decided to continue pursuit.

The chase continued through busy downtown rush-hour traffic with the fleeing vehicle exceeding the speed limit and running several red lights. While proceeding westbound on Madison, the offenders' vehicle struck a Mercedes

Benz sports utility vehicle at Madison and Des Plaines. The offenders' vehicle then continued through the intersection and onto the sidewalk at the intersection's southwest corner, where it struck pedestrian Qing Chang. Her small body was thrown 40 feet in the air and landed under a car in a nearby parking lot. She was transported to Northwestern University Hospital, where she was later pronounced dead of massive internal injuries.

Police reports indicate that the time between the theft's occurrence, the police pursuit, and the fatal crash was less than three minutes. For the theft of a wallet, a brilliant, innocent lady lost her life. It was later revealed, following an autopsy by the Cook County Medical Examiner's Office, that Qing Chang was pregnant with her first child – a fact that even her husband had not known.

Police arrested the three offenders involved in the theft and attempted getaway. They were identified as Lakesha Smith, 24 years old, who was the driver, and Tamika Wilson, 22 years old, and Larry Scott, 34 years old, the two who stole the wallet. All were charged with first-degree murder, felony murder, burglary, and reckless homicide of an unborn child. Smith was also charged with aggravated fleeing and eluding police.

At the same time that Qing Chang had begun establishing her life's course at the age of 15 years at the University of Peking, the three offenders were establishing their lives' courses as small-time criminal violators and petty thieves. Police records indicate that by the age of 22 years, Wilson already had five arrests for crimes including battery, criminal trespass to a vehicle, and retail theft; by age 24, Smith had 11 arrests for theft, assault, shoplifting, criminal trespass to a vehicle, and possession of cocaine; and by age 34, Scott had accumulated 23 prior arrests for theft, battery, criminal trespass to a vehicle, possession of a controlled substance, and assorted other crimes. In total, the trio had 39 prior arrests.

Superintendent Terry Hillard called the death of Qing Chang a tragedy, stating,

> A bright, young woman was tragically killed after a vehicle pursuit. An officer was attempting to apprehend a group of fleeing offenders who had just stolen a wallet. The woman wasn't an offender. She wasn't part of the pursuit. She was simply a woman walking down the street on her way home from work. This is a tragedy because we had petty criminals eluding the police. We had a pursuing officer with nothing but good intentions and acting in good faith. The end result was that a woman's life was cut short. (Chicago Police Department, 2003a)

The problems posed by police pursuits have gained national attention over the past decade, in large part because of the staggering statistics associated with the dangerous police practice. It is estimated, according to the National Highway Traffic Safety Administration, that more than 3,000 people died in crashes involving police pursuits in the past ten years. Nearly one-third of those killed in police pursuits were innocent bystanders; the other deaths were of fleeing offenders or police officers themselves. Geoffrey Alpert, a professor of criminology at the University of South Carolina, points out,

Research "debunks the myth" that most suspects chased by police are serious criminals. . . . Most are deadbeats making stupid decisions to avoid being caught for not having a license or some offense that would be very minor compared to what happens when they initiate a pursuit. (Alvord, 2003)

According to Alpert's research, approximately 40% of all police pursuits result in a crash, 20% result in an injury, and 1% result in death. Alpert says that "these percentages are accurate for departments throughout the country and over a period of years, even when the numbers of police pursuits fluctuate" (PursuitWatch.org, 2004). In Chicago in 2002, there were 625 police pursuits, and nearly 30% of those ended in a crash.

It is important to note that police are equipped with two types of deadly weapons – one is a firearm and one is a vehicle. It is a fact that deaths resulting from high-speed police chase incidents exceed deaths related to police discharge of firearms. A two-ton vehicle used in an inappropriate manner can become a deadly weapon, as is evidenced by the 40,000 to 50,000 people killed annually in the United States in automobile accidents. When police officers receive instruction in the basic training academy on "the use of deadly force," they also receive training on police driving and related potential physical threat and legal liability.

The police are employed to catch the bad guys. Most citizens accept this proposition. The bartender at the Redfish Restaurant and the patron whose wallet was stolen expected the sergeant on the street to chase down the thieves, arrest them, and return the wallet and its contents. If the sergeant had told them that it was only a wallet and that it was too dangerous to chase the suspects through the city streets, the officer would have been judged to be lazy, a coward, or just unwilling to perform his duties. Furthermore, a message would have been sent to the perpetrators and other would-be thieves that police won't come after them for simply stealing a wallet. This is the dilemma that police officers face. If police give chase and everything goes fine and no one is hurt, the police did well; however, if police initiate a chase and an innocent person is injured or killed, it is the police officer who faces criticism, possible disciplinary action, and legal liability. And finally, like most police decisions, the totality of the facts surrounding the incident must be considered within a matter of seconds.

In recognizing the inherent danger of police vehicle pursuits, law enforcement agencies across the nation have developed policies and procedures to help officers and their supervisors make decisions about when to pursue and when to terminate a chase. In fact, more than a year before Qing Chang's death, Superintendent Hillard had ordered a comprehensive review of the Chicago Police Department's policies and procedures concerning vehicle pursuit. The CPD studied vehicle pursuit policies in other major cities and reviewed its own policies with an eye toward enhancing accountability throughout the chain of command. Hillard had directed the study committee, convened by Karen Rowan, the department's general counsel, to make recommendations on how the department could create a sound policy that would increase public safety without making the police officers' already difficult job more difficult.

On April 24, 2003, just three months after the death of Qing Chang, Superintendent Hillard held a press conference to announce a new vehicle pursuit policy. In a prepared statement, Hillard said,

> The new policy includes a balancing test our officers must apply in making that split-second decision on whether to pursue or not. In short, they must decide whether the need to apprehend a fleeing suspect outweighs the level of inherent danger created by the pursuit. The policy builds in accountability throughout the ranks. It clarifies when an officer should pursue a fleeing vehicle. It gives more guidance in determining when to cancel a pursuit. The new policy brings back the Traffic Review Board, which will review the circumstances involved in all pursuits and determine whether the officer's actions were appropriate. (Chicago Police Department, 2003b)

Hillard concluded the press conference by pointing out the difficult job that police face with regard to pursuits:

> It is our obligation to strike a balance between our efforts to make our streets safe from criminals with the public's expectation to track down and apprehend criminals who victimize innocent citizens. And, our officers know, that is a difficult line to walk. On the one hand, citizens have every right to move about our streets safely. However, that same public expects the police to make every reasonable effort to hold criminals accountable for their actions. (Chicago Police Department, 2003b)

The new pursuit policy implemented in Chicago was not as restrictive as those in Boston, Miami-Dade County, or Memphis. In those departments, police pursuits are only authorized in cases involving suspected felons. The Chicago police pursuit policy bans officers from initiating a chase for a minor traffic infraction such as a broken headlight. In addition, unmarked police vehicles are banned from chases involving traffic violations. Officers are also prohibited from continuing a chase if the fleeing driver is suspected of simple theft or a traffic violation such as running a red light or stop sign except in cases of DUI.

Under the new policy, Chicago officers may chase suspected felons who run a red light or a stop sign, but they must determine whether the need to catch the suspect outweighs the danger of the chase using a "balancing test" that considers speed, volume of traffic, road conditions, and other factors. Police lieutenants and watch commanders, for the first time ever, are now responsible for listening to their police radios at all times so that they can monitor potential pursuits and act to terminate them if the conditions are too dangerous or the chase is unwarranted. Hillard also called for the entire department to receive training on the new vehicle pursuit policy.

Finally, Hillard and the city of Chicago called upon the Illinois General Assembly to pass more restrictive legislation that would make fleeing police a felony instead of a simple misdemeanor. Hillard said, "Every pursuit has at least two players – the criminals who are fleeing the police and fleeing justice and the police trying to bring them to justice." As one citizen wrote in a letter to the editor appearing in the *Chicago Sun-Times* on Wednesday, January 22, 2003:

> I propose that lawmakers finally take pursuits seriously and enact the following tough laws instead of always blaming the police: Anyone fleeing from police [receives] a 5-year prison sentence; if property damage or minor injuries occur, 10 years; and, if major injuries are inflicted or any death occurs, life imprisonment without parole. I believe this will curtail many police pursuits. (Belpedio, 2003)

Notwithstanding extensive lobbying efforts to enhance penalties for fleeing police, Illinois law has not changed. Fleeing and eluding police remains only a misdemeanor.

A public memorial organized by Thoughtworks was held for Qing Chang at the University of Illinois at Chicago with more than 200 people in attendance. Following the service, Qing's husband, father, mother, and sister planned to return her cremated remains to Shandong, China, where her life began. In just 25 years, this lovely, kind, intelligent woman had accomplished so much and touched so many lives. She had traveled to the United States to learn, to grow, and to contribute. Her husband said, "I think she liked the U.S. very much, even when she was in China. The life here very well fit her character. . . . There's more freedom, opportunities, and challenges here" (Sadovi, 2003). A life so filled with promise was reduced to ashes, and a future once filled with hope ended in a split-second because of the recklessness of petty criminals. This is the danger of police pursuits.

Qing Chang's husband, Yong Huang, filed a wrongful death lawsuit against the city of Chicago. James Montgomery, former corporation counsel for the city, said,

> This should be a bank breaker. . . . The damages depend a lot on who the victim was, and economic loss the family sustained. . . . If you take somebody who is in the field she is in, calculate her earnings over a lifetime, you probably end up with $7 or $8 million right there. Add to that the fact that her family has lost her association, and that's worth whatever a jury is willing to give them, $10 or $15 million. (Pallasch, 2003)

The critical issue to be determined in the Chang wrongful death civil suit is whether the officer's decision to pursue the fleeing vehicle contributed to her death. The case is currently pending.

Police Brutality – The Jeremiah Mearday Case

Charges of police brutality almost always generate intense media coverage and community outcry, particularly in cases in which minorities are the alleged victims. News headlines of police brutality and charges of excessive use of force draw the public's attention. Whether the allegations have merit is irrelevant in the initial reporting of these incidents. Perception often becomes reality, and a cursory review of story headlines that link "police" and "brutality" often resonates with the public, even if the charges are later found to be unsubstantiated.

The streets of Chicago are rough, combining gangs, guns, and drugs with flat-out "bad ass" characters. Police officers take an enormous risk every time they report for duty. The people police routinely deal with are not the most congenial among us; in fact, they are the most dangerous of the dangerous, nonconforming element of society – they simply don't play by the rules. They would just as soon shoot police officers as look at them. The truth is that police officers in Chicago are assaulted and battered by the citizens they serve on an average of more than 1,350 times per year – police are shot, stabbed, punched, kicked, bitten, and intentionally run down by vehicles. They are cursed, threatened, and spat upon, and such incidents of aggressive assaults on police are rarely reported by the press unless an officer is killed in the line of duty. Incidents of assault and battery against Chicago police officers increased by 25% from 1999 through 2002. Police collectively wear the scars of citizen abuse, both physically and emotionally, and the remembrance of fallen officers who have been killed in the line of duty is ever-present in their minds.

By definition, criminals do not play by the rules. Police officers, on the other hand, take a professional oath of office and swear to play absolutely by the rules. Police officers must, at all costs, guarantee that citizens' constitutional and civil rights are protected, and the vast majority of officers honor that pledge. In any given year, more than 2,600 complaints are filed against Chicago police officers for excessive use of force. From 1999 through 2002, 10,846 excessive use of force claims were filed against the Chicago police and were investigated by the Office of Professional Standards. Of that total, 644 (less than 6%) of the complaints were sustained, meaning that the allegation was supported by sufficient evidence to justify disciplinary action. The other 94%, or 10,202 of the complaints, were either unfounded or not substantiated, or the officer was exonerated.

While most officers obey their oaths, occasionally there are documented incidents wherein individual police officers step over the line and engage in excessive use of force. In such cases, the police department must take necessary disciplinary action, up to and including termination, to ensure that such disregard for the law on the part of officers will not be tolerated.

One of the most highly publicized cases of police brutality in Chicago occurred on September 26, 1997, during the arrest of a 17-year-old African-American Chicago resident named Jeremiah Mearday. Police officers James Comito and Matthew Thiel of the Grand Central District were on patrol in a marked police vehicle when they stopped to question four black males standing on the sidewalk at 1306 N. Pulaski Avenue. While attempting to conduct a field interview, the officers requested that the four subjects approach them. Three of the individuals complied, but Jeremiah Mearday refused. Mearday became loud and abusive toward the officers and began to hit Officer Comito repeatedly when the officer attempted to pat him down for protective purposes. Officer Thiel then grabbed Mearday in an attempt to assist his partner. The police officers later reported that during the struggle with Thiel, Mearday and the officer fell against a car and then onto the pavement. The fall allegedly caused lacerations to Mearday's head and face. According to police reports, the officers then placed Mearday into custody and transported him for medical attention. The three other subjects with Mearday fled the scene. Mearday was charged with resisting arrest and battery.

Mearday had a different version of his encounter with police on that day. He said that he was walking with friends to a Walgreens drugstore to purchase medication for an allergic reaction when the police stopped to question him and his friends. Mearday said he was walking ten to 20 yards in front of his friends. He heard the police shout that if he continued walking or running, he would be shot. He turned around to find Officer Thiel pointing a gun at him. Mearday said he went down on his knees as the two officers approached, but both officers began beating him on the head with their flashlights and kicking him. Mearday was screaming to his friends to get his father when the officers lifted him off the ground, and Officer Thiel hit him across the mouth with his flashlight. Mearday said he then fell over the squad car and started coughing and gagging up blood. The police officers allegedly continued to hit him on the head and kick him even after he was handcuffed.

Mearday filed formal complaints against Officers James Comito and Matthew Thiel, alleging that they beat him, used excessive force, and violated his civil rights. Mearday had a broken jaw and underwent reconstructive surgery at Cook County Hospital. According to medical reports, five of his teeth were loosened, and he suffered several lacerations to the head.

The alleged beating of Mearday garnered national attention, and community groups organized local protests. On October 7, 1997, at the urging of the Reverend Paul Jakes and the Chicago Committee Against Police Brutality, Attorney General Janet Reno initiated an investigation of the Mearday case through the Civil Rights Division of the United States Department of Justice. In addition, the Cook County State's Attorney's Office conducted an investigation to determine whether enough evidence existed to bring criminal charges against the officers. The report of two white police officers beating an unarmed, law-abiding black teenager on the streets of Chicago had potential national news interest equal to the Rodney King case in Los Angeles.

On October 22, 1997, then Superintendent Matt Rodriguez took action to suspend Officers Comito and Thiel after reviewing investigative reports issued by the Office of Professional Standards. Furthermore, he recommended to the Chicago Police Board that the officers be fired for their actions in connection with the Mearday case. Rodriguez's actions were applauded by the minority community but were chided by the Chicago Fraternal Order of Police as a sign that the city and the department did not support working police officers. Rodriguez's disciplinary actions occurred quickly, just 26 days after the incident. Most cases involving claims of excessive use of force by police take several months, if not years, to fully investigate.

On March 12, 1998, following a thorough hearing, the Chicago Police Board announced its findings regarding the disciplinary actions against Officers James Comito and Matthew Thiel. Board President Demetrius Carney said,

> The Chicago Police Board today found two Chicago police officers guilty of using excessive force during an encounter with Jeremiah Mearday on Chicago's West Side last fall. The Chicago Police Board takes charges involving the use of excessive force very seriously. Above all, our responsibility to the people of Chicago is to ensure that our procedures are thorough, fair, and beyond reproach. I am proud of the job that the police board and its staff have done in this case.... In the Mearday case, Board members considered more than 1,100 pages of hearing transcript, including the testimony of 15 witnesses. (Chicago Police Board, 1998)

It was the determination of the Chicago Police Board that the officers violated several departmental rules by engaging in the physical maltreatment of Mearday and then conspiring to cover up the incident. Both officers were fired from the Chicago Police Department.

On April 9, 1998, Cook County State's Attorney Richard Devine issued a press release regarding his office's investigation of the incident. The press release, in part, read,

> After an extensive investigation, misdemeanor charges of resisting arrest against Jeremiah Mearday have been dropped . . . and no charges will be filed against two Chicago police officers in the September 26, 1997 incident. . . . We need reliable evidence to charge a defendant and to prosecute a case. But at every step in this incident, we find inconsistencies and contradictions that would make pursuing this case on either side an exercise in futility. . . . Devine noted that while a report by the Office of Professional Standards resulted in the firing of the police officers, the State's Attorney's Office has a higher standard to meet – proof beyond a reasonable doubt (vs. preponderance of evidence) – to prosecute the officers for alleged criminal offenses. (Cook County State's Attorney's Office, 1998)

The announcement by Cook County State's Attorney Devine put to rest any criminal prosecution against Mearday or the police officers.

This might have been the end of the story involving Jeremiah Mearday and the Chicago Police Department, but there was more to come. On March 19, 1998, just 19 days prior to Devine's announcement that the charges against Mearday were to be dropped and just one week after the two officers were fired, the paths of Mearday and Chicago police officers crossed once again. Grand Central Police Officers Joel Bemis and Michael Brosnan, accompanied by Lieutenant Wayne Thompson, were canvassing a West Side neighborhood in an unmarked police car searching for a suspect who had shot a police officer in the early morning hours. At approximately 1:00 PM, the officers approached Mearday, who was standing near his home, and asked whether they could speak with him. Mearday turned and ran onto the porch of his home, attempting to turn the doorknob to get inside. Mearday said that he feared for his life because of his earlier experience with the police and their threats against him. According to Mearday, he was so nervous that he could not turn the doorknob as the police approached with their weapons drawn. Mearday said he wiggled his body to avoid being handcuffed but that he did not hit or kick the officers.

The police officers had a different story. They alleged that Mearday refused their orders to stop and that as they approached him, he had his left hand concealed underneath his coat, leading the officers to believe that he may have had a weapon. As Officer Bemis grabbed Mearday's left arm, Mearday elbowed and punched Bemis in the face, and he kicked Brosnan in the groin as the officers struggled to handcuff him. It took four officers to finally subdue and handcuff Mearday according to police reports. The offender was arrested and taken into custody by Chicago police and charged with two counts of aggravated battery for striking and kicking the officers and one count for resisting arrest.

Community groups and defense attorneys for Jeremiah Mearday claimed that his March 19 arrest was in retaliation for Officers Comito and Thiel being fired. The arresting officers were from the same police district as Comito and Thiel – the Grand Central District. According to reports from the *Chicago Tribune,*

> Defense lawyers contended the firings made Mearday – who emerged as a prominent symbol of the problem of police brutality and the tensions between the police and the black community – a marked man. They said he had every reason to fear the police when they approached him outside his home on March 19, 1998, just a week after the officers were dismissed. (Hanna, 2001b)

On March 8, 2001, Mearday's trial was concluded with a verdict of not guilty. In an unprecedented display of compassion following the announcement of the verdict, the presiding judge and members of the jury hugged Mearday and wished him well.

In two separate incidents between Chicago police officers and Jeremiah Mearday, two police officers were fired for using excessive force, and all charges against Mearday were dropped or found to lack evidence necessary for conviction. Two civil rights lawsuits against the city of Chicago by Mearday are pending. The reaction by Bill Nolan, president of the Fraternal Order of Police, regarding the Mearday case and the general lack of support that the Chicago police officers received was pointed and direct. He said, "I'm sick and tired of our police officers getting punched and pummeled and kicked. Some punk gets cracked because he resists arrest, and everybody makes him out to be a 'hero'" (Roberts, 1997). Obviously, there are two sides to every story, and in the rough and tumble streets where police and criminals do battle, the truth is often hard to determine.

The extensive investigation by the Cook County State's Attorney's Office regarding the September 26, 1997, altercation between Mearday and the Chicago police and their subsequent finding of conflicting and contradictory accounts of the incident is not uncommon in such cases. Who was right? Who was wrong? These are questions that often can never be fully answered. The truth is that when police officers encounter a suspicious person on the street, the stress level on both sides is elevated, and personal defense mechanisms immediately kick in. One harsh word or act of disrespect can incite anger and fear, which can, within a matter of seconds, lead to physical contact resulting in injury or death. A confrontation between a citizen and the police, which most often lasts no more than one minute from beginning to end, can take years for the courts to resolve.

The alleged September 26, 1997, beating of Jeremiah Mearday occurred prior to Hillard's appointment as superintendent, but the case played itself out during his tenure. Hillard has a saying that, "If you mess up, you fess up and you clean up." As a matter of course, he gave officers the benefit of doubt unless evidence proved that they were at fault. If they were at fault, he would go after them in order to restore both the professional image of the department and the public's trust.

Police Brutality – The Cabrini Green Incident

On April 17, 2003, Chicago police officers conducted a routine traffic stop during daylight hours. Police reported that the four African-American occupants of the van they had stopped refused police orders to step out of the vehicle. The stop occurred in front of the Cabrini Green Public Housing complex. According to citizen accounts of the incident, police broke the van windows, pepper-sprayed the passengers, dragged them out of their vehicle and to the ground, and beat and kicked them even after they were handcuffed. Numerous residents of Cabrini Green gathered to watch the incident unfold. The mother of one of the suspects protested police actions and was beaten so badly that she spent four days in the hospital. More than 40 officers surrounded the van as the crowd looked on. A Cabrini Green resident shot an 8-minute videotape from the upper level of the housing complex recording all police actions.

Superintendent Hillard immediately obtained a copy of the videotape and called together his entire command staff to view it and assess the incident to determine whether the actions of the police were appropriate and consistent with department policies and procedures. After viewing the videotape, there was a consensus among Hillard's command staff that department policies and procedures appeared to have been violated. Hillard immediately called a news conference to discuss police actions and assure the public that a complete investigation would ensue. He said,

> I viewed the tape, and I'm personally upset about what I've seen. The Chicago Police Department has worked far too long and too hard in all our communities to build a very strong relationship with our residents. These incidents undermine that relationship. (Garcia, 2003)

Lori Lightfoot, Chief of the Office of Professional Standards, discussed her office's pending investigation of the incident, saying, "We're going to follow the facts where they lead us and take the time that's necessary to make sure we do a thorough job" (Garcia, 2003). Hillard said that in addition to conducting an internal CPD investigation, he would send a copy of the videotape to the U.S. Attorney's Office in Chicago and to the Cook County State's Attorney's Office for their review and determination as to whether the police action violated state or federal laws.

When he became superintendent, Hillard vowed to work with the community to ensure that all police actions were aboveboard and not detrimental to Chicago's law-abiding citizens. The forums that Hillard conducted with leaders of the minority community were conducted in good faith with the expressed intent of improving police-minority relations. The incident at Cabrini Green was a test of the superintendent's commitment to monitor police actions closely and to come down hard when the police were at fault. When Hillard held a press conference just hours after the Cabrini Green incident, the minority community took him at his word that he was upset and embarrassed by the police actions and that he would undertake the necessary steps to investigate the incident thoroughly and, if warranted, to discipline officers for any wrongdoing. By going out front to address the Cabrini Green incident and releasing the videotape, Hillard had quickly allayed major public concern that Chicago police officers could operate at will, without the oversight of department review. True to his word, Hillard made sure that the department fully investigated the incident and took corrective action.

Summary

A review of the details of the major cases presented in this chapter should make apparent that police organizations are open institutions: all of their actions are subject to critical review by the media, politicians, the community, and the courts. Although extensive and detailed department policies and procedures are put in place to protect the department, the officers, and the citizens they serve, many police decisions are made within a matter of seconds and affect life and liberty. With the exception of police corruption, which is a premeditated choice made by an officer, the other categories discussed involve the use of a considerable degree of individual discretion and instant decision making based upon rapidly unfolding events. In any altercation that police officers have with a citizen, the line between appropriate physical response for purposes of self-protection and the use of excessive force is very thin and not well-defined. The same is true of police chases.

The vast majority of police officers are honest and do their best to perform a most difficult job in a professional manner. Unfortunately, no matter how many department policies and procedures are written to guide police action, the nature of police work is such that officers' individual discretion and split-second personal judgment will either hold them in good stead or lead them into trouble. The next chapter tells the stories of two incidents involving Chicago police officers who chased fleeing suspects and used force that resulted in the deaths of two African-American citizens.

Chapter 10

DEALING WITH A NIGHT FROM HELL

The chief of any large police agency will acknowledge two facts. First, every police department will at some time experience a night from hell – a night when everything that could go wrong does. Second, it is always risky for the chief to leave town. Even with the deputy chief in charge, it is not the same. When things go to hell, the mayor, the media, and the public expect to see and hear from the top police official.

On June 5, 1999, Superintendent Hillard was on his way to Sun Valley, Idaho, to attend the summer conference of the Major City Chief's Association. He was scheduled to catch a connecting flight from Denver to Boise. Before deplaning, the stewardess announced over the intercom that the captain had a message for Superintendent Hillard and that he should come forward to the cabin. The captain told Hillard that he must immediately call his office before boarding his connecting flight.

Hillard exited the plane and walked to the terminal where two uniformed Denver police officers were waiting for him. A picture of him had been faxed by the Chicago Police Department, so they recognized him instantly. The officers escorted Hillard to an office where he made the call. When Hillard talked to personnel in his office, he was informed that there had been two separate incidents in which Chicago police officers had shot and killed young African-American citizens. The black community was up in arms. Hillard was told, "The mayor wants you back in Chicago now!" The Denver police had already made arrangements with the airlines to get Hillard on the next flight back to Chicago. They told him that they would intercept his luggage and send it on to him. Hillard jetted back to Chicago to deal with what would become one of the most difficult crises of his tenure. Chicago police officers had shot and killed LaTanya Haggerty and Robert Russ in two separate traffic stops only hours apart.

The Case of LaTanya Haggerty

LaTanya Haggerty was a good student and had graduated from Southern Illinois University in Carbondale, Illinois. At 26 years of age, LaTanya was establishing herself in her professional life as a computer analyst working in downtown Chicago. She worked for Encyclopedia Britannica, Inc., and was living with her family in the South Side Chicago neighborhood of Brainerd. She had recently become engaged to be married.

On June 4, 1999, Haggerty worked all day before being picked up by a long-time college friend, 24-year-old Raymond Smith. What had begun as a typical day in the life of this young professional woman would soon turn into tragedy.

Officer Michael Williams and his partner, Serena Daniels, began the second work shift at the Chicago Police Department by going through roll call. They were on patrol in their South Side district shortly after LaTanya Haggerty caught her ride home. At 88th and South Cottage Grove, Officers Williams and Daniels observed Raymond Smith's vehicle pulled over on the wrong side of the street, where Smith had stopped to talk to a friend.

Observing Smith's obvious traffic violation, Officers Williams and Daniels approached the vehicle and asked Smith for his driver's license and insurance card. Smith ignored the request of the officers, engaged his vehicle, and drove away from the police. The officers pursued Smith for nearly 30 blocks. At approximately 5:18 PM, the officers notified the police dispatcher that they were pursuing a vehicle and that they were eastbound on 95th Avenue.

Another police unit, driven by Officer Carl Carter and accompanied by his partner, Officer Stafford Wilson, was in the area of the pursuit and had heard the dispatch. They responded to assist Officers Williams and Daniels. Officers Carter and Wilson intercepted the fleeing vehicle at 95th and Cottage Grove and positioned their squad car in such a manner as to force Smith to stop his vehicle. Officers Williams and Daniels then pulled up behind the Smith vehicle. All officers exited their vehicles and ordered the occupants out of their car. Smith again refused to comply, maneuvered his car free, and fled.

The four officers later reported that they felt their lives were in danger during the stop at 95th and Cottage Grove and that Smith had used his vehicle in such a manner as to threaten the officers and place them in harms' way. (This point would later be disputed by civilian witnesses.) As Smith drove away from police a second time, Officer Daniels fired two shots at the tires of the Smith vehicle, and Officers Williams and Wilson each fired one shot in similar fashion.

Smith and passenger Haggerty proceeded northbound, nearly 30 additional blocks, with both police units in pursuit. At 64th and King Drive, Smith finally stopped his vehicle, unlocked the doors, and put his hands in the air while remaining in the vehicle. Officers Carter and Williams opened the driver's door and pulled Smith from the vehicle. After a brief struggle, he was subdued and restrained.

Officer Daniels then turned her attention to Haggerty, who was sitting on the passenger side, looking straight ahead and talking on a cell phone in her left hand. Daniels ordered Haggerty to put her hands up and to drop the cell phone. Daniels was on the driver's side of the vehicle between the front and back doors with her weapon drawn and pointed in Haggerty's direction. According to Daniels, Haggerty then turned in her direction and raised her right hand. When Haggerty turned, Daniels said she observed a silver object in her hand and thought the silver object was the barrel of a handgun. Daniels fired one shot through the driver's side rear window. The bullet entered Haggerty's upper left arm and proceeded through her body in a downward direction, hitting several vital organs. The wound was fatal. Officer Wilson, who had positioned himself near the rear door of the vehicle on the passenger side, quickly pulled Haggerty from the vehicle, not knowing whether or not she had been hit by gunfire.

The facts and differing accounts of this encounter, which began and ended in less than 15 minutes, would be argued for years to come. What was immediately obvious was that a young professional woman, who was an innocent passenger in a vehicle initially being stopped for a minor traffic offense, was shot and killed by police. Furthermore, the shooting victim was found to be unarmed. Police later found a silver padlock on the front passenger side floorboard of the Smith vehicle, which Officer Daniels claimed was the silver object she observed in Haggerty's right hand.

Officer Daniels made a split-second decision to shoot at Ms. Haggerty. It was reported that immediately after shooting Haggerty, Daniels said, "I'm sorry, I didn't mean to." And as Daniels approached Haggerty, she said, "We're going to get you some help" (Devine, 2002).

As one might suspect in a police shooting of this type, the scenario described is only the beginning. Facts of the incident would be variously described over the coming months and years by participating officers and observing witnesses who were involved in the chain of events that led to Haggerty's death. Those accounts and recollections would, however, be remembered in very different ways and with very different emotions. What caused this young lady to be shot by police? Who was at fault – the police or those who fled? It was clear that answers would be demanded and that fault would eventually be determined.

Several facts relevant to the Haggerty shooting would soon be known. First, all four officers and both suspects involved in the chase were African-American. Second, both Officer Daniels, who fired the fatal shot, and Haggerty were female. These facts may not seem significant, but when white officers shoot African-American victims, it is immediately assumed that racism may have played a role. Furthermore, it is often assumed that male officers may be more aggressive than female officers. While race and gender may not have played a part in this incident, differing impressions and interpretations of facts create their own spin.

There is no doubt that Raymond Smith's decision to ignore police direction and commands contributed to the fatal conclusion of this encounter. It was later discovered that Smith was driving on a suspended driver's license and that he was in possession of marijuana at the time of the encounter with police. He was also on court supervision stemming from a previous arrest. Smith had reasons for not wanting to be apprehended by police.

As for LaTanya Haggerty, she was an innocent victim, simply seeking a ride home from a person she thought to be a friend.

As with any citizen shooting by police, the department immediately launched a full-scale investigation through the Office of Professional Standards (OPS). The focus of this investigation was to reconstruct the incident and complete a thorough review of the facts that led to the shooting and death of La-Tanya Haggerty at the hands of police. The focal concern of the investigation was ultimately to determine whether the involved officers followed proper police procedure.

On July 12, 1999, about five weeks after the incident, Superintendent Hillard issued a press release in which he announced that based on the investigation of the incident by OPS, he was recommending to the police board that all four officers involved in the incident be fired. Rules and regulations violated included the following:

- Failure to obey the direct order to terminate a police pursuit
- Firing at a vehicle without justification
- Failure to properly notify a supervisor that shots had been fired
- Improper use of deadly force

In a departmental press release pertaining to the incident, Superintendent Hillard stated that when he was appointed superintendent, he made it clear that if an officer tried to do the right thing and made an honest mistake, he would stand by that officer and do whatever was within his power to offer that officer additional training, counseling, supervision, and direction. He also stated, however, that when an officer was intentionally involved in corruption or deliberate misconduct, he would take swift disciplinary action. In the July 12 press release, Hillard stated, "After reviewing the [Haggerty] case, I am convinced that department rules and regulations were intentionally ignored, and the four officers involved must be held accountable for their actions" (Hillard, 1999c).

The conclusions of the OPS and the superintendent were based upon the findings that the officers did not properly communicate with the police dispatcher about the chase, ignored a sergeant's request to terminate the chase, shot at the victim's vehicle, did not immediately report shots fired, and, in the case of Officer Daniels, used deadly force improperly. Through various procedural hearings before the police board, and later in circuit court and civil court, these findings would be vehemently disputed and extensively argued.

The police board took action to fire Officer Daniels, Officer Williams, and Officer Wilson and to suspend Officer Carter for a period of one year. Upon review of the police board actions, a Cook County circuit court judge later affirmed the police board firing of Daniels, remanded the police board to rehear the cases of Williams and Wilson, and reversed the police board ruling on the suspension of Officer Carter, ordering him back to work with back wages, benefits, and seniority. In commenting upon these rulings, Circuit Court Judge Aaron Jaffe stated,

> Officer Serena Daniels was a police officer who should not have been in control of a deadly weapon. Being a police officer is a stressful and dangerous job. Individuals who cannot responsibly handle these situations should not control deadly weapons or be police officers. (Case 00-CH-06091, Circuit Court of Cook County, 2001, p. 15)

The shooting death of LaTanya Haggerty was also investigated by the Cook County State's Attorney's Office and the Northern Illinois District Office of the U.S. Attorney General to determine whether criminal charges should be filed against the officers for criminal intent or civil rights violations. State's Attorney Dick Devine stated that "there are no more difficult cases to investigate than police shootings, where split-second deadly decisions must be made." He further concluded that "the shooting was a horrible mistake, but not a crime" (Devine, 2002). The U.S. Department of Justice, in a separate investigation, concurred, finding there was insufficient evidence to conclude that the victim's civil rights had been violated (Strausberg, 2002).

The last decision reached in this case was in response to a civil action involving a survival claim and a wrongful death suit. The family of LaTanya Haggerty retained the legal counsel of James D. Montgomery and, more notably, Johnnie Cochran, of the O. J. Simpson defense team. Although the case was scheduled to go to trial, the city of Chicago settled by agreeing to pay the Haggerty family an unprecedented monetary award of $18 million. Chicago Corporation Counsel Mara S. Georges commented on the settlement, saying, "I feel this is a very good settlement for the city. We've got a very volatile situation that I felt was necessary to close, and it was in the best interest of the citizens of Chicago to close this chapter" (Strausberg, 2001a). In voting to approve the settlement offer, Alderman Freddrenna M. Lyle said, "We do not want human life arbitrarily taken based upon improper judgement taken by the police department and that is the message being sent" (Strausberg, 2001b).

Following the settlement, Johnnie Cochran was asked "whether the dynamics in the case, political and legal, would have changed if the officers who killed Haggerty were white." Cochran responded, "We weren't interested in race. We were interested in a tragedy and a loss of life and respect for life. That knows no racial boundaries, and I think that's what was important in this case" (Kass, 2001).

This story was tragic for everyone involved. LaTanya Haggerty died long before her time and left a family who loved her. The jobs of four police officers were either lost or placed in jeopardy. The city of Chicago and its citizens paid an $18 million settlement. Also disturbing is the fact that a petty criminal named Raymond Smith was charged and convicted of only minor criminal violations.

Superintendent Hillard was cautious, yet deliberate, in taking administrative action to resolve this case. Once the investigation was completed and it was clear that Chicago police officers were at fault, Hillard did not hesitate to take appropriate disciplinary action.

The Case of Robert Russ

Robert Russ was a Division I-A athlete, having played defensive tackle for the Northwestern University Wildcats football team. He was 22 years old and just days from graduating with a bachelor's degree from the highly respected academic institution. "According to his family, Russ was a funny, compassionate, young man: homecoming king at his south suburban high school, a member of the National Honor Society, and a singer in his Baptist church choir" (Mendell, 2003b). He was considering joining the Peace Corps after graduation.

In the early morning hours of June 5, 1999, at approximately 1:00 AM (just hours, in fact, after Chicago police had shot and killed LaTanya Haggerty), Russ was driving southbound on Lake Shore Drive. He was purportedly heading home to Calumet City to be with his girlfriend, who was six months pregnant with their son. According to police reports, Officer Philip Banaskiewicz observed Russ's 1986 Chevrolet Celebrity maneuvering in an erratic manner. The officer reported that Russ's vehicle almost hit a motorcyclist. Officer Banaskiewicz activated his emergency equipment and attempted to stop Russ. At Lake Shore Drive and Balbo, Russ's vehicle came to a stop due to a red light and backed up traffic. Banaskiewicz exited his vehicle and approached Russ's car. Because of the heavily tinted windows, the officer could not see inside the vehicle, so he knocked on the window. Suddenly, Russ locked the doors and drove on, forcing his way through the heavy traffic. Officer Banaskiewicz immediately notified the police dispatcher of the incident and indicated that he was in pursuit of the fleeing vehicle.

Upon hearing that Banaskiewicz was in pursuit, two more Chicago police officers in separate marked units responded to offer assistance. The Chicago officers joining the pursuit were Officers Van Watts IV and George Renner. Also joining the chase was off-duty Cook County Sheriff's Investigator Robert Helson, who had heard the pursuit over his radio and observed the chase firsthand. Helson was in an unmarked county vehicle.

Russ's vehicle exited Lake Shore Drive via the Stevenson exit ramp, proceeded west on I-90/94, exited that ramp, and traveled southbound on the Dan Ryan Expressway. The marked police vehicle driven by Officer Watts, with police emergency lights activated, pulled alongside. Russ rammed him three times in his attempt to escape. Russ finally spun out of control and came to a stop.

All responding officers, now consisting of four police units, positioned their vehicles so as to box-in Russ's vehicle. Russ then accelerated his vehicle in an attempt to flee once again and struck one of the police vehicles. The officers exited their vehicles and gave repeated demands for Russ to put his hands in plain sight and exit the vehicle. Russ did not respond, and officers could not see inside the vehicle because of the darkly tinted glass. The officers opened the passenger side door of Russ's vehicle and observed Russ sitting motionless with his hands between his legs. At the same time, Officer Watts attempted to open the driver's side door, but it was locked. So Watts smashed the rear driver's side window with a tire iron to gain access to the vehicle. With his service weapon drawn, Watts again ordered Russ to raise his hands and exit the vehicle. He could see Russ sitting motionless but could not see his hands. According to Watts, he had his service weapon pointed at Russ through the broken rear window when Russ, in a quick and assertive motion, reached around his left shoulder with both hands, grabbing the officer's hands and gun. Watts attempted to pull his gun back, and during the short struggle that ensued, the weapon discharged. Russ was struck in the chest with a single bullet. Banaskiewicz and Cook County Investigator Helson pulled Russ out of the vehicle by his legs and handcuffed him. They did not realize he was hit. Robert Russ was dead at the scene. No weapons were found in Russ' vehicle – he had been unarmed.

Even though the Robert Russ and the LaTanya Haggerty shooting incidents may appear to have similarities, there were many differences. Indeed, both began as simple traffic stops, only hours apart, and both resulted in a Black police officer's shooting an unarmed Black civilian, but the Office of Professional Standards, after an extensive investigation, issued a finding that the shooting of Russ was accidental.

In a press release on February 11, 2000, Superintendent Hillard announced that he had completed his review of the investigation surrounding the death of Robert Russ on June 5, 1999, and ordered that Officer Watts be suspended for 15 days. The superintendent also ordered that Officer Watts undergo additional training at the academy on departmental policies for handling a weapon and pursuing fleeing vehicles (Hillard, 2000). Hillard noted that Watts was a ten-year veteran of the Chicago Police Department and that this was the first disciplinary action taken against him; in fact, Watts had received 35 department commendations and honorable mentions. Officer Watts accepted the disciplinary action, deciding not to challenge the superintendent's decision either through the department's internal review system or through the police board.

This case was not over by any stretch of the imagination because a civil suit was brought in Cook County Circuit Court by Erin Lewis, the victim's fiancée. She gave birth to Robert Russ, Jr., on September 26, 1999, just three months and 21 days following the shooting death of his father at the hands of police. The wrongful death suit against Officer Watts and the City of Chicago was brought by Lewis on behalf of her son.

In the civil trial, city attorneys argued that Russ's shooting was caused by his actions to avoid the police and to grab Officer Watts's service weapon, causing the gun to accidentally discharge. Attorney Donald Shapiro, representing the Russ family, contended that Officer Watts concocted the tale of a struggle for his weapon. Shapiro said Watts willfully and wantonly shot Russ at point blank range after Watts lost his temper when the chase ended (Mendell, 2003b). Testimony from observing witnesses indicated that Officer Watts was "pretty charged up" and repeatedly used obscenities as he yelled at Russ to get out of the car. Civilian witnesses also testified that they did not see a struggle for the weapon (Caldwell, 2003).

Attorneys for the Russ estate also called numerous expert witnesses, including Dr. Michael Baden, a renowned pathologist, who had been called to examine forensic evidence surrounding the shootings of Reverend Martin Luther King, Jr., and President John F. Kennedy. Dr. Baden, after reviewing all of the evidence, concluded "that Russ could not have grabbed the gun barrel when he was shot," and that "the evidence was not suggestive of a struggle going back and forth" (Caldwell, 2003).

The plaintiffs' attorneys also called James Fyfe, a noted expert on police shootings and deputy commissioner for the New York City Police Department, who testified as a witness on Russ's behalf. Fyfe told jurors, "Officer Van Watts IV and other officers mishandled everything from the pursuit of Russ to how they conducted themselves when the chase ended." Fyfe stressed repeatedly that "the officers should have stayed behind their car doors and tried to talk Russ out of the car, rather than approaching the car, screaming profanities, and smashing the window" (Mendell, 2003a).

On Friday, October 17, 2003, a Cook County jury ordered the city of Chicago to pay the estate of Robert Russ, Jr., $9.6 million. According to news sources, "In the end, the jurors felt the officer 'was lying' when he claimed his gun discharged during a struggle with Russ" (Strausberg, 2003). The jury did find Robert Russ, Sr., to be 20% at fault for his own death because he eluded police and refused to comply with the officers' orders. The original award by the jury was $12 million, but it was reduced to reflect Russ's responsibility.

Another fact that was not allowed to be introduced at the civil trial was that Russ had a previous arrest and pleaded guilty to battery in a run-in with Evanston police in October 1998. Police reports of that incident indicated that Russ behaved in a bizarre manner, battered several persons including police, and caused criminal damage to property.

The Effect of the Haggerty/Russ Incidents

Following the shootings of LaTanya Haggerty and Robert Russ in June of 1999, the community reacted immediately, charging police with shooting unarmed African Americans for little or no cause. The Reverend Jesse Jackson, representing the Rainbow Coalition, issued a press release two days after the shootings. It read, in part,

There is a new wave of terrorism sweeping across America. Police brutality and excessive use of force is one of the most serious, enduring, and divisive civil and human rights violations in the United States. Today, in Chicago, it is LaTanya and Bobby; yesterday it was Amadou Diallo in New York, Johnie Grammage in Philadelphia, and Tyisha Miller in Riverside, California. It bothers me that no matter what the circumstances – whether you are asleep in your car; or walking down the street; or coming out of your apartment; or simply driving home from school or work – that as an African American, you pose a threat to law enforcement. African Americans deserve equal protection under the law. We are not second class citizens. All people of goodwill must organize and rally together to fight against this wave of terrorist behavior. (Jackson, 1999)

Other protesters commented that police were not sensitive to racial diversity and that "racism is hardly confined to white cops." Critics proclaimed that "racial sentiments provoke black-on-black confrontations as well" (McLaughlin, 1999, p. 1). As Reverend Paul Jakes claimed, "It matters less the color of the skin; it's blue vs. black, and it needs to be rectified" (Strausberg, 2002).

In the wake of the Haggerty/Russ shootings, the City Council conducted public hearings on June 17 and June 24, 1999. Superintendent Hillard addressed the committee, saying he "had listened to many people expressing concerns about the damage the Robert Russ and LaTanya Haggerty incidents have caused in the relation between people and police." Hillard said, "The Chicago Police Department has a long history of working proactively with the community to identify problems and to find solutions." Hillard's remarks to the committee called for cautious and judicial review of the facts surrounding the shootings and warned against hasty conclusions and stereotyping of all police officers based on the actions of a few.

Hillard also indicated that the Chicago Police Department had reached out to the families of Haggerty and Russ and that he personally met with the Haggerty family and community leaders including ministers, elected officials, community activists, and countless others in order to have dialogue and reinforce the bonds of trust and confidence that the Chicago police and the people of Chicago had worked so diligently to develop over the years. The superintendent gave his assurance that the Chicago Police Department was forever committed to reviewing police practices with an eye towards improving services to the community and maintaining the trust and confidence of the citizenry. He said, "We have built a strong relationship between police and community – and we can't allow that relationship to suffer as we work together to determine all the facts surrounding these incidents."

Moreover, the superintendent was well aware of the potentially damaging effects that these two incidents might have had on the morale of the more than 13,000 officers of the Chicago Police Department and the fact that increased media and public attention on two negative police-citizen encounters often can be projected upon the entire force. Hillard stated, "There have been suggestions that [these two incidents] reflect a broader pattern of police misconduct –

and I strongly disagree. They were two isolated incidents that are not reflective of police activity as a whole." He further emphasized that "on an everyday basis, the vast majority of the men and women of the Chicago Police Department do their job professionally – with sensitivity, good judgement, and skill – and given the continuing challenges they face each day, that should be acknowledged" (Hillard, 1999b).

Of course, it is critical that the police department stays engaged with the media and the community when tragic events occur. As the storylines surrounding events emerge, impressions will be shaped by what people know and don't know. Obviously, sensitive investigations require careful evaluation and consideration of facts; however, the public demands information, even if it is just a general update or status report. The public needs to know that the police are working on the case and that they are taking it seriously. In the Haggerty/Russ cases, Superintendent Hillard was reactive in a forthright manner, and his leadership projected a serious, deliberate, and honest tone that engendered public trust and confidence. He stated that the facts would be gathered and that corrective action would result if the police officers were at fault. He was also straightforward in assuring the community that he would evaluate current police practice, policy, and procedure to identify any shortcomings and that he would be willing to bring change and reform for purposes of improving police service.

In the days, months, and years that followed the Haggerty/Russ shootings, Hillard implemented myriad administrative actions designed to review police practice and improve service. Johnnie Cochran, commenting on the unusually large settlement of $18 million paid by the City of Chicago to the Haggerty family, said, "This is an expensive lesson for the city. Police have to treat people with respect. They can't be profiling. They can't shoot at cars" (Spielman & Pallasch, 2001). While one could interpret his comment as arrogant banter from the victor, there is an undeniable element of truth in his words.

In the aftermath of the Haggerty and Russ shootings, Superintendent Hillard announced a new partnership between the Chicago Police Department and the John Marshall Law School to review the Chicago Police Department's policies, rules, and regulations, including use of force. He also invited a team of experts from the Federal Law Enforcement Training Center to conduct a comprehensive review of the Chicago Police Academy training curriculum. These actions resulted in concrete recommendations clarifying guidelines for police during traffic stops, high-speed pursuits, and other high-risk calls for service and set in place revised academy curriculum and procedures.

Other significant changes implemented by Hillard included reorganizing the Office of Professional Standards (OPS) and providing additional training for all OPS investigators to ensure a timely and objective review by civilian investigators of citizen charges of police misconduct; raising the recruiting standard for police recruits and extending their training and probationary periods; reviewing the feasibility of adding more video cameras in police vehicles to monitor vehicle stops; distributing materials developed by the NAACP and the National Organization of Black Law Enforcement Officers that explained to citizens their rights during police stops; and developing mandated roll call training for police on cultural diversity, racial profiling, and showing courtesy and respect in traffic stops.

In editorials that appeared in the *Chicago Tribune* on May 9, 2001, and the *Chicago Sun-Times* on May 10, 2001, Superintendent Hillard was praised for the reforms he brought to the department. Both editorials focused attention on the fact that Hillard identified and emphasized the importance of the initial police-citizen interactions – that the initial approach and exchange between the citizen and the police largely dictates the tenor and outcome of the entire encounter. Courtesy, respect, and civility matter. The *Chicago Tribune* commented that "it's important for all of us – police and citizens alike – to remember that we share control of those first fragile 15 seconds" ("Learning," 2001). The *Chicago Sun-Times* concluded its editorial with these words: "We're mindful of the difficult job police have, but disrespect – from either side of the blue line – can escalate routine stops into tragic confrontations" ("Awareness," 2001).

Chapter 11

THE LIFE OF CHICAGO COPS

Heroes

The men and women who wear the badge
are heroes one and all
To serve and protect with honor and pride
they answer trouble's call

From village to village, county to state,
they stand ready, willing and prepared
To respond at once, by day or by night,
giving protection, comfort and care

What they see and what they hear can
be painful, ugly and mean
As danger pervades from call to call
with little relief taken in between

Protecting the weak, our elderly and
youth, from sinister deeds of those who would harm
Vigilant they stand, together they serve,
when injustice sounds the alarm

Their appearance is neat with polish
and shine; their manner remains polite
But appearance can mask broken
spirit and heart, caused by significant struggle and fight

When heroes we meet, we often misjudge
the credentials that must be brought
To distinguish between those who truly deserve,
and those who clearly do not

But the policemen I see who serve and
protect, who fight for justice for one and for all
Deserve nothing less to qualify best
for the naming of heroes we call.

– Thomas J. Jurkanin

In our society, law enforcement officers are alternatively praised and ridiculed by the citizens they serve. Police officers may be labeled as overly aggressive, incompetent, and corrupt one day and be heralded as heroes the next. Officers of the law are expected to possess the accommodating and compassionate skills of a trained psychologist on the one hand, while concurrently being expected to employ the aggressive intervention tactics of a commando on the other. They are expected to provide citizen protection and mediate highly volatile situations wherein angry words can escalate into physical violence within a matter of seconds. Police officers accept minimal pay to confront the meanest of the mean, the antisocial criminal element that is so obnoxiously aberrant that the average citizen could never fully appreciate or understand its level of depravity. Police officers kiss their spouses and children goodbye and report to the job every day, not knowing if this will be their final shift. Police officers are protectors, caregivers, and referees on the streets; they alone maintain the thin blue line between peace and anarchy, between right and wrong, between good and evil.

Some people who are unfamiliar with the conditions under which police officers work may contend that it is overly dramatic to call police officers heroes. But how many people really know that the daily actions of police officers make a real difference in improving the quality of life for all? How many men and women are willing to risk their own lives for the good of their fellow man? How many would subvert personal gain and monetary reward for public good and service? The heroic acts of police officers do not have to be embellished because they are documented day after day, year after year on the streets of America. The following incidents are real and offer just a few examples of the bravery and heroism of Chicago police officers.

A Day in the Life of a Chicago Police Officer

POLICE INCIDENT I: On August 28, 2001, at approximately 10:00 AM, Chicago Detective Joseph M. Airhart, Jr., a member of the FBI's Violent Crime Task Force, attempted to serve a warrant on Daniel E. Salley. Salley was a suspect in two robberies of the Charter One Bank located at 3250 West 87th Street in Chicago. On August 17, 2001, Salley allegedly made off with $16,719, then robbed the bank a second time on August 24, 2001, taking $239,000. In both robberies, Salley used a firearm.

Police had information that Salley was staying at his girlfriend's residence, a third floor condominium at 1307 South Wabash Street. Airhart, a 19-year decorated veteran of the department volunteered to lead the FBI Task Force into the apartment by posing as a deliveryman. When Salley opened the door, Airhart greeted him and handed him a package. Unfortunately, Salley did not buy into the ruse and quickly threw the package inside. A struggle ensued, and the FBI Task Force immediately stormed the door. Unable to hold off the agents, Salley ran into a nearby bedroom. Salley had a .45 caliber semiautomatic pistol in his hand and grabbed a second handgun for reinforcement. Airhart followed Salley into the bedroom and said, "You don't want to do that." The two exchanged gunfire, and Detective Airhart was shot once in the head, falling just inside the bedroom door. In the exchange of gunfire, Salley was shot three times in the leg and once in the chest. The offender closed the bedroom door and took Airhart hostage, threatening to kill him if agents came any closer.

Police negotiated with Salley for more than two hours before he agreed to surrender to police and allow Detective Airhart to receive medical attention. Police reporter Paul Meinke of ABC Channel 7 assisted the police in negotiating Salley's surrender. Airhart and the offender were transported to area hospitals. Salley was arrested and later charged with two counts of attempted murder, three counts of assaulting federal officers, two counts of armed bank robbery, one count of hostage-taking, and one count of illegally possessing firearms. Police found a stockpile of weapons including a .45 caliber semiautomatic pistol, a .44 caliber revolver, a .762 caliber rifle, a 10-gauge shotgun, and a .30 caliber rifle.

A bullet fired by Salley struck Detective Airhart in front of his left ear, passing through his brain's left temporal lobe and into the back of his brain. After two operations to remove the bullet and blood clots, Airhart remained in a coma for two months and suffered permanent, disabling injuries. Retired police officer Lorenzo Jackson, one of Airhart's closest friends, said of Airhart, "He's the kind of cop you want to take to the back alley with you. . . . He has a sixth sense of how to deal with people, how to get people to tell him things. . . . He treats people with respect. . . . He's what a law enforcement officer should be" (Simpson & Kaiser, 2001).

POLICE INCIDENT II: On November 14, 2001, four plain-clothed tactical officers – Daniel Gorman, Edward May, Sean Ryan, and Jerome Turbyville – were on patrol and paying special attention to the Humbolt Park neighborhood. The police were aware that there had been an escalating gang war between the Vice Lords and the Gangster Disciples over the control of drug turf in the area. The four tactical officers stopped to question five suspected gang members at Christiana Avenue and Heron Street. During the course of the stop, one of the suspects dropped a bag of cocaine to the ground and was immediately placed into police custody. While police were escorting the offender to the police vehicle and attempting to question the other suspects and witnesses, four gang members emerged from a nearby alley and began firing upon the officers. Although the officers announced their affiliation with the Chicago Police Department, the offenders continued to fire, and the police officers fired in return. The gang members were armed with a .30 caliber M1 carbine semiautomatic rifle, a 20-gauge Remington shotgun, and a .45 caliber Colt semiautomatic pistol. In total, more than 20 rounds were fired at the officers in ambush style. In the exchange of gunfire, Officer Ryan sustained a gunshot wound to his forearm, and Officer Turbyville suffered a laceration to his arm.

In addition, one offender and two witnesses were shot and later received medical attention.

Police Incident III: On March 15, 2003, at approximately 2:00 PM, Tactical Officer Wilfredo Torres, Jr., was patrolling with his partner in an unmarked police vehicle in the 3400 block of West Belmont. The two officers were summoned by a citizen exiting the D&L Snack Shop. The citizen informed the officers that a man had come into the shop to confront his girlfriend over an ongoing domestic dispute and had taken her hostage, threatening to shoot her and anyone who interfered. Torres instructed his partner to cover the back entrance and indicated that he would go in the front door of the shop. As Torres entered the front door, he encountered an armed suspect who was holding a woman hostage with a gun pointed at her head. Torres announced his office and ordered the offender to drop his weapon. The offender replied, "Someone is going to die today!" At that instant, the offender turned his weapon on Torres, while still holding the hostage with his arm around her neck. Officer Torres quickly pushed a male patron to the ground and out of the line of fire. The offender fired shots at Torres, striking him in one leg and then the other. Torres went down and then quickly popped back up. Despite his injuries, Officer Torres returned the gunfire, striking the offender once in the head and killing him instantly.

POLICE INCIDENT IV: On September 11, 2003, at about 2:00 in the afternoon, Chicago Police Officers Federico Andaverde and Andrew J. Dakuras were working an undercover assignment as members of the Area 5 Narcotics Enforcement Team. While driving westbound on Grand Avenue from Austin, the officers heard several gunshots coming from the direction of West Belden Grade School. The officers drove to the location of the shooting and noticed numerous elementary school children across the street on the playground. Two offenders had been firing at rival gang members. The officers, while still in their vehicle, announced that they were the police and demanded that the offenders drop their weapons. The two offenders disobeyed the officers' orders and immediately fired into the police vehicle. One of the offender's bullets struck Andaverde in the upper right leg. The officers then exited their vehicle and returned fire, hitting one of the offenders and knocking him to the ground. The second offender fled. Although injured, Officer Andaverde approached the offender who had been shot. The offender still had possession of a loaded .25 caliber semiautomatic pistol. As Andaverde approached the offender, he realized that his service weapon had been emptied in the exchange of gunfire and was locked in the slide position. In order to give the impression that he had a loaded gun, Andaverde placed his thumb on the slide lock lever, quickly releasing it, and pointed the empty gun at the offender. The wounded man allowed himself to be disarmed and taken into custody. Meanwhile, Officer Dakuras had taken up foot pursuit of the second armed offender. After a short chase, the gunman turned to fire upon the officer. Officer Dakuras returned fire, striking the offender, who fell to the ground. The offender, realizing that he was in danger of dying, surrendered his weapon and was apprehended by Dakuras and an assisting officer. The two offenders were transported by ambulance to area hospitals and were charged with the attempted murder of a police officer.

POLICE INCIDENT V: Salvadore Tapia was an angry man. The 36-year-old immigrant from Mexico had a long history of violence and alcohol abuse. Tapia had been arrested by police a dozen times for offenses that included domestic battery, aggravated assault, and possession of illegal weapons. He was so abusive to his girlfriend that she abandoned her home and possessions and moved out of state to escape his violence. In March 2003, Tapia was fired from his job at Windy City Core Supply, an auto parts warehouse on the city's South Side, because of excessive tardiness and absenteeism.

On the morning of August 27, 2003, five months after being fired from his job, Tapia returned to Windy City Core Supply at 3912 S. Wallace Street to exact revenge. Tapia entered the warehouse as the company's owners and employees were arriving at work about 8:00 AM.

Tapia methodically executed six employees as they arrived for work, using a .380 caliber semiautomatic Walther PP. For reasons unknown, Tapia spared the life of a seventh employee. He bound the victim's wrists with rope and tied him to a railing near a basement stairwell. Tapia then retreated into the warehouse to hide and wait for two other employees to arrive, who were running late for work. At about 8:35 AM, the employee who had been tied up managed to free himself and escape through the front door. He immediately flagged down a citizen, informed him of what was going on inside, and asked him to call the police. As several squads of beat officers arrived at the scene, Tapia exited the building twice to exchange gunfire with the officers.

The Chicago Police Department, recognizing that several company employees had been shot and others may be in danger, activated the Hostage Barricade and Terrorism (HBT) Team. The team assembled outside the warehouse at 10:00 AM and was ordered to make an assault on the building. The plan called for an emergency entry, assault, and rescue operation. Officer Luis Maldonado was assigned to be the "point man." Maldonado was directed to enter the warehouse in the lead position and locate, isolate, and neutralize the offender.

The officer, with his police service weapon drawn, carefully worked his way through a maze of crates, barrels, and boxes while attempting to locate the gunman. The electricity at the warehouse had been shut off, so it was difficult for the officer to see through the darkness. After working two-thirds of the way through the warehouse, Officer Maldonado spotted Tapia, with gun in hand, hiding behind a stack of crates. Maldonado ordered Tapia to drop his weapon. Tapia disregarded Maldonado's order and attempted to escape by quickly taking cover behind more boxes and crates. This time, however, Tapia was cornered. Officer Maldonado again ordered Tapia to surrender his weapon. Ignoring the officer's request, Tapia emerged from hiding and turned to face Maldonado at a distance of five yards with his weapon drawn. Officer Maldonado fired several rounds into the body of the offender, immediately incapacitating him. Tapia later died from the gunshot wounds.

Seven people died during that summer morning – six innocent victims and one deranged gunman. Many more people could have died if not for the quick and effective response of the Chicago police. The courage and tactical skills of Officer Maldonado not only saved his own life but possibly the lives of other officers at the scene that morning.

Recruitment

The Chicago Police aggressively recruit qualified people to serve as members of their department. Like any major corporation, the quality of the product – in this case, public protection – is contingent upon the quality of the people recruited and retained. The attrition rate for the Chicago Police Department is over 5% per year, which means that in a ten-year period, half of the Chicago Police Department will be replaced with new officers. Recruiting therefore becomes important. Although ten years may seem like a long time to change the culture and professional orientation of any major bureaucracy, the time span is actually quite short. The opportunity for upgrading and enhancing the overall quality of personnel within this period is appreciable.

Recruitment materials distributed by the Chicago Police Department state the following:

> We are looking for talented men and women who want to be a part of one of the nation's largest police departments and, most importantly, help make a positive difference in the lives of our residents. Do you have what it takes to be among the best? Are you a problem solver, able to think and react quickly to a variety of situations? Are you a leader, a strategic thinker? Do you have personal initiative, self-discipline, integrity? Do you enjoy helping people, improving your community? If you answered "yes" to these questions, you are the person we want. You are ready to take the challenge. (Chicago Police Career Information, 2005)

Applicants to the Chicago Police Department undergo a rigorous review, including a written examination, a physical fitness test, drug screening, a psychological test, a background investigation, and a medical examination. Only the most qualified applicants advance through the screening process to become eligible to attend the Chicago Police Academy. The initial training consists of 20 weeks of classroom instruction and practical exercises on such diverse topics as human behavior, criminal law, firearms and physical training, report writing, criminal investigation, patrol procedures, defensive tactics, and numerous other related topics. Police recruits are tested and evaluated throughout their training at the academy and during their one-year probationary period.

A Chicago police officer's starting salary is $36,984 in the first year, increasing to $47,808 after one year, and to $50,538 after 18 months. The employment benefits are good: paid health insurance, paid sick leave, 20 days' vacation, 13 paid holidays, a prescription drug plan, a retirement plan, and tuition reimbursement. While the employment benefits are generous, the hazards of the job are numerous and include much more than just physical danger.

When a young person takes the oath of office to become a police officer, he or she enters a new world characterized by an environment of fear, anger, conflict, violence, danger, mistrust, and death. Whatever life a new police officer leaves behind, it is doubtful that it was as chaotic and unpredictable as the one he or she will now assume. Police officers live a life of extremes. From their first day as rookie cops until the day they retire, police officers are on a roller coaster of emotional highs and lows, regulated by factors largely outside of their control. For all the hype surrounding community policing, problem-oriented policing, and preventive patrol, police work, for the most part, is reactive. Police officers respond to calls for service when a crime is in progress or shortly after a crime has occurred.

Police officers patrol in vehicles that are marked with city emblems, signifying authority. The vehicles are equipped with emergency lights and sirens and a caged backseat for transporting suspects. The officers wear distinctive uniforms displaying departmental patches, a symbolic silver star, and the customary equipment: firearms, handcuffs, flashlights, and batons. Police are trained to respond to and neutralize emergency situations, and they are prepared for the extreme. Whether responding to a call of a barking dog, a minor traffic accident, a complaint of loud noise, or a shooting in progress, police respond fully equipped, ready to employ all necessary force.

As police officers begin each shift, they are uncertain about the course of events that will unfold in the ensuing hours. The police radio and portable data terminals direct them to certain locations to interact with known and unknown persons and to intervene in potentially dangerous situations. Police dispatchers will regulate the priority assigned to each call and the frequency with which each unit is dispatched. In the majority of cases, the communication center is unable to inform responding officers of any potential dangers that might lie ahead. A domestic dispute can quickly turn into a murder-homicide. A suspicious person call can escalate into shots fired at the police officer. And a call regarding a missing child can become a case of criminal sexual assault and murder. On patrol, police may initiate a routine traffic stop for a minor offense and suddenly find themselves in the middle of a gun battle or a high-speed pursuit through city streets. Tactical officers execute search warrants and may kick down doors, not knowing what dangers await them on the other side. Narcotics officers work undercover, always aware that their identity might be revealed at any moment, thus placing their lives in immediate jeopardy. Officers working gang assignments are forever aware that they are just one misstep away from walking into the line of enemy fire. In each and every episode, officers may be exposed to dangers that will cause their adrenaline to surge, immediately increasing their heart rate and blood pressure, and initiating other biological "fight or flight" responses. These innate biological stress responses exact wear and tear on the body that, over time, may lead to physical and psychological deterioration.

In addition to the dangerous, violent, chaotic, and unpredictable aspects surrounding the police work environment, law enforcement officers face a multitude of other work-related stressors. These stressors are not overt or immediate threats to their personal well-being, but are nonetheless dangerous. A healthy lifestyle requires moderation, regulation, and consistency in matters of personal care. Eating right, getting enough sleep, maintaining family relationships, and cultivating friendships and interests outside of work are all measures conducive to living a balanced and healthy life. For most police officers, this "ideal" lifestyle is nearly impossible to maintain.

When police officers join the force, they know that from the day they sign on until the day they retire some 20 or 30 years later, the police department will never shut down. Police work is 24 hours a day, seven days a week, 365 days a year, year after year after year. Whether working days, evenings, midnights, or rotating shifts, police officers become accustomed to interrupted sleeping patterns. Police are on duty when their kids are asleep, participating in scouts, playing sports, or performing in a school play or band concert. Important family functions such as birthdays, holidays, graduations, and reunions have to be missed or rescheduled to accommodate police work schedules. Many police officers work second jobs to supplement their income and provide added levels of comfort for their families. A police officer's sacrifice of time, family togetherness, and sleep takes its toll on the officer and his or her family.

Unlike the majority of the population, police officers are isolated by their work. This assertion may seem odd to the general public given that police officers interact daily with a diverse cross-section of people and perform their duties largely within community view. It must be emphasized, however, that the people police most often encounter are not friendly, law-abiding, model-citizen types. Such people do not require police attention. Rather, police babysit people like drunks, drug addicts, and other derelicts who throw up, urinate, and defecate on themselves. They deal with problem people who do not obey the law, those who are violent, disrespectful, and problematic. Surveys consistently reveal that the vast majority of citizens support and respect the police and that only a small percentage of citizens consistently show disdain and disrespect for police and what they represent. It is this small percentage, however, of noncompliant, recidivist criminals and derelicts that police deal with routinely. Exposure to friendly, law-abiding folks is limited as the police concentrate their attention on problem people. Police psychologist John G. Stratton describes this phenomenon as developing a "microcosmic view of the world":

On the job, law enforcement personnel deal consistently with a very small percentage of the population – about 5%. What they see most often is tragic, demeaning, and criminalistic – in experiencing this, the officer begins in time to see the entire world as a magnification of what he or she encounters each day, and that population frequently views him or her in a degrading way as the "man" or "pig." The contact with the larger segment of the population who would reinforce the public service image is lacking. The officer working in this atmosphere often sees the situation as "me against the world." (Stratton, 1975, p. 44)

Police commonly express the notion that the world is black or white, "us" against "them"; however, it is inaccurate to say that "the police" are against "the world." Rather, the police are diametrically opposed to those few violent and dangerous criminal predators that freely roam the city streets, striking without a sense of conscience or remorse. In this context, police should be proud to say it is "us" against "them." Nevertheless, the "us" against "them" working environment serves to polarize and isolate the police from *everyone* who is not "us," thus further contributing to a police culture that extends far beyond the streets and into the day-to-day lives of the officers.

Police officers often have a difficult time separating work from other aspects of their lives. Police are the police 24 hours a day, and yet human emotions cannot be regulated by the hours in a shift. Traumatic events and less-than-appealing images are replayed in the officers' minds long after they sign off for the day. At home, police officers usually remain silent about their day, not wishing to expose their families to the horrible things they have seen. They may stare at their children across the dining room table and remember re-trieving a lifeless, mangled body, as small as that of their own child's, from an abandoned building. They might engage in casual conversation with their spouse, choosing not to divulge the details of a dangerous drug bust they are scheduled to execute later that night. In short, police officers often struggle to maintain a positive attitude toward life after years of being beaten up and worn down by the negative influences of the streets; therefore, for the protec-tion of their families, police officers often choose to remain silent, and their silence further isolates them from both their families and mainstream society.

Police officers are further isolated by the friends they choose. Police culture dictates that only a police officer can truly understand another police officer, so officers gather after work and on their days off in bars, around card tables, or on fishing trips to commiserate and share camaraderie. In one respect, these sessions are healthy because police officers are allowed to freely vent their emotions and discuss troubling events that they would never discuss at home. On the other hand, these off-duty activities further inculcate them into the police culture – they are exposed only to the mindset of other cops. The police brotherhood at once provides a support group and a safe haven from the chaotic and dangerous world that officers share while further isolating them from society at large.

Police officers have bars that they call their own – hidden away places where they can retreat at all hours of the day. These are places that accommodate their odd shift assignments, places where the few civilian regulars know to leave them alone. One journalist described a popular police bar named Ira's in the 1100 block of West Madison:

> Ira's is marked by an Old Style Beer sign out front, a 50-cent-a-game pool table lit by a Budweiser lamp and bumper stickers on the wall that read, "Proud to be a Union Sheet Metal Worker," and "If You Love Your Freedom, Thank a Vet." A Confederate flag hangs inconspicuously on the wall near the back door. A life-size stuffed pig wears a Chicago Police cap and has a gun strapped to its front right leg.

> Though the bar doesn't serve breakfast, it opens at 7:00 AM, in part to accommodate cops on every shift. Most of the patrons are white men, and they come in all ages, shapes, sizes, and ranks, talking, laughing, cursing and draining beer after beer and leaving the empty bottles to stand in mute congregation on the heavy wooden tables. (Kaiser, 1999a)

Duggan's, an Irish bar in Greek Town, is another police hangout. Duggan's proudly displays a 5' × 4' picture of the Old Mayor Daley and sells a 50¢ draft beer to anyone buying a police tee shirt. These bars are an integral part of the police culture, offering relaxation, brotherhood, understanding, and drink.

The irregularities of working long hours and rotating shifts also negatively affect the diet of police officers. They tend to drink too much coffee and soda, capitalizing on the caffeine energy boost each provides. They grab breakfasts at doughnut shops, lunches or dinners at fast food drive-ups, and snacks at gas station convenience stores because breaks may be interrupted at any moment. When they finally get home, some heat up leftovers from the family meal and chase them down with beer. Police are forced by their jobs to eat on the run, consume the wrong kinds of food, and take antacid tablets to calm their upset stomachs.

In addition to those stressors already discussed, police report high levels of frustration and stress related to what they perceive as unfair and unreasonable administrative practices – such matters as job assignment, restrictive departmental policies and procedures, discipline, and other bureaucratic matters. They often cite the lack of administrative backing and support as a major cause of work-related stress. Similarly, police report frustration related to the courts. Police believe that no matter how many times they arrest a person, no matter how many good pinches they make, the courts simply cut the offenders loose with a mere slap on the wrist.

Police officers are trained to be in control at all times. When a situation has deteriorated beyond their verbal control or they lose control because of some intervening factor, they are trained to take physical control. As adept as police may be at dealing with the chaotic and volatile encounters they face on the street, however, they are often less prepared for and less capable of resolving the internal emotional turmoil that slowly builds up inside of them. Like a pressure cooker, one traumatic incident after another exacts an emotional toll on officers, and without appropriate venting or resolution, the pressure builds to the point of manifestation, sometimes explosively. Police experience depression, burnout, alcoholism, divorce, health problems, and suicide at a disproportionately high rate when compared with people in most other occupations.

Notwithstanding their popular public image – tough as nails, fearless, emotionally callous, and always in control – the police are people first. As human beings, they experience the same sensitivities, vulnerabilities, fallibilities, and frailties as anyone else; they just happen to be police officers. The following poem captures the human side of the police.

Tears of a Cop

I have been where you fear to go . . .   *The one you bring your troubles to . . .*
I have seen what you fear to see . . .   *All these people I've been for you . . .*
I have done what you fear to do . . .   *The one you ask to stand apart . . .*
All these things I've done for you . . .   *The one you feel should have no heart . . .*
I am the one you lean upon . . .   *The one you call the man in Blue . . .*
The one you cast your scorn upon . . .   *But I am human just like you . . .*

                                                   – Author Unknown

One prominent figure in the field of human stress research was Dr. Han Syle, an internationally distinguished endocrinologist, biochemist, and philosopher. Syle reported the following:

> Some occupations are more likely to cause stress-related maladies (for example, high blood pressure, cardio-vascular disease, gastric ulcers, mental disturbances) than others. . . . Stress manifests itself not only in health disorders, but several other forms, including emotional and psychological disorders, which lead to such problems as divorce, alcoholism, drug addiction, poor job performance, boredom, cynicism, and even suicide. (Syle, 1978, p. 7)

Policing has long been recognized as a high-stress occupation prone to produce several of the work-related maladies described by Syle. The incidence of police suicide is the most shocking of all stress-related outcomes. Nationally, more than twice as many cops – as many as 400 annually – commit suicide than are killed in the line of duty. The following data demonstrate surprisingly high numbers:

> The Fraternal Order of Police studied suicide among its members and found a suicide rate of 22 deaths per 100,000, while the national suicide rate is 9 per 100,000 people, according to the Center for Disease Control and Prevention. In Chicago, from 1990–1998, 12 officers were killed in the line of duty, while 22 officers killed themselves (a rate of 18.1 suicides per 100,000; 50% above the national average). (Schwab, 2004)

According to Dr. Daniel Goldfarb, incidents of police suicide are most commonly precipitated by a combination of four factors: (1) divorce, (2) alcohol use, (3) depression, and (4) failure to seek help in the form of counseling (Gold-farb, 2004). Also contributive to the high incidence of suicide among police is their easy access to firearms. One study found that nearly 95% of all police suicides involved the use of a firearm, whereas only 56% of suicides among the general population involved firearm use (Violanti, 2004). Furthermore, it is widely believed that hundreds of police suicides go unreported or are mis-classified by police as "incidents involving the accidental discharge of a weapon." Police have a propensity to protect other officers' families so that they can collect death insurance benefits and so that all affected parties may be spared the embarrassment associated with suicide. In 1983, a Chicago Police Department study found that as many as 67% of all police suicides had been misclassified (Lynn, 2004).

While police suicide may be the most dramatic outcome of police stress, other symptomatic outcomes are equally as troubling. According to Dr. Gold-farb, "Research shows that police officers suffer a substantially higher divorce rate than the general population. While the national divorce rate is 50%, police officer divorce rates are estimated to be between 60 to 75%" (Goldfarb, 2004). In a comprehensive 40-year study of police stress and mortality, Violanti (2004) found that the average age of death for police officers is 66 years. Comparatively, "the life expectancy in the United States is 74.4 years for men and 80.1 years for women" (CIA, 2002). In an article entitled "Dying from the Job: The Morality Risks for Police Officers," Violanti (2004) reports on his research:

- Younger officers under conditions of high stress and other risk factors may be at higher risk for arteriosclerotic heart disease.
- There is a significantly elevated mortality risk for all malignant neoplasms in police officers. Specifically, (we found) a significantly increased risk of all di-gestive and hematopoietic cancers among officers employed 10–19 years.
- Twenty-five percent of police officers have been found to be dependent on al-cohol, and a significantly strong positive relationship was found between stress and alcohol use among police. Alcohol is [a pervasive] problem in police work and may lead to other work problems such as high absenteeism, intoxication on duty, complaints by supervisors and citizens of misconduct on-duty, traffic accidents, and an overall decrease in work performance. There was a signifi-cantly elevated risk of cirrhosis of the liver among police officers, a disease which has been related to alcohol use.
- Approximately 40% of police officers smoke cigarettes. (Our) findings indi-cate officers have a significantly high risk of esophageal cancer, which has been related to alcohol use and smoking.
- The significant suicide risk among police officers (in our study) denotes the possibility that chronic job stress leads to emotional numbing in officers and makes death easier to accept as a coping solution.

Superintendent Terry Hillard understood the multitude of pressures that police officers face on the job. As an officer on the street and as a supervisor,

Hillard witnessed officers struggling with personal problems and saw first-hand the devastating effect of ruined lives and careers, both on officers and their families. One of Hillard's top priorities as superintendent was to ensure that police officers received the necessary departmental support to identify, address, and overcome personal, family, and work-related problems.

Chicago police officers are fortunate in that they have access to counseling services provided by St. Michael's House. St. Michael's House is a not-for-profit corporation whose mission is to provide comprehensive services that enhance the emotional and spiritual well-being of police officers and their families. St. Michael's House is staffed by mental health professionals who specialize in law enforcement issues. Services are strictly confidential and include individual, marital, and family group counseling for such problems as depression, anxiety, job stress, alcoholism, eating disorders, marital dysfunction and divorce, and domestic violence. St. Michael's House is located in a four-story facility at 1759 West Adams. The building was obtained through the Asset Forfeiture Program, wherein the Chicago Police Department seized the real estate holdings of a drug dealer. Police officers and their families have unrestricted access to the services provided by St. Michael's House, which include long-term residential treatment programs.

Hillard strongly supported the work of St. Michael's House and encouraged Chicago police officers to take full advantage of the assistive medical and psychological services it provided. In an open letter to all Chicago police officers, Hillard wrote,

Dear Fellow Officers:

Every one of us who has walked the beat, chased the bad guys, locked up the criminals, or run toward the sound of gunfire to keep our neighborhoods safe knows the stress a police officer faces every day. It's a part of the job, but it doesn't have to work against us.

At St. Michael's House in Chicago, officers can find a safe haven, a place where they can feel comfortable and get the confidential counseling and treatment they need to deal with health problems such as alcoholism or depression.

The Chicago Police Department has been working with St. Michael's House for several years and strongly supports the good work being done there by the highly trained, professional staff who have a special understanding of the needs of the police. There is no shame in an officer admitting he or she needs help or in that officer seeking help. What is senseless is ignoring a problem and letting it fester into a crisis.

It's second nature for officers to chase bad guys or run toward the sound of gunfire, but it's not so easy for us to pay attention to what's happening inside. When it comes to our mental and emotional health, we need to be as vigilant as we are when we are walking the beat. St. Michael's House is one place where officers can feel safe and get the help they need. (Saint Michael's House, 2003)

During his tenure, Superintendent Hillard initiated many suicide and alcohol awareness programs for police officers and their supervisors. Hillard knows that police supervisors and colleagues are often reluctant to report fellow officers suffering from emotional and alcohol problems because they fear that the department will place the officers on medical leave or take immediate disciplinary action. Hillard attempted to create a more understanding and compassionate approach to dealing with such problems. His message was clear when he said, "We recognize that the job of policing is stressful and that officers suffer the effects of job stress. Our objective is to help officers facing difficult problems, to counsel and rehabilitate them, not to fire them." In his first year as superintendent, Hillard, concerned about the number of police suicides, transmitted a radio dispatch to Chicago officers just before the Thanksgiving holiday, urging them to seek help if they were depressed or were having suicidal thoughts.

In addition to assistance and counseling provided by the Chicago Police Department, the Chicago Fraternal Order of Police (FOP), Lodge #7, is a strong and vibrant organization that provides a plethora of assistive services to its members and their families. The mission of Chicago FOP is stated as follows:

> We pledge ourselves to promote the health and welfare of all Chicago law enforcement officers and their immediate families: to raise and maintain the professional standards of the Chicago law enforcement officer; and to represent Chicago police officers in affairs relative to the administration of the department. (Fraternal Order of Police, 2004)

Chicago police officers depend upon their strong union to ensure that their best interests are represented and safeguarded. The Chicago FOP intervenes with respect to individual and collective matters of concern to Chicago police officers, thereby providing a high level of support for officers on the street.

Although police officers face difficult challenges and occasionally suffer the maladies associated with high-stress occupations, the vast majority of officers learn to cope with such stressors appropriately and continue to lead healthy and productive lives throughout their careers. After all, police officers are selected through an extensive screening process whereby they are required to demonstrate their psychological fitness, emotional stability, and general propensity to manage high-stress situations appropriately. Police officers as a group embody an uncommon set of attributes, abilities, and commitments that set them apart from the general population. Individuals are selected as police officers because they are exceptional, strong, and capable of effectively handling high-stress situations.

The vast majority of police officers have productive and satisfying careers because they find meaning and purpose in their work. They gain a personal identity based upon that meaningfulness and purposefulness, so they are extremely committed to performing their job professionally and serving the public to the best of their ability. Police officers have chosen this noble occupation in part because they recognize the unique beauty and the unique tragedy of human behavior, with all of its inconsistency, unpredictability, and contradiction. For better or worse, law enforcement officers would not be content performing other jobs. The constant exposure to people and their behaviors, the opportunity to assist people in trouble, and the ability to interact and solve human problems are all factors that make the job of policing interesting and worthwhile. Police officers know full well, and reconfirm on a day-to-day basis, what it is they wish to contribute as productive members of society. The fact that they are police officers speaks clearly about commitments and concepts that they see as important in life – things like justice, equality, the protection of human freedom and life, and the protection of human rights and dignity.

Police officers meld their special and unique characteristics, sensitivities, talents, and abilities within the structure of their working environment. In this sense, they do not just react; they interact. They become active agents in each and every situation they handle. Their approach, attitude, and demeanor dictates to a large degree the outcome of each encounter. Their reaction can either escalate a situation into crisis or, alternatively, bring about a calm and peaceful resolution. Police officers understand that the environment in which they work is always fluid: it fluctuates day by day and hour by hour. The human behavior they observe reminds them of the goodness of men and women; however, their hope is forever countered by the inhumane injury and pain they often see inflicted by one person upon another. They are reminded that human beings are as capable of hatred as of love, that human beings can give and sacrifice to protect another's life, and that human beings can just as quickly take a life without remorse.

Police officers are in a position to observe contrasts in human behavior up close and on a more frequent basis than people in any other profession. Unlike professional psychologists, police officers deal with human behavior in the trenches, where a missed diagnosis can result in death or injury to themselves or innocent citizens. Police don't have the luxury of taking a personal history, running a battery of psychological tests, or seeking a second opinion from a colleague. Situational assessment and response by the police must be made within a matter of seconds – and always balanced against aggravating risk factors. A split-second decision made in the dark of the night is often the difference between life and death.

Police officers seldom ask for understanding or sympathy because they accept both the good and the bad of policing. They represent a chosen few who have the devotion, compassion, courage, and emotional stability to carry out the critical function of public protection. Police officers are aware of the dangers of the job, but their primary desire to serve and protect carries them through with pride. Author Ambrose Redmoon wrote, "Courage is not the absence of fear . . . but rather the judgement that something else is more important than fear." Police are not fearless, but they are courageous. If others fail to respect them as dedicated public servants, they themselves have no such doubts – because police officers feel good about what they do.

Every year in the United States, between 150 and 165 law enforcement officers are killed in the line of duty. Buried behind these grim statistics are stories that are seldom told – from uplifting stories of courage and service, to stories of shattered families and shattered lives. The names, faces, memories, and circumstances of every police death forever remain with the families and partners of the fallen officers, but many people fail to take notice or care to remember.

Six Chicago police officers were killed in the line of duty during Terry Hillard's tenure as superintendent, and four additional officers died in the performance of duty. As one police official said of Hillard, "You have to understand these are his kids; this is his family; when a police officer dies, a piece of all of us dies with them." Hillard said that losing so many officers – officers with promising lives and careers, who left grieving families – was far and away the toughest part of his job. These were senseless acts of violence against those whose only desire was to protect others. Hillard said, "In this cynical time when heroes have feet of clay, our fallen officers emerge as the true role models." Following are brief details regarding each of the officers who were killed in the line of duty during Hillard's tenure as superintendent.

Officer Michael A. Ceriale – Killed in the Line of Duty

Star Number: 17429
Age: 26 years
Date of Appointment: May 5, 1997
Date of Death: August 21, 1998
Survivors: Tony and Mary Ceriale, parents; Anna Retelskyj,
    grandmother

Incident Summary

At approximately 3:45 AM on August 15, 1998, Officer Michael A. Ceriale was shot while working in Wentworth, a neighborhood that has one of the highest crime rates in Chicago. Ceriale and his partner, Officer Joseph Ferenzi, both just 10 months out of the academy, were in plain clothes working the night shift. They were observing possible drug dealing activity at the Robert Taylor Homes, a Chicago Housing Authority high-rise building at 4101 S. Federal, known to be the drug market for the Gangster Disciples. The officers were hiding in a cluster of trees when they were spotted by gang members. Two offenders emerged from the building, and one fired a single shot in the direction of the officers. The shot fired from the .357 magnum revolver struck Officer Ceriale in the abdomen, just below his bullet-proof vest. Officer Ceriale struggled for his life for six days, and after five operations and 200 pints of blood transfusions, he lost his fight for life. Police later arrested and charged the 16-year-old shooter and several accomplices.

Tributes

Mayor Richard M. Daley – Speaking at Ceriale's funeral services with tears in his eyes: "Less than 2 years ago, [Michael] stood at Navy Pier. He raised his right hand; he stood by that motto: we serve and protect. He was taken from us. Blessed are the peacemakers for they will be called sons of God" (Kass, 1998).

Friend Robert Robles – "It's just surprising for such a new cop, an officer with such little time, that he did so well. . . . He really wanted to work. He was a good all-around kid. He had a great attitude. He was going to be one of the up-and-coming great cops" (Pallasch & Wilson, 1998).

Officer John C. Knight – Killed in the Line of Duty

Star Number: 5119
Age: 38 years
Date of Appointment: December 26, 1989
Date of Death: January 9, 1999
Survivors: His wife, Joan; two sons, Matthew and Brian; a daughter,
    Lauren; his parents, Anna Marie and Charles L.; two brothers,
    Stephen and Charles; and a sister, Mary McAvoy

Incident Summary

On Saturday, January 9, 1999, at approximately 2:45 PM, Officer John Knight and his partner, Officer James Butler, were investigating two suspicious men in a parked car. As the officers exited their squad car to investigate, the offenders sped off. During the ensuing chase, the offenders' vehicle crashed. Before either officer could exit their squad car, Officer Knight was shot by one of the offenders at point-blank range through the windshield of his squad car. The assailant, 23-year-old James Scott, was armed with a 9-mm semiautomatic Ruger handgun with a laser scope. Scott fired the weapon at least 25 times, hitting Knight in the head and shoulder. Butler, wounded in the hip, returned fire, hitting Scott twice. Officer Knight was transported to the hospital but was pronounced dead upon arrival. Scott was charged with first degree murder and attempted first degree murder. Scott told police later that he was waiting in the car with the other occupant to buy drugs when Officers Knight and Butler came to investigate. Superintendent Hillard had worked with John Knight's father as a young police officer.

Tributes

Superintendent Terry Hillard – Hillard recalled how Knight proudly took his retired father's Star Number 5119, when he joined the police force: "He was determined to follow in his father's footsteps. John was an exceptional police officer whose zest for life brought joy to everyone he met" (Hillard, 1999a).

Mayor Richard M. Daley called the loss "a senseless act of violence that affects every child in this city and in this nation. Any attack on a Chicago police officer is an attack on our society as a whole" (Sullivan, 1999).

Officer James H. Camp – Killed in the Line of Duty

Star Number: 3934
Age: 34 years
Date of Appointment: May 31, 1994
Date of Death: March 9, 1999
Survivors: His wife, Opal; three brothers, John Major, Rodney Davis Major, and Tony; a sister, Mary Galloway; and a stepfather, Meredith Palmer

Incident Summary

At approximately 2:00 PM on March 9, 1999, Tactical Officers James Camp and Kenneth King were on foot at 3807 S. Cottage Grove and observed a black 1987 Chevrolet Caprice parked with two occupants in the front seat, one male and one female. The vehicle was parked near the Albert Einstein Elementary School while classes were in session. The officers walked past the vehicle and observed that the vehicle was running without a key in the ignition – a sign that the vehicle may have been stolen. Camp approached the male subject on the driver's side, while Officer King walked around to the passenger side of the vehicle. The male subject immediately exited the car and engaged Officer Camp in a physical confrontation. During the struggle, the offender was able to gain control of Camp's weapon and fired one shot into the officer's face. When Officer Earl Carter arrived at the scene to assist, he observed the struggle and the shooting. Carter fired five shots at the offender, thereby incapacitating him. Camp and the offender were transported to the hospital. The officer was pronounced dead at 2:30 PM. The offender, Kevin Dean, survived and was charged with first degree murder and multiple other offenses. The vehicle had been stolen from Indiana.

Tributes

Alderman Ed Smith – "The shooting death of Officer Camp was horrendous. It shows that the moral fiber of this country is just gone. Somewhere down the line someone dropped the ball" (Washington, 1999).

Superintendent Terry Hillard – "James Camp was a gentle giant who used his strength for good. Not just his physical strength – which was impressive – but his strength of character. Review the life of James Camp and you find a man

of toughness and integrity . . . always using his strength for the forces of good"
(Hillard, 1999b).

Officer Brian J. Strouse – Killed in the Line of Duty

Star Number: 15806
Age: 33 years
Date of Appointment: January 3, 1995
Date of Death: June 30, 2001
Survivors: Paul and Anne Marie Strouse, parents; sisters, Kathleen
   Nuncz (a Chicago police officer), Cynthia, and Paula

Incident Summary

Officer Brian Strouse was working 12th District Tactical (plain clothes) in
the Pilsen Neighborhood at 2:00 AM on Saturday, June 30, 2001. He and two
other officers responded to a report of a sporadic gang-related gunfire on the
1300 block of West 18th Place. The three responding officers exited their vehicles and began to search the area. Strouse left the other officers so that he
could get a closer look. Sixteen-year-old Hector Delgado, acting as security
for drug dealers of the Ambrose Nation Gang, spotted Strouse behind a
parked van and opened fire with a .40 caliber handgun. Although Strouse was
able to yell "police," Delgado continued to shoot, hitting Strouse twice, once
in his bulletproof vest and once in the head. Officer Strouse was transported
to the hospital where he later died. Delgado was arrested for first degree
murder, tried as an adult, and is serving a mandatory life sentence.

Tributes

Superintendent Terry Hillard – "I stand here feeling a mixture of strong emotions. I am deeply saddened. I am frustrated at the senseless violence. And, I
am proud. When gunshots are fired in the community, most people run away.
In contrast, Brian is the type of man who runs to the sound of gunfire because
he knows someone needs help" (Hepp & Janega, 2001).

Mayor Richard M. Daley – "Another valiant, courageous man has been taken
from us in an act of mindless violence. . . . We must do everything we can to
eliminate the circumstances that led to the loss of one of Chicago's finest"
(Main, 2001).

Officer Eric D. Lee – Killed in the Line of Duty

Star Number: 16947
Age: 37 years
Date of Appointment: December 16, 1991

Date of Death: August 19, 2001
Survivors: Wife, Shawn; daughter, Erica; parents, Anna and Bobby;
    brothers, Mark (Isslee) and Steven (Shanita); sister, Michelle;
    grandmother, Anna Bates

Incident Summary

At about 9:20 PM on Sunday, August 19, 2001, Tactical Officer Eric Lee was
working in the Englewood District on a narcotics investigation with four other
officers. He and two other officers responded to a call of a man being beaten in
an alley at 6330 Aberdeen. When Lee and his partners identified themselves,
one of the individuals involved in the altercation displayed a handgun and fired
at the officers, striking Lee in the head. All three of the suspects fled. Officer
Lee was transported to the hospital where he was pronounced dead at 10:02
PM. Police later apprehended Aloysius Oliver, aged 26 years, and charged him
with first degree murder. Oliver was a gang member with a two-page arrest
record. The gun Oliver used to kill the officer, a Ruger .357 caliber revolver,
was reported stolen in Waukesha, Wisconsin, on New Year's Day 2001.

Tributes

Shawn Lee – "My husband's death was a senseless act of violence that must
challenge the people of Chicago to demand action, to stand up and say, 'This
must end.' . . . to show our children a better way of life . . . to end senseless violence in our communities ("Officer's Wife," 2001).
    Chicago Tribune – "Officer Lee chose to work in Englewood rather than
pulling seniority and transferring to a safer district because it is where he grew
up. He wanted to help people in his community" (Kaiser & Kapos, 2001).

Officer Donald J. Marquez – Killed in the Line of Duty

Star Number: 8620
Age: 47 years
Date of Appointment: February 1, 1982
Date of Death: March 19, 2002
Survivors: His wife, Maria; daughters, Maria, Carla, and Alana;
    son, Donald; grandson, Antony; parents, Daniel and Mary;
    brothers, Daniel, Dave, and Dean; and sisters, Donna and Deanna

Incident Summary

Officer Donald Marquez was a 20-year veteran of the Chicago Police Department. A former gangs crime investigator and tactical officer, Marquez was
detailed to the City's Law Department, where he served subpoenas and made

arrests for violations. At approximately 10:00 PM on March 18, 2002, Marquez, attempted to serve a warrant at the Logan Square Apartments in the 25th District. The owner of the apartment building, 77-year-old Henry A. Wolk, had failed to appear in housing court after he was fined $14,500 in 2001 for 29 housing code violations. After several attempts to convince the owner to open the door, Marquez made a forced entry into the apartment using a sledge hammer. Immediately after gaining entry, the building owner fired at Marquez with two .22 caliber semiautomatic handguns, striking the officer twice in the chest and once in the head. The offender was later shot and killed by responding officers. The fallen officer was transported to the hospital where he died the next day.

Tributes

Superintendent Terry Hillard – "When Donald was growing up on the city's South Side, he suffered through the deaths of several of his friends at the hands of gang violence. That's when he made a decision to become a Chicago police officer. He wanted to make a positive difference in his life" (Hillard, 2002a).

Illinois State Senate Resolution – "Officer Marquez will be remembered as an honest, hard-working cop who died a hero in his efforts to make the city of Chicago a safer place for all" (Ninety Second Illinois General Assembly, SR-0364).

Officers Ceriale, Knight, Camp, Strouse, Lee, and Marquez, all good officers, were killed defending the city of Chicago and its citizens. Each of them was killed with a firearm by individuals who had no regard for human life. Ceriale, Knight, and Strouse were white; Camp and Lee were black; and Marquez was Hispanic. Their skin color didn't matter; what mattered was that they were all men of Blue. As one Chicago columnist wrote, "[They] were willing to put their lives on the line to try to restore simple civility in neighborhoods locked in a battle between good and evil. And the evil isn't just gangs and drugs. It is disrespect, hatred, and wanton behavior" (Mitchell, 2001, p. 14).

Superintendent Hillard kept a memorial card of each officer killed during his administration on a credenza behind his office desk. In addition to the officer deaths documented previously, the following Chicago police officers died in the performance of duty while serving the citizens of Chicago while Hillard was superintendent.

1999, Officer Myles M. Smetana, Star # 14658
2000, Sergeant Alane Stoffregren, Star # 1203
2001, Sergeant Hector A. Silva, Star # 1760
2002, Officer Benjamin Perez, Star # 12225

Hillard wanted to be reminded constantly of their heroism and service, of the families that they left behind, and of their loss and sacrifice. Hillard took the death of each officer personally.

Hillard said that he and the Chicago Police Department made some mistakes in how officer shootings and deaths were handled early in his administration but were able to correct them later on. They learned that the colleagues of injured officers needed to be kept informed of their medical status, as well as the status of the on-going investigation. One tragic event was particularly revealing.

On September 18, 2002, at 6:30 PM, Officer Benjamin Perez and his partner were conducting a narcotics investigation on the city's West Side, just north of Cermak Road, in the 2000 block of Spaulding Avenue. The two uniformed officers were on a trestle of the Burlington Northern/Santa Fe Metra Railway attempting to surveil narcotics trafficking below. Metra Train #1285 was westbound, and Perez was unable to get out of the path of the train. Officer Perez was killed instantly, and his body was dismembered and scattered in parts along the railroad yard.

As Hillard and his command staff arrived at the scene, a large group of Chicago police officers assembled in the distance, prepared to recover the body of their fellow officer. After consulting with Hillard, his command staff determined that they would not allow the officers to recover the body. Officer Perez was their colleague and friend and exposure to the carnage would be too painful and traumatic for the young officers. After inspecting the scene, Hillard and his command staff approached the group of officers and explained that the supervisors would recover the body, but that once the body bags were prepared, they (the officers) would transport the officer to the waiting ambulance. The command staff told the officers, "You need to remember Benjamin how he was, not as he is now." Hillard and his command staff went to their cars, got their flashlights and gloves, and recovered the body of Officer Perez. Hillard praised Officer Perez, who died in the performance of duty as "a gifted policeman, who shared those gifts with his community and colleagues. . . . Officer Perez, a quiet, but professional officer, understood that we are fighting a war – a war against crime, a battle against guns and gangs. . . . He was a brave young man" (Hillard, 2002b).

Hillard explained that when an officer is shot or seriously injured, his or her partners and fellow officers respond in mass to show their support. At the hospital, concerned officers fill the waiting rooms, hoping to gain information on their wounded colleague's status. In the past, the superintendent and command staff would talk to the doctors and talk to the families but would leave all other officers out of the loop. That policy was soon changed. Based on the recommendation of First Deputy Superintendent John Thomas, once the command staff had all of the information concerning the officer's status and the direction of the investigation, all officers gathered would be briefed by Superintendent Hillard. Hillard said,

> What we knew, they knew. And, we would give them the straight-skinny; we wouldn't sugar coat anything. If we were withholding information from the press, the officers would be told to keep it quiet. This policy change was the right thing to do; after all, this was their partner, their colleague, their friend; the officers had a right to be kept informed.

Superintendent Hillard's sensitivity to fallen officers, their families, and partners is legendary. Several days after Michael Ceriale was shot in the abdomen and was struggling in a coma to survive, Michael's father entered his hospital room in the middle of the night and found Superintendent Hillard standing quietly by Michael's side. Others talked about Hillard buying birthday and Christmas gifts for children of fallen officers, and Hillard always spent hours consoling the families, forever concerned about their welfare.

The *Chicago Tribune* related a story told by Officer Joe Ferenzi, Michael Ceriale's partner, the night Michael was shot. Officer Ferenzi was in the waiting room of the hospital when Superintendent Hillard arrived. The Superintendent walked up to Ferenzi, introduced himself, and offered him words of comfort. Hillard then asked Ferenzi, "Are those boots heavy?" The question caught Ferenzi off guard. He was trying to determine whether the superintendent's question had a deeper meaning. As Ferenzi struggled to formulate an appropriate response, Hillard repeated the question, "Are those boots heavy?" Finally, Officer Ferenzi looked down at his feet and said, "Yes, they are heavy." Superintendent Hillard nodded and told Ferenzi, "The Department was thinking of testing some lighter athletic shoes for the officers" (Kaiser, 1999a). Even in this most difficult time, Hillard was just trying to make the shaken officer relax and think about other things.

Between 1972 and 2002, 4,449 police officers were killed in the line of duty in the United States – 2,553 were killed feloniously and 1,896 were killed accidentally (Sourcebook of Criminal Justice Statistics, 2002). Ceriale, Knight, Camp, Strouse, Lee, Marquez, Smetana, Perez, Silva, Stoffregren, and more than 460 other Chicago police officers lost their lives while on duty between 1854 and 2002. All were heroes. The *Chicago Defender*, in an editorial published on August 23, 2001, noted, "The gladiators in Blue are society's last line of defense against the insanity in this world. We are thankful for their dedication and passion to protect us, and we mourn heavily when we lose them, especially to foolish venal acts" ("Remembering," 2001).

A *Chicago Tribune* article, written by John Kass and published on March 16, 1999, aptly captures the life and death of Chicago police officers:

> Today there will be bagpipes, and the Mayor and the brass and a baton salute. Chicago is burying another police officer. . . . Despite the concerned community groups and the political law-and-order speeches and the official sympathy when one of them is buried, they (the Police) know one thing. They know they are alone. . . . We curse them until we need them. Then we call them heroes. . . . They wade through the stupid brutality of crime and clean up the human garbage and get dirty. We don't really want to know how it gets done and what they do. And they wouldn't tell us anyway. Here's what they do. They pick up dead infants, frozen in plastic bags left on the back of a wooden porch. They listen to a man explain why he stabbed his brother to death over a 98-cent cigarette lighter. They hear the reasons of the monsters who lure children on playgrounds. . . . Nobody but their own would understand. They gather at funerals . . . then go off with their own kind. . . . They're cops and they are alone. (Kass, 1999)

Chapter 12

SUPERINTENDENT HILLARD'S LEGACY: ACCOMPLISHMENT AND LEADERSHIP

As superintendent of the Chicago Police Department, Terry Hillard enjoyed a high-profile public presence, and, because of his friendly and easy-going demeanor, he was well liked by the citizens of Chicago. Hillard was recognized everywhere he went. His frequent appearances on local television promoted a positive public persona, and citizens felt comfortable approaching him at various events, in restaurants, and on Chicago streets. He frequently participated in community events, anticrime marches, and parades, often accompanying Mayor Richard M. Daley. As with many high-profile public officials, Hillard was provided with drivers and a security detail and was often accompanied by a number of departmental personnel, depending on the type of event he was scheduled to attend. The trappings that accompanied his high-profile position only added to the mystique of his celebrity status. In the end, however, it was Hillard's humble personality and quiet Tennessee-bred charm that endeared him to the people he met.

One of Hillard's management team members and close friend Frank Radke recalls accompanying the superintendent when he marched in the Bud Billiken Day Parade, the nation's largest African-American parade and the largest parade in Chicago, drawing a crowd of nearly one million people annually. The parade is a 75-year-old celebration offered as a salute to children and their return to school. The parade includes hundreds of marching bands, floats, performers, and politicians. On this particular occasion, Radke remembers,

> Thousands of people were chanting something as we walked, and it was difficult to hear what they were saying. Finally, I figured it out; they were chanting "Terry," "Terry," "Terry," and mothers were holding their young children up to get a close look at the superintendent. That's how popular he was.

Radke says that he and Hillard would go to the opening day White Sox game, and it would take them several hours to walk to and from their seats. As Radke said, "Terry would just keep telling me '20 more minutes, 20 more minutes,' and 2 hours and 20 minutes later, we would finally get out of there. People just flocked to him, and Hillard loved to stop and talk to people."

Two amusing stories regarding Hillard's popularity were conveyed by his staff. On one occasion, Superintendent Hillard was scheduled to attend a visitation for the adult daughter of a Chicago police officer who had died. Hillard's security detail arrived at the funeral home to take a look around so that they could provide the superintendent and his drivers with details regarding the arrangements because there were several visitations taking place at the funeral home concurrently. When Hillard arrived, he went to the end of the line and waited his turn to show respect to the officer and his family. Hillard stood in line patiently, but as he looked around, he did not see any other cops and became suspicious. As the line advanced, it became clear that he was in the wrong line, but it was already too late to step out of line without showing disrespect and drawing attention to himself. As Hillard approached the casket and the family, he saw an old lady lying in state. The deceased's husband looked at Terry and said, "Superintendent, I didn't know you knew my wife. Thanks so much for coming. It would've meant a lot to her." Hillard gave his condolences and moved on.

On another occasion, Superintendent Hillard was out in public dressed in a suit and tie, as often was the case, and was surrounded by people wanting to shake his hand and talk to him. One young man observed the crowd of people around Hillard and decided to approach to ask for an autograph. Hillard politely took a pen and signed his autograph. The young man then held the autograph at arm's length to examine it and then said, "Terry Hillard? I thought you were (baseball legend) Ernie Banks." Terry's staff were often amused by such stories and used them to good-heartedly tease their boss.

Accomplishments

For years, Chicago police operated out of an antiquated headquarters at Eleventh and State Streets. The building was old; the offices were small and cluttered; and any attempt to properly maintain the rundown structure was futile. When Hillard was appointed superintendent, one of his assignments was to oversee the construction of a new Chicago Police Headquarters. Mayor Daley and the City Council had approved the money for the new headquarters, and plans had already been developed. Between 1998 and 2000, the city of Chicago constructed a magnificent 390,000 square foot building on a ten-acre site at 3510 S. Michigan Avenue. The new Chicago Police Headquarters was a beautiful, modern structure and became the most technologically advanced police facility in the country. The Public Building Commission of Chicago issued a press release stating,

> The jewel of police headquarters is the command center, a high-tech hub where daily activities of the police department can be carried out – or strategy for managing a crisis can be carefully plotted. Eight 50-inch screens spread across the

front of the room; each can project different visual images. . . . From his seat in the command center, Superintendent Hillard can participate in roll call at any of his district stations via video links. Or, he and other police officials can track crime throughout the city, spotting patterns in certain neighborhoods and creating a proactive link of attack. (Public Building Commission of Chicago, 2000)

In addition to producing a police headquarters equipped with the most sophisticated technology, the architectural plans incorporated a design to promote police-community interaction. At the direction of Mayor Daley, the new five-story police headquarters included a 500-seat public auditorium on the first floor for members of the community to use in furtherance of the Chicago Alternative Policing Strategy (CAPS) program.

While Chicago laborers carefully laid each brick to construct a world-class police facility, Superintendent Hillard and his management team set out to organizationally structure a police department that would stand on an equally solid foundation and meet the current and emerging public safety needs of the city.

President Theodore Roosevelt once said, "The best executive is one who has sense enough to pick people to do what he wants done and self-restraint enough to keep from meddling with them while they do it." Hillard surrounded himself with talented and capable individuals. He knew their strengths and would encourage them to work creatively and with a sense of independence. As Deputy Superintendent Barbara McDonald said, "His management style was such that he didn't bother you. He knew what you were working on, but he left you alone. His whole focus was to give you the support you needed to get the job done." Peter Drucker said, "No executive has ever suffered because his subordinates were strong and effective." Hillard always proclaimed that any successes attributed to him as superintendent were actually the work of his management team and the entire force.

The programs and initiatives introduced during Hillard's tenure were significant and far reaching. Hillard's organizational and management initiatives reflected an ongoing commitment to community policing, technology, and accountability, while concurrently employing aggressive crime-fighting strategies designed to battle guns, gangs, and drugs. Outlined below is a summary of just a few of the initiatives spearheaded by Hillard and his management team:

- Hillard's commitment to community policing was strong and enduring. Through the community forums and other community-based initiatives, Hillard's message was clear: "The Chicago Police Department's mission [is] to work closely with residents to build lasting foundations for safe neighborhoods – foundations built to survive fluctuations in the crime rate" (Chicago Police Department, 1999/2000).
- Hillard forged a strong partnership with local, state, and federal law enforcement agencies to combat guns, gangs, and drugs through intergovernmental investigative task forces and the sharing of intelligence

information on ongoing crime problems and potential security threats related to terrorism.

- Hillard implemented Citizen Law Enforcement Analysis and Reporting (CLEAR). The department, through CLEAR, utilized information technology to police smarter; to share information with other agencies; and ultimately, to better identify, analyze, and combat crime.

- Hillard reorganized the Detective Division into three strategic operational units: (1) Homicide/Gang and Sex Crimes Unit, (2) Property Crimes Unit, and (3) Special Victims Unit. The reorganization allowed the department to make the best use of available resources to solve crimes on the street. In addition, Hillard created an elite 100-officer cadre called the Targeted Response Unit (TRU). These officers were trained to quickly saturate areas plagued with problems of gangs, guns, and drugs. TRU officers worked flexible hours to hit hot spots at the peak of criminal activity.

- Hillard initiated the purchase and installation of video cameras, strategically placed in public areas and street corners where gangs congregated to sell drugs. From blocks away, police could use monitoring devices the size of a briefcase to watch and record drug buys and other illegal activities and to gather intelligence and evidentiary information.

- Hillard implemented a revised Department General Order regarding the use of force by police officers. The policy provided officers with guidance and options with respect to how to apply force in maintaining public order. The policy also made individual officers more accountable for their actions. A new restrictive policy on police pursuit was also implemented to better define situations in which police could pursue fleeing suspects. Both policies incorporated training, supervision, and accountability measures.

- Hillard introduced taser technology to give sergeants the option to use force that is short of deadly force. In addition, Hillard implemented computerized video simulation technology to train officers better on "shoot, don't shoot" decision making.

- Hillard reorganized the Office of Professional Standards (OPS) and appointed a former assistant United States' Attorney to run the office. The charge of the office was to get at the truth in allegations against police officers and to ensure that all investigations are conducted fairly and expeditiously. In addition, Hillard directed the office to open a dialogue with the community to describe the functions, responsibilities, and procedures of OPS to the Chicago citizenry.

- Hillard implemented the Ambassador Program, which enlisted the assistance of minority community leaders, teachers, business owners, and the clergy, for purposes of recruiting high-quality applicants to the department. The goal was to achieve diversity among the ranks of the Chicago Police Department to ensure that the Chicago Police Department is comprised of officers who reflect the communities they serve. From 1998 through 2002, the Chicago Police Department increased its minority representation to 42%. Over a two-year period, nearly 50% of all new hires were minorities. In addition, more women were hired, bringing the total percentage of women on the force to nearly 25% of sworn personnel; and more women than ever before were promoted to command positions.

- Hillard implemented a new policy prohibiting Chicago police officers from engaging in acts of racial profiling and requiring each of them to complete additional training on cultural diversity. All command officers were required to sign the following pledge: "As members of the Chicago Police Department, we reject racial profiling as a law enforcement tactic. We do not encourage, tolerate, or condone the use of racial profiling. We are committed to the use of sound police strategies based upon reasonable suspicion, probable cause, the judicious use of police discretion, and the continued development of community relations" (Chicago Police Department, 2001).
- Hillard recruited and hired Lieutenant Colonel Gary Schenkel from the United States Marine Corp to take charge of the Chicago Police Academy, to revise and enhance basic and inservice training programs, and to instill pride and discipline in the academy setting.
- Hillard increased hiring and promotional standards related to education. Additional education and training opportunities were provided to all officers regardless of rank.
- Hillard created the Office of Management and Accountability to ensure that police managers were held accountable for issues of crime and disorder in their respective areas of assignment.

No matter what organizational changes may occur to enhance police operations and response, a superintendent of police and the department as a whole will always be judged by comparative increases or decreases in crime. After all, the majority of people believe that the sole responsibility of the police is to control crime. If the Sunday newspaper carries a front page headline that reads "Violent Crime Is Up by 20% Over Last Year" or "Sexual Assaults Have Doubled," the public takes notice, and they assuredly will be alarmed. The bells and whistles of newly implemented crime-fighting technologies and the cute acronyms used to identify elite crime-fighting units or special police operations are no longer impressive when crime is on the rise. From the public's view, such initiatives have apparently failed, or else crime would be going down.

Prior to Terry Hillard's assuming the superintendency in 1998, reported crime in Chicago had experienced a significant and sustained six-year decline, beginning in 1991. During Hillard's 5½-year tenure, crime continued to decrease. In Chicago between 1991 and 2002, violent crime declined by 49%; murder went down 30%; robbery, 58%; criminal sexual assault, 45%; and aggravated assault and battery, 41%. In the same time period, property crime was down 36%, including a 47% decrease in motor vehicle thefts, a 51% decrease in burglaries, and a 27% decrease in thefts (Skogan, Steiner, & the Chicago Community Policing Consortium, 2004, pp. 52–54).

Crime data from Hillard's tenure as superintendent show that crime continued to decrease year after year, with one exception. Murder declined 10% from 1998 through 2000 and then went up slightly, 2.6%, from 2000 through 2002. From 1998 through 2002, robbery decreased 30%; criminal sexual assault, 24%; aggravated assault and battery, 35%; motor vehicle theft, 25%; burglary, 44%; and theft, 21%. Overall, during Hillard's superintendency, violent crimes decreased 32.5%, and property crimes decreased 27%.

In general, Chicago's dramatic decline in the rate of reported crime from 1991 through 2002 parallels national crime rates and those experienced in other major cities including Detroit, Phoenix, Houston, San Antonio, San Diego, Dallas, Philadelphia, and New York. The only exception was murder. While Chicago's murder rate fell by 33% from 1991 through 2002, the combined murder rate of other major cities declined by 50% (Skogan et al., 2004, p. 74). As discussed previously, Chicago is unique in terms of problems related to guns, gangs, and drugs, and this trio of factors could partially account for the lagging decline of murders in Chicago when compared with other major cities.

The fact that reported crime is down significantly in Chicago is undoubtedly good news; however, the news gets better. Recent research conducted by the Chicago Community Policing Evaluation Consortium found that the "fear of crime" among the majority of Chicago residents was also down from 1994 through 2002 and that Chicago citizens rated the "quality of police service" as better in 2002 than they did in 1994.

In a longitudinal survey distributed to Chicago citizens from 1994 through 2003, researchers asked the respondents to answer the following question: "How safe do you feel being alone outside in your neighborhood at night?" Citizens could respond *very safe, somewhat safe, somewhat unsafe,* or *very unsafe.* The survey results revealed,

> Fear was down 10 percentage points or so among men and younger people. In 1994, 30% of the men surveyed reported they would be afraid to go out after dark; in 2003, the comparable figure was 20%. Levels of fear among the city's whites dropped by half, from 34% to 17%. However, fear was down more – by 20 percentage points or so – among African Americans, women, and older residents of the city. (Skogan et al., 2004, p. 70)

In addition to reporting that Chicagoans felt less fearful in their neighborhoods in 2003 than in 1994, researchers also reported that "public confidence" in the police had improved from 1993 to 2003, particularly on measures of "police responsiveness" and "police performance." The research report concluded that, in general, "Chicagoans are happier about their police . . ." (Skogan et al., 2004, pp. 39–41).

It has been emphasized that the overriding goal of Chicago's Alternative Policing Strategy (CAPS) is to improve "the qualify of life" for all citizens of Chicago. Three positive outcomes, as reported by the Chicago Community Policing Evaluation Consortium, indicate that significant progress has been made: (1) reported crime went down; (2) citizens were less fearful in their neighborhoods; and (3) public confidence in the police improved. All of these positive changes occurred during the tenures of Superintendent Hillard and his predecessor Superintendent Matt Rodriguez and were concurrent with implementation of (CAPS) community policing.

Leadership

The legacy of Terry Hillard will not be the declining crime rates realized during his tenure; nor the improved status of police in the eyes of the public; nor the many innovative organizational, operational, and technological advances he brought to the department. The legacy of Terry Hillard will be his effective leadership ability and style. There are thousands of executives managing private and public enterprises throughout the world, but there are a limited number of leaders. Terry Hillard is a true leader.

The superintendent's former staff spoke glowingly of Hillard as a man of principle, Hillard the boss that they loved, and Terry their respected, trusted friend. There is no greater tribute to a leader than the respect and admiration of people he once led. Marjorie O'Dea, Hillard's administrative sergeant, may have said it best:

> Terry Hillard is a rare human being. He is a man with a well-designed moral compass, someone you can count on to do the right thing. He is extraordinarily smart and holds very strong personal beliefs about what is right and what is wrong. He is a person who has great personal integrity and expects others to act the same way. And he is genuinely disappointed when they don't. In the six years I worked for him, I never saw him lose his temper or even raise his voice. He was always composed and treated everyone with great respect and kindness. He possesses an inner strength of character that everyone who meets him recognizes.

Terry Hillard's leadership is his legacy. In many respects, the principles upon which he based his leadership style are straight-forward and easy to understand, at least in a conceptual sense. What distinguishes Hillard from others, however, is that he never deviates from his ethical and moral principles. Hillard knows the difference between right and wrong, and he has the focus and discipline to always do the right thing. As Ellie Foster, his long-time friend and aide, said, "Terry would always tell us, if you keep your priorities straight and do the best you can, what more could be asked of you?" From Hillard's perspective, leadership is that simple. Outlined below are ten principles that best define Superintendent Hillard's leadership philosophy and style.

Leadership Principle One

The secret of a leader lies in the tests he has faced over the whole course of his life and the habit of action he develops in meeting those tests.
– Gail Sheehy

Hillard was a leader before he became superintendent. There is little doubt that he was selected by Mayor Daley because the mayor recognized his extraordinary leadership qualities. Hillard had the fortune and misfortune of many life experiences. Being born in the segregated South and being one of ten children, becoming a Marine and serving in Vietnam, joining the police force and being shot in the line of duty, and surviving cancer – all presented exceptional opportunities for personal growth and maturity. And Hillard took advantage at every turn in order to strengthen his character as a person and to become a leader. As one of Hillard's colleagues said, "One thing we all know; Terry set his priorities right sometime early in his life. God, family, the Marine Corps and the police department – they were all important in shaping his life, his beliefs, and his commitments." All of these factors made Terry Hillard a better leader.

Leadership Principle Two

He who has never learned to obey cannot be a good commander.
– Aristotle

From his earliest days as a child cleaning up his mother's kitchen and doing chores around the house, Terry learned to obey, and in the Marine Corps, he followed orders explicitly and adhered to his training because he wanted to get out of Vietnam alive and return home to his family. Then, he joined the Chicago Police Department and found himself following orders once again. Fred Miller was his sergeant. When Hillard was assigned to the Gangs Crime Unit, Miller recalled how Hillard performed, saying, "I never met a more loyal officer who was so focused on what he was doing. He was never distracted when he was working. You could count on him being at a location if you told him to be there. You could go to the bank with that." Miller also said, "In the Gangs Crime Unit, when we executed search warrants, Terry was always the first one in, not because he was trying to be macho, but because it was his assignment and he was always concerned with protecting his partners." Hillard was lauded as a "Cop's Cop." He had been on the streets; he had taken a bullet for the city; and he would not ask anyone in the department to do anything he wouldn't do. As one officer said, "Terry Hillard was a police officer who happened to be superintendent; Hillard cared about the officers on the street because he came up through the ranks."

It is a fact that Chicago police officers do not automatically trust and respect a person just because he or she has the title of superintendent. Trust and respect must be earned, and Chicago cops saw Hillard as a leader who was one of their own.

Leadership Principle Three

The respect that leadership must have requires that one's ethics be without question. A leader not only stays well above the lines between right and wrong, he stays well clear of grey areas.

– G. Alan Bernard

Hillard always told his people, "Just do what is right. Always take the high road." To him, integrity and trustworthiness were not options but absolute necessities for all who worked for him. In a job interview with a person whom Hillard later hired on his command staff, Hillard said, "You're never going to have to lie for me because I'll never put you in that position; however, remember, I'm never going to lie for you, either." According to his staff, people never had to worry about Superintendent Hillard sending mixed messages either. He told people exactly what he meant, even if it was uncomfortable for him to do so. As one staff member said, "When Superintendent Hillard faced the press, he wasn't going to be ducking, dodging, and doing all that spin-doctor stuff on them. He said what he had to say in clear and simple terms, and he would tell them straight-out if he could not release information." Hillard's word was his bond, and he would not compromise his integrity for purposes of taking the easy way out. During Hillard's superintendency, there was not one hint of a scandal. As one of his staff said, "The worst thing they could ever accuse Terry Hillard of was getting his shoes shined on company time." George Van ValkenBurg stated, "Leadership is doing what is right when no one is watching." In terms of professional ethics and personal integrity, Hillard saw no grey areas. Because he had such a strong moral compass, it appeared easy for him to set a good example by simply being himself and doing the right thing.

Leadership Principle Four

A leader takes people where they want to go. A great leader takes people where they don't necessarily want to go, but ought to be.

– Rosalynn Carter

Superintendent Hillard's genius was in his ability to recognize good, talented people and to place them in the positions where they could do their best work. One of Hillard's administrative assistants, Tom Argenbright, said, "Superintendent Hillard made a genuine effort to promote qualified, highly talented individuals." Just a few years after being appointed superintendent, Hillard promoted Barbara McDonald to deputy superintendent of Administrative Services. McDonald was a civilian whom Hillard met in 1992 when she was director of the department's Research and Development Division. McDonald had spearheaded the CAPS Program and was one of the innovators of CLEAR. According to McDonald, Superintendent Hillard had met with her and told her he wanted to appoint her as one of his six deputy superintendents. McDonald initially told Hillard that she was not very interested in the job, but Hillard was insistent, saying, "Well, I want you to take it anyway – I need you to do this." McDonald accepted the position and never regretted it for a second. Similarly, Hillard promoted 30-year-old patrolman Ron Huberman to assistant deputy superintendent because of what he knew and what he could contribute to the organization. It didn't matter whether a person was male or female; white, black, Hispanic, or Asian; civilian or sworn; young or old; an old friend or a new acquaintance. It was talent and management ability that Hillard sought for his administration. As Argenbright observed,

> The people that Superintendent Hillard promoted and surrounded himself with tended to be a reflection of his style of management. Terry Hillard's top promotions consisted of people who had excellent interpersonal skills and were good managers. A person who tried to motivate employees by yelling, screaming, and intimidation did not get very far with his administration.

In one case, a commander made derogatory remarks about women. Hillard took offense saying, "My mother, wife, and daughter are women." Shortly thereafter, the commander was no longer part of Hillard's administration.

Finally, Hillard felt that people who attempted to gain promotion through political connections, as opposed to merit, were not even worthy of consideration.

Leadership Principle Five

> *Stand with anybody that stands right, stand with him, stand with him while he is right and part with him when he is wrong.*
>
> – Abraham Lincoln

Terry Hillard trusts people to do the right thing and is disappointed when they do not. Foremost, he believes in loyalty, but he knows that loyalty is a two-way street. As superintendent, he would never tolerate people who placed personal gain above the good of the department. *American Police Beat*, a national law enforcement publication, ran a feature article on Hillard, stating,

> Although he'll stand by his officers when they make an honest error, it's a different story when they cross over the line. Brutality, racial profiling, corruption – if these charges hold up, Hillard is not subtle, "Engage in any of these activities and we'll come after you." Superintendent Hillard related, "On [one] Monday morning, I spent the morning giving out awards for heroism at Police Headquarters. These were officers who survived shootouts, who ran into burning buildings to save people, who volunteered for extremely dangerous assignments. Two hours later, I was at the U.S. Attorney's Office at a press conference where they announced the indictments of several Chicago police officers. . . .

The good guys in the department work way too hard for me to tolerate corrupt cops." (Brown, 2003, p. 67)

Leadership Principle Six

> *A successful man is one who can lay a firm foundation with the bricks others throw at him.*
>
> – David Brinkley

In a very real sense, the life of Terry Hillard was blessed. He was born into a family with rock-solid values and was taught from an early age by parents who understood life's struggles and challenges. Good parents know that they will not always be by their children's sides to protect them, so they must inculcate values, attitudes, and personal skills that will enable their sons and daughters to survive in the world. Terry Hillard experienced racism in his life; however, he is forever unwilling to acknowledge this fact because to do so would also be an admission that other people's aberrant behavior may hold influence on the person he chose to become. His mother taught him that words have no power to hurt unless you let them hurt you and that people who wish to hurt you with words are not worthy of your emotion and anger.

Ellie Foster tells the story of accompanying Superintendent Hillard to a City Council meeting when the city was in an uproar about several incidents of alleged police brutality. The City Council held a public hearing that lasted for seven hours while citizens vented their complaints, outrage, and anger. When the meeting was over, protesters were crowding the streets and yelling insults as the superintendent struggled to get to his car. Foster said, "Terry Hillard took it in stride." Hillard realized that people were upset, but he also knew that when he took the job as superintendent, he would become the designated target for their anger and frustration. Most of the time, Hillard's staff would be more hurt and upset by the personal insults inflicted upon the superintendent than Hillard himself. Hillard would tell them during these trying times, "It's all about family. As long as these people don't come on my front lawn and try to bang on my door, and try to intimidate my family or myself, I can handle it." As Assistant Deputy Superintendent James Molloy said, "Terry Hillard is a gentleman. He is a caring and considerate man who is comfortable with himself and his place in the world."

Hillard knows through experience that people who resort to anger and personal attacks are not the ones who are willing to be part of the solution. Indeed, Superintendent Hillard was very concerned about police brutality, but he also understood that eliminating it meant working in a collaborative manner with both concerned community leaders and the police in a civil and enlightened manner. Hillard's tireless work through community forums and other proactive and progressive initiatives proved to be successful. As Foster said, "Hillard is a gentleman; he's kind and considerate, and people sometimes underestimate him. But don't mistake his kindness for weakness because he is a very strong person." When bricks were thrown at Terry Hillard, he knew instinctively as a leader that it was unproductive for him to throw bricks back in an angry display. Superintendent Hillard's goal was to elevate the level of discussion, to choose the high road, to do the right thing, and to work productively with concerned citizens in an attempt to make things better.

Leadership Principle Seven

Great leaders are almost always great simplifiers, who can cut through argument, debate, and doubt to offer solutions everyone can understand.

– Secretary of State Colin Powell

As superintendent, Hillard was intelligent enough to know that he did not have all the answers. One of his greatest assets was being able to bring the necessary people to the table for discussion and dialogue on important issues. Hillard firmly believes that tough problems can be solved through proper research, review, and an honest airing of ideas and opinions. As discussed in Chapter 8, each morning upon arrival at Police Headquarters, Hillard would hold a "morning meeting" with his command staff and whoever else he thought could contribute to the discussions of the day. Hillard led the morning meetings, but his real purpose was to listen. He would methodically go around the table asking each person for his or her input. In the process, the superintendent would take copious notes. As one staff person said, "It was not unusual for us to be in a group discussion for an hour or more, and then the superintendent would start flipping back through the several pages of notes he had taken and say, 'Commander so and so, earlier in the meeting you said this' [quoting almost verbatim]. 'What did you mean?'" According to staff, note-taking was a very important and effective tool that Hillard used because it sent a clear message to all that he was listening carefully and considering their opinions as an integral part of the decision-making process. It also meant that the superintendent was evaluating their input and holding them accountable for their contributions. Hillard did not care if people disagreed with him. In fact, he welcomed disagreement so long as his dissenters were contributing to the best of their ability and for the good of the organization. Hillard would always make the final decision, but in almost every instance, his decision reflected the consensus opinion of his staff.

Dr. Chuck Wexler, executive director of the Police Executive Research Forum, worked with Hillard on several projects including the Community Forums, and he observed, "Terry Hillard's true genius lies in his ability to take a wide variety of ideas and opinions and then craft them into written policies that result in change" (Brown, 2003, p. 58). Hillard was careful and deliberate in arriving at important decisions because he wanted to be sure that all options had been fully explored and that nothing had been overlooked. On the other hand, he did not see the need to complicate an issue that seemed to have an obvious and clear solution. A true hallmark of Hillard's leadership was tackling difficult problems and coming up with practical solutions.

Leadership Principle Eight

A good leader takes a little more than his share of the blame and a little less than his share of the credit.

– Arnold Glaslow

Hillard never spoke of the good work and successes of the Chicago Police Department without minimizing his role and emphasizing the contributions of his management team and the officers on the street. All accomplishments were the accomplishments of the Chicago Police Department, not of Terry Hillard or any one individual. Hillard is by nature a modest man and delights in the accomplishments of others. As Barbara McDonald said, "Superintendent Hillard is a guy that is so caring that his favorite times were when he handed out departmental awards. He loved to give the men and women of the department their just dues." Tom Argenbright said that Hillard "created the prestigious O. W. Wilson Award (for outstanding contributions to law enforcement) and would personally review all of the candidates before selecting the winner. This was one additional way in which he could recognize the exceptional contributions and heroic acts of the troops." On one occasion, during a department awards ceremony, Hillard learned from his staff that one of the award recipients was unable to attend the ceremony because of a serious illness. The officer was in the advanced stages of cancer and was not expected to live much longer. After the ceremony, Superintendent Hillard arranged for the officer's entire tactical team to report to the man's home. Hillard then went there and, in the presence of the officer's family and police partners, presented him with his award.

In an interview with a reporter, Hillard was asked to comment on his countless successes as superintendent. Hillard, in his modest, soft-spoken manner, said, "I have a lot of good people here. From the officers out on the street to the sergeants and lieutenants, right up to my command staff, this is a very talented department" (Brown, 2003, p. 67).

In policing, public criticism is offered more than public praise – that is just the nature of the business. Hillard would accept responsibility when the department or one of its officers was wrong but would vehemently defend the department and its officers when they were right. In a newspaper commentary in the *Chicago Sun-Times,* Cindy Richards made the following observation:

> His 5 years at the helm of the Chicago Police Department were not without controversy, but it was good to know that Terry Hillard was in charge. He never shied away from the microphone, even when the questions were tough, and he never stopped supporting his troops with his calm demeanor. (Richards, 2003)

Good leaders are ones who realize that their time in the spotlight is temporary and fleeting, and it is the institution that must survive for better or for worse. In the 170-year history of the Chicago Police Department, Terry Hillard is just one of 52 superintendents who have come and gone. He has a tremendous sense of who he is as a person and his time and place in the bigger scheme of things. Hillard's goal was simply to improve the department, not to embellish and aggrandize his list of personal accomplishments. Religious leader Charles H. Spurgeon said, "Humility is to make the right estimate of oneself." Because of his humility, Hillard took less credit for the successes of the department and accepted blame on behalf of the department when it was appropriate to do so.

Leadership Principle Nine

The act of progress is to preserve order amid change and to preserve change amid order.
– Alfred North Whitehead

The complexities of overseeing and managing a major police agency are nightmarish at best. The department's every move is monitored and critiqued by the public, the press, and politicians. Police missteps provide fodder for the naysayers, while police triumphs are merely acknowledged as "the police doing what they ought to be doing." Complicating matters is the fact that police agencies operate within the context of a larger societal environment that is forever changing. In order to remain effective, police agencies must remain flexible enough organizationally to adapt to such changing conditions. Law enforcement officials, probably more than those of any other profession, experience the effects of these changes first as they work face to face with people and their problems. Police agency management is affected by several factors including the changing conditions, needs, and values of the communities they serve; changes in the degree and type of criminal behavior; changes in law and legal interpretations; and changes brought on by emerging data, research, knowledge, and technology. As with any organization, police agencies must continuously reinvent and renew themselves in order to keep pace within the context of a rapidly changing society.

Superintendent Hillard recognized that there is a delicate balance to be maintained in concurrently pushing for progressive change while maintaining a level of comfort and stability in the day-to-day operations of the department. As one commentator said,

> Police agencies must strike a balance between retaining and refining organizational elements that have proven effective, and taking the risks necessary for continuous innovation, renewal, and organizational rebirth. Stated in other terms, police agencies must remain traditional, when traditional methods have proven effective, but must be willing to abandon traditionalism when the old way of doing things is no longer effective. (Jurkanin, Hoover, Dowling, & Ahmad, 2001, p. xiii)

The Chicago Police Department has a strength of nearly 17,000 personnel including sworn and civilian staff. The department will not realize change overnight just because the superintendent issues an order. For real change to occur, employees must collectively be convinced that such change is not only necessary, but that it is in the best interest of the department and conducive to the conditions under which they work. Hillard knew that change must be managed effectively and that employees at all levels of the organization, especially those working the streets, needed to be consulted throughout the process.

Superintendent Hillard implemented change incrementally and always strove to gain the necessary support of the troops and the community at large. For purposes of effectuating lasting change, patience is a virtue. Initial goals, objectives, and timelines often must be revisited and revised in order to achieve the much broader goal of instituting progressive and lasting change. The marquee programs and initiatives spearheaded by Hillard – especially community policing, information technology, and accountability – were all successful because of attention paid to the process of change.

Leadership Principle Ten

> *What wisdom can you find that is greater than kindness.*
> — Jean-Jacques Rouseau

One of Terry Hillard's greatest strengths as a leader came from always exhibiting kindness and heartfelt compassion toward other human beings. Hillard truly cares about the welfare of people. As his friend and colleague John Eschoo said,

> No one could pass by Terry Hillard without receiving a warm greeting and being asked how they were doing. It didn't matter whether they were a boss, a patrol officer, or a cleaning person in the building. Terry looked through titles and facades and always showed a genuine concern for the person as an individual. Whether he did it with his caring words or with his signature smile, the person he was speaking to always knew that, in that moment, Terry had their interest in mind and that he really wanted them to tell him how they were doing.

Stories of Terry Hillard's kindness are countless. He repeatedly demonstrated an appreciation and sympathy for the difficulties others were going through. From officers injured or killed on the job to associates and friends struggling through personal and family crises to citizens who fell victim to crime, he always took the time to care.

Superintendent Hillard's staff said that one morning he came to work very somber about something he had read in the newspaper. A white man, walking with his family to see a White Sox game at Comiskey Park, was attacked by a black man who had jumped out of a vehicle and begun beating the man for no apparent reason. The man's daughter and grandchildren witnessed the beating.

The victim was in critical condition at the hospital, so the superintendent got in his car and went over to visit the man and his family. Hillard's staff said that when he returned, he was even more upset because he felt that the only reason the man was beaten was that he was white. Hillard gave his personal credit card to his staff and told them to order lunch for the family and have it sent to the hospital. Two days later, the man died. The Superintendent could not stomach the thought of a man being beaten and dishonored in front of his daughter and grandchildren; neither could he tolerate the thought that race and hate had been the motive for the assault. As Hillard's friend and former Sergeant Fred Miller said, "I don't think Terry has a vicious bone in his body. He always treated everyone the way he would want to be treated."

It may seem odd that a person as caring and compassionate as Terry Hillard would choose a profession in which he would be exposed to so much suffering and pain. Although many police professionals become emotionally callous and insensitive during the course of their careers, Hillard never did. In fact, Hillard incorporated kindness and compassion as a tenet of his leadership style. He knew that it was all right to be kind and that there was no shame in showing compassion, even if you are a tough, seasoned cop.

A particularly descriptive quote regarding Hillard's kindness came from a citizen. Following the shooting death of a Chicago police officer, a reporter learned that Superintendent Hillard had spent a considerable amount of time comforting the family of the officer, as he always did. The reporter asked the aunt of the slain officer what she thought of Superintendent Hillard. She said, "He's a very, very nice guy. Being so soft-spoken in this crazy city we live in" (Heinzmann & Bush, 2003).

Summary Thoughts: Having a Vision and Seeing It Through

Leadership is the capacity to translate vision into reality.
                                                                    – Warren Bennis

Through a unique combination of ability and skill and by adhering to the leadership principles discussed above, Superintendent Hillard brought progressive change to the Chicago Police Department. Hillard's well-developed personal skills and attributes allowed him to carefully build a consensus for change among both the community and members of the force. In the end, Hillard not only implemented innovative programs and initiatives to improve police operations, but also accomplished something much more difficult and exceedingly more important. Superintendent Hillard changed the culture of the Chicago Police Department. Through his leadership, Hillard demonstrated to everyone concerned that the police department cannot operate effectively within a vacuum, that the police department must be open and interactive with all factions of the community, and that service and accountability to the public are necessary in building community partnership and trust. Hillard knew that if the public better understood the police and the police better understood the public, the common goals of reducing crime and improving the quality of life for all citizens were much more achievable.

Futurist writer Alvin Toffler once said, "You've got to think about the big things while you're doing the small things, so that all small things go in the right direction." Hillard knew where he wanted to take the Chicago Police Department. His vision had to do with inclusiveness, openness, accountability, service, and partnership. In the process of change, he also created an atmosphere of mutual respect, compassion, and care within both the department and the community. His vision, by all accounts, became reality. That is leadership.

Chapter 13

THE DECISION TO RETIRE

I don't know what your destiny will be, but one thing I know:
the only ones among you who will be really happy are those who
will have sought and found how to serve.
— Albert Schweitzer

The most infectiously joyous men and women are those who
forget themselves in thinking about others and serving others.
Happiness comes not by deliberately courting and wooing it but
by giving oneself in self-effacing surrender to greater values.
— Robert J. McCracken

When Mayor Richard M. Daley appointed Terry Hillard as superintendent, he told him two important things, both of which seemed to be orders rather than friendly advice. First, the mayor made it clear that Hillard would have free reign to run the police department and that he (the mayor) would handle the politics. For the superintendent, this was good news. Not only did the mayor's operating philosophy insulate the superintendent and the department from outside political influences, but it provided Hillard with the opportunity to concentrate his attention on improving the police department. Daley is a popular and powerful politician, and his insistence on handling the politics made it clear that he took sole responsibility to protect the department from other politicians who wished to meddle in police matters. The second directive that Daley gave to Hillard was to take Sundays off. The mayor warned Hillard that the superintendent's job would be all-consuming and that there simply were not enough hours in the day to honor all of the requests and demands that would be placed upon him. The mayor told Hillard to spend Sundays with his family, to relax, and to forget about the department for just one day a week. The mayor told him that taking Sundays off would be critical to his survival in such a high-pressure job. It was apparent that the mayor was speaking from experience.

Hillard never had to be convinced about the importance of family and friends. Throughout his entire career, he relied heavily upon family and

friends for solace and strength. Although his new commitments as superintendent left him with limited free time, Hillard never isolated himself from his
family and friends. John Eschoo, one of Terry's partners from the Terrorism
Task Force days, said,

> You know, Terry has so many friends. Terry is that kind of guy. While all of us
> make friends throughout our life and careers, things change – assignments
> change, some people are promoted, and others retire. But with Terry, he would
> never give up old friends. He would just keep adding new ones. Terry depended
> upon his friends, and he knew that his friends depended upon him.

People have different strategies for handling stress. Some people exercise;
some play golf, or boat, or garden, or build things in the garage. Hillard has
trouble articulating in specific terms how he handled the stresses of the job
other than to say that he liked to take walks when he was particularly stressed,
that he enjoyed staying home with his family, and that he enjoyed cooking.
Eschoo's comment about Hillard and the importance of friendship brings
everything into perspective. Of course, friends were the way Hillard handled
stress. He was always just a phone call away from dozens of people whom he
cared about dearly and who genuinely cared about him. He understood explicitly that friendship was a two-way street. His friends said that Hillard enjoyed giving much more than receiving and that, on any occasion, when his
friends needed him, he was there without even being asked. John Eschoo,
Jerry Lewis, and Tommy Raines, former Terrorism Task Force members, all
tragically lost their sons, and Terry Hillard, their friend, was there for each of
them in their time of need. Hillard found comfort in the network of friends
he developed over the years in the same way that he found comfort within his
family. Each day that Hillard ventured out to face the chaotic, dangerous,
angry, and unforgiving world of crime and law enforcement, he knew that he
had a safety net secured by family and friends.

It is not surprising that the average tenure of most big city police chiefs is
only two to three years. If they are lucky enough not to be derailed by politics,
departmental scandal, or a lack of support from either the community or the
officers under their command, they may survive three years. After three years
as superintendent, Hillard beat the odds. He still had the strong support of the
mayor, of the community, and of the troops under his command. Although
the department had not been without controversy during his tenure, Hillard's
personal integrity and his commitment to do the right thing had never been
called into question.

Those police chiefs not fortunate enough to survive the three-year mark are
not in a position to enjoy the fruits of their labor. As discussed previously, meaningful organizational change often requires several years to be fully implemented. The several initiatives that Hillard implemented in his first two to three
years as superintendent were coming to fruition in the fourth and fifth years of
his tenure. When a new head coach is introduced to change the direction of a

sports franchise, owners and fans should not expect a complete turnaround in year one or year two, but after three years, improvement better be noted. Superintendent Hillard had implemented progressive change and had survived long enough to see the measurable results of his actions. As with any good coach, Terry Hillard was able to take pride in the successes and accomplishments of his team.

The seasons of life change quickly. It is an irrefutable fact that one's time on earth is limited, so each person must carefully calculate how he or she wishes to live life. If people's lives are to remain satisfying throughout, they must involve themselves in a continuous process of evaluation and revaluation, assessing both personal and professional priorities. They can be satisfied and content, yet there can still be a nagging doubt concerning the next step; staying in one place too long is a constant risk. Knowing when to move on or when to initiate change requires an accurate, honest, and timely assessment of priorities.

In the fifth year of his superintendency, Terry Hillard had committed 39 years of his life to public service – four years in service to his country as a member of the United States Marine Corps and 35 years in service to the Chicago Police Department. He had done his time. Out of more than 13,000 Chicago police officers, Hillard had risen to become Number One. He started as an inexperienced patrol officer and advanced to superintendent, and not because he had political connections. In fact, Terry Hillard considered himself apolitical. He became superintendent because he earned it through dutiful service and years of gaining the respect of those who knew and worked with him.

Keeping a schedule of 14 hours a day and being on call throughout the night would be difficult for any man. Hillard was approaching 60 years of age, but he was fit, ate right, did not smoke, and did not drink to excess. In short, he took good care of himself; however, over time the wear and tear of the job began to take its toll. Colleagues close to Hillard said they began to notice that the superintendent often appeared tired, especially in his fifth year; and, while it may seem glamorous to be in the public spotlight, the chief of a major police department is most often in the spotlight regarding bad news, not good news. Regardless of the type of crime committed or the parties involved, the superintendent is called upon to give details and to answer questions. These media events are tense, with reporters asking probative questions and second-guessing every response. In such a high-profile position, it is virtually impossible to simply walk out of Police Headquarters at 5:00 PM and turn everything off. For the superintendent of the Chicago Police Department, there is no downtime. At any moment, the phone may ring, and within 30 minutes, the superintendent might be talking to scores of reporters, rushing to the hospital to be at the bedside of a dying cop, or on scene at a major crime or disaster. It doesn't matter whether it is 7:00 PM, 3:00 AM, or even Sunday afternoon.

There are certain events in everyone's life that become so significant that they markedly alter the way we think and feel about life from that day forward. These singular events are indeed life-changing in that they cause personal introspection and a reordering of one's priorities. Two such dates played a major role in Terry Hillard's decision to retire. It is ironic that the two events that ultimately convinced him to retire were two issues that he faced every day as a police officer – issues of life and death.

On July 22, 2002, Terry Hillard had served as superintendent of the Chicago Police Department for four and a half years. More significantly, however, on that date, a new life began with the birth of Danae Hillard. Danae was the newborn daughter of Dana, Terry and Girl's son, and the Hillards' first grandchild. From the day of her birth, this healthy, bright-eyed girl changed the way Hillard thought about life.

As a Chicago cop, Hillard had seen everything, and a lot of what he had seen was bad. He had been shot, had confronted violent offenders, had chased down gang members, had seen children beaten and sexually abused, had broken up domestic disputes, had recovered bodies, had kicked down doors to execute search warrants, had buried police officers, and had told far too many families that a loved one was dead. Such ugliness takes its toll on police officers and influences the way they perceive the world. After 34 years of dealing with bad things, the cute, sweet, innocent, smiling face of a new granddaughter offered a stark and appealing contrast.

Family had always been important to Hillard, and with the birth of Danae, his family had a new member to love. Because Hillard's son Dana was still in college, Danae and her parents lived with Terry and Girl. As a result, Terry got to be with Danae every day. As he spent time watching Danae grow, he realized that he wanted to spend even more time with her. He wanted to play a significant role in her life. Over the course of the next year, when Superintendent Hillard traveled to attend out-of-state meetings and conferences, Girl and Danae would often accompany him. Deputy Chief Barbara McDonald observed that Danae's effect on Terry was amazing: "She was clearly the apple of his eye. The superintendent would just beam with joy when Danae was with him."

Nearly eight months after Danae's birth, a second major event occurred that changed Hillard's thinking: he lost his police partner. John Thomas was Hillard's first deputy superintendent. He died unexpectedly on March 6, 2003, of a massive heart attack at 53 years of age. The death of John Thomas saddened and shook Hillard as much as any other single event in his life.

In the Chicago Police Department, the first deputy superintendent is second in command and maintains a powerful position. According to police spokesperson David Bayless, "Although he reports directly to the superintendent, the first deputy pretty much is in charge of the day-to-day operations of the department. The meat and potatoes of that is the Patrol Division, which is about 10,600 officers" (Heinzmann, 2003).

The life and career of John Thomas was similar in many respects to the life and career of Terry Hillard. Neither man was native to Chicago. While Hillard was born in a small town in Tennessee, Thomas was born and grew up in a small town in Southern Illinois. As such, they shared a set of values and beliefs commonly associated with rural life – they were not big city boys. Hillard joined the Chicago Police Department in 1968; Thomas joined in 1970. Both men came into the department without a college degree, and both went back to school part-time to earn their degrees. Both men advanced steadily through the ranks and earned the respect of other Chicago cops. Neither considered himself to be political by nature – they both advanced by working hard, maintaining their integrity, and getting the job done.

Although both men were long-time employees of the Chicago Police Department, the two did not meet until the mid-1990s when Hillard was chief of detectives and Thomas was district commander of the 17th District. One of Thomas's men, a young Hispanic officer who worked a high-risk detail, was confronted by a gang banger one night when he was off-duty. The officer was shot and killed, and the gang banger fled. Hillard said that Thomas took the death of his officer very hard, so Hillard promised him that they would get the guy who did the shooting. Hillard was so impressed with the fine character of John Thomas that he quickly promoted him to commander of Area 5 Detectives.

In February 2002, Jack Townsend, who had served as the department's first deputy during Hillard's first two years as superintendent, retired after 40 years on the force. The first person Hillard thought of as his replacement was John Thomas. He called Thomas one night and told him that he needed to meet with him to discuss some issues.

Superintendent Hillard always liked to meet people in obscure locations to discuss confidential matters. The two men met near an auto repair shop with which they were both familiar. When the superintendent told Thomas the news that he wanted to make him first deputy, Thomas was shocked. Usually the appointment of the first deputy came directly from City Hall, but Hillard felt so strongly about Thomas's abilities that he went directly to the mayor with his recommendation. The mayor agreed, and Thomas became first deputy.

By all accounts, Thomas was a workaholic who loved the Chicago Police Department and cared deeply about Chicago cops. When he became first deputy, he instituted new operational procedures to take more of the load off the superintendent. For example, Thomas did not think it was appropriate for the superintendent to be called out of bed in the middle of the night unless an officer had been seriously wounded or a major incident had occurred that required the superintendent's immediate attention. Thomas became a buffer for the superintendent. He was the one to decide whether or not to call the superintendent out of bed. First Deputy Thomas was also a master at dealing with delicate matters involving the press and City Hall. Hillard had full confidence in Thomas as a partner and as a friend and trusted him implicitly to make important decisions.

Hillard and Thomas would talk eight or nine times a day, either in the office or by phone. The superintendent's office and the first deputy's office are adjacent to one another, and at about 4:30 PM every day the two would meet in the superintendent's conference room and talk casually. Sometimes they would talk about the job, sometimes about family, and sometimes they would just muse about how two country boys were now leading the Chicago Police Department. Hillard says that he and Thomas were not the type of friends who went out for a beer or to dinner or the ball game, but the time they shared one-on-one was special because the two had a lot in common. At about 10:00 PM every night, Hillard and Thomas would talk one last time on the phone to share information. Usually, Hillard was at home lying across his bed and Thomas was at home on the couch. The men told each other everything that they knew – there were no secrets between them.

In giving the eulogy at Thomas's funeral, Hillard spoke of a man and partner who was a remarkable public servant. He said, "John Thomas was intelligent, firm, humorous, dedicated, and, above all else, compassionate. John cared deeply about Chicago police officers." Just a week after First Deputy Thomas was buried, the superintendent addressed a graduating class of new Chicago police officers, and said,

> When you talk about police officers having courage, we usually think about brave confrontations with armed offenders. Another equally difficult type of courage is always making the right decision . . . to live a life of integrity. As John Thomas showed us, your measure as a police officer will be determined by the depth of your convictions . . . and the reach of your love. For those who are willing to work hard and have the moral fiber, there is great opportunity within the Chicago Police Department. (Hillard, 2003a)

Following the death of her husband, Candice Thomas asked Hillard for a special favor. Hillard says, "She made me promise to get a physical examination and to ask all of Chicago's command staff to get one as well. Candice wanted to make sure that what happened to John did not happen to others." Hillard made sure that Candice's request was honored. While the results of the superintendent's physical examination were good, the emotional impact of his dear friend's death had sounded warning signals.

In times of trouble, Hillard would often retreat to the beautiful shore of Lake Michigan to take long walks and clear his mind. From the paths that run along the lakeshore, one can marvel at the complexity of the city to the west and be comforted by the simplicity of the crashing waves to the east. When John Thomas died, Hillard walked for miles along the lakeshore and found himself looking mostly to the east. Although other factors played a role in his decision to retire, it is not coincidental that he announced his retirement exactly six weeks after John Thomas's death. In the end, it was Danae's life and Thomas's death that helped convince Hillard that it was time to retire.

The retirement of the superintendent of police is big news in Chicago. In considering his retirement, Hillard first talked to Girl and his family and then to the mayor. When he met with Mayor Daley on Thursday, April 16, 2003, he had already decided to retire, but he knew that the mayor would want him to stay on for several additional months to provide adequate time for the police board to initiate a search for his successor. Hillard and Daley agreed that the superintendent's retirement would be effective August 15, 2003.

Speculation regarding Hillard's impending retirement dominated the Chicago news media. Hillard contacted his long-time friend Michael Sneed, a *Sun-Times* correspondent, to give her the story. The next morning, he held a press conference to make his announcement official.

Although Hillard was announcing one of the most important decisions of his life, his comments at the press conference were brief and reserved. As was his style, he kept his remarks short for two reasons. First, he had always felt most uncomfortable when the focus of attention was on him instead of the department. Second, he was feeling a great deal of emotion about his decision to leave the department and the people he loved. As a result, he struggled to keep his composure and his emotions in check. After all, this was a very personal decision that by necessity had to be announced in a public forum.

In various statements to the press regarding his retirement, Hillard said,

> The loss of Deputy Superintendent John Thomas hit me hard. . . . I'm 59 years old. This is my sixth year in this position. You can stay somewhere too long. The lifetime of a big-city chief is between two and four years. I've done my time. (Spielman & Main, 2003, pp. 1, 6)

> I've probably buried more police officers than any other superintendent I can remember. That's because of the proliferation of gangs, guns, and drugs. Each time it was heart wrenching. (Spielman & Main, 2003, p. 7)

> I'll be 60 come August 11. I've got a few more good years, and I'm going to enjoy them. (Bradley, 2003, p. 4)

The *Chicago Tribune* ran a story on April 20, 2003, about Hillard's retirement press conference, and reported,

> When Police Superintendent Terry Hillard was asked what he wanted people to remember about his 5½ years as Chicago's Top Cop, he couldn't find the words. Always quick to attribute accomplishments to "us" instead of "me," Hillard said he wanted people to know that "we cared." But then his eyes filled with tears and he abruptly ended the Friday morning news conference. (Heinzmann, 2003, p. 1)

The reason Terry Hillard retired – the *main* reason – was the love he had for his family. He knew that the stresses of the job would eventually overcome him. He had a gut feeling that enough was enough. He wanted to relax, to be with his family, to enjoy his new grandbaby, and to help take care of his 80-year-old mother. It was time to relinquish his role as superintendent so that he could spend more time being a good husband, son, father, brother, and grandpa. Terry Hillard would leave on top, without a trace of controversy, without being forced out. When he retired as superintendent, he bowed out on his own terms and left the citizens of Chicago wanting more of him. He had decided that he had given all that he could give.

In a press statement released the day before he retired, Superintendent Hillard wrote,

> It has been an honor and privilege serving as superintendent of the Chicago Police Department. I extend a personal thank you to every dedicated police officer and citizen who has helped improve the quality of life in Chicago. I share your pride in our many successes, including the drop in both overall crime and violent crime in Chicago for 11 straight years. . . . I leave my office knowing that the quality of life in Chicago, the city I love, will continue to improve. I have seen first-hand the commitment of its officers, citizens, elected officials, and our mayor. (Hillard, 2003c)

Words of appreciation and thanks for Superintendent Hillard's stellar leadership poured in from politicians, colleagues, community leaders, citizens, and the media. Hillard, through his quiet and strong character, had earned the respect of the entire Chicago community. Mayor Daley said,

> Every resident of Chicago owes Terry Hillard a debt of gratitude for his outstanding leadership. . . . He was a leader of unquestioned honesty and integrity, a police officer's police officer who earned the respect of not only the 13,500 men and women of the Chicago Police Department but also the three million Chicagoans they serve and protect. (Hack, 2003)

It would have been much easier for Daley if Hillard had stayed. The mayor and superintendent worked well together. They were men who shared a strong work ethic, a love for the city, a commitment to family, and the belief that loyalty and trust are cornerstones to maintaining effective partnerships. Although Terry Hillard was a strong leader who was loved by the community, his popularity was not a threat to Daley; indeed, the mayor was popular in his own right. There was also a recognition, however, that Hillard would never attempt to capitalize on his popularity to promote any personal agenda. He had simply wanted to be the best superintendent he could be and, in the process, make the mayor and the city proud of the Chicago Police. When Daley was asked at a press conference what qualities he was looking for as he began his search for a new police superintendent, the mayor did not say a word; he simply pointed to Superintendent Hillard. Later, Mayor Daley said, "Hillard's accomplishments could fill a book. . . . He will be tough to replace in one of the most difficult and demanding jobs in Chicago" (Spielman, Main, & Lawrence, 2003b).

On August 20, 2003, just days after Superintendent Hillard's retirement, Carol Marin wrote an article for the *Chicago Tribune* entitled "Leadership 101: You Don't Have to Be Showy to Get Noticed." In her article, Marin referred to a favorite saying of one of her friends: "The true tests of parenthood aren't the good times; they come late at night when your kid is throwing up." Marin, drawing an analogy to leadership, said, "Likewise, the true tests of leadership comes when things fall apart." Marin praised Hillard's leadership in the bad times he faced, not just the good times. She made reference to a book on leadership entitled *Good to Great: Why Some Companies Make the Leap and Other's Do*

Not, written by Jim Collins. Marin summarized several key factors identified by the author that make companies great:

> In every case, the organization had a leader who was disciplined, low-key, and pragmatic. Someone who gave credit rather than took it. Someone who worked to get rid of the wrong people and recruit the right ones. Someone who knew success was not achieved in a "miracle moment" but usually over a long time. Someone who didn't ask another to do what he wouldn't do.

Marin reflected upon Terry Hillard's leadership and said, "It's always the walk, not the talk that tells the story of who's a leader and who is not. I guess that's why I've had Terry Hillard on my mind lately. [However], even the best leaders need a rest" (Marin, 2003).

A *Chicago Tribune* editorial published on August 14, 2003, stated,

> When Mayor Daley appointed Terry Hillard in 1998, the *Tribune* hailed Hillard as a leader of high integrity and concluded: An expectant city bids him good luck. On Friday a city better off for his leadership bids Hillard farewell – with gratitude for his work to ease tensions, to modernize his department, and to attack the horrific levels of violent crime that persist in Chicago. . . . A law officer's primary job is to keep the peace. Terry Hillard has kept the peace, moving his department past an era of persistently testy relations with key elements of the city it serves. ("Terry Hillard's Legacy," 2003)

The Reverend Michael C. Pfleger, pastor of St. Sabina Catholic Church, wrote,

> Police Superintendent Terry Hillard will be deeply missed by the citizens of Chicago and by law enforcement nationally. . . . Hillard was the first Superintendent of Chicago and perhaps of any major city who opened the doors of communication between the public and the department on equal grounds and with equal respect. . . . He is a decent man. Even when you disagreed with him, you knew he believed in his heart what he was doing was right and always gave you his very best. (Pfleger, n.d.)

Another *Chicago Tribune* article proclaimed, "As Chicago's top cop, retiring police Superintendent Terry Hillard has been the steady hand that has guided a department weathering scandal and struggle to reform" (Heinzmann & Bush, 2003, p. 1).

Hillard's reputation as a cop's cop was memorialized in a statement by Deputy Superintendent James Maurer, who was chief of the patrol division:

> He is by far the best superintendent we have ever had. He took better care of the troops than anybody. He didn't have a selfish bone in his body or an ulterior motive for anything. The job of the city came first. (Spielman, Main, & Lawrence, 2003a, p. 9)

And finally, a *Sun-Times* editorial praised Hillard with these words:

> Whatever you think of Terry Hillard's performance as a police superintendent – and we think he did a fine job in the face of countless obstacles and trying circumstances – he proved that it was possible to be both a forceful presence in the fight against crime and a good guy. ("Top Cop," 2003)

On his last day as superintendent, Hillard walked out the front door of Police Headquarters as hundreds of Chicago Police personnel gathered to give him applause for a job well done. Military jets flew in formation over Lake Michigan to acknowledge his distinguished career of service. Hillard gave a proud wave and salute to all; he and Girl got into an antique Chicago Police Department vehicle and were driven away, signifying the end of one life and the beginning of another.

When people meet Terry Hillard for the first time at the supermarket, at a restaurant, or at a friendly gathering, their initial impression is often, "Wow, this is just one heck of a nice guy." His gentle and polite manner, his engaging smile, and his genuine interest in other human beings make him an instant friend to all who meet him. What is remarkable is that Terry Hillard, the person, never changes. Although important positions of power and authority have the tendency to change people, making them less patient, more focused on self, and less concerned with others, that clearly was not the case with Hillard. He never compromised nor confused his identity as a person with his position as superintendent. Terry Hillard was Terry Hillard long before he became superintendent and throughout his superintendency, and he will remain Terry Hillard in retirement. At his retirement celebration, he and his guests viewed a special video program documenting his many successes. The video presentation appropriately concluded with a quote from Ralph Waldo Emerson: "What lies behind us and what lies before us are tiny matters compared to what lies within us."

Terry Hillard always knew what lay within him. From his early days of growing up in South Fulton, Tennessee, he learned that life is not always fair. He learned that the color of his skin determined where he could eat, where he could sit in the theater, and which sports he could play; however, listening to radio broadcasts of the Brooklyn Dodgers with Jackie Robinson in the line-up gave him hope – as it did for all African-Americans – that change would eventually come. As one of ten children, he learned that a strong family served as an institution of guidance and protection from the outside world. He and his siblings were fortunate to have parents who were aware of discrimination but did not hold it out as an excuse for their kids not to succeed. He learned that family, religion, hard work, and education were important, as were personal qualities such as fairness, politeness, and treating others with respect.

As a young Marine, Hillard was dedicated and committed to fighting for his country at a time when many American youths were protesting the Vietnam War and race riots were destroying American cities. His four years in the Marine Corps and 13 months in Vietnam did not leave him bitter; to the contrary, his service in the Marines taught him the importance of maturity and discipline. As a young Chicago cop, he was shot on the Chicago streets, and his response was not to call it quits, but to rehabilitate himself so that he could return to the work he loved. As a dedicated Chicago police officer, he worked hard, pursued his education, and steadily advanced with progressive experience.

When colorectal cancer threatened Terry's life late in his career, he fought back once again and survived to become superintendent of police for five and a half years. He distinguished himself as one of the most respected big city chiefs in the nation and as one of the best superintendents in the history of the Chicago Police Department. Finally, Terry Hillard knew when to call it quits. Indeed, Hillard always knew what lay within him.

Terry Hillard, the man, attempted to live a life guided by principles which were larger than life. He knew that living in a world that is imperfect does not mean that one should refrain from striving for better things. In the law enforcement profession, it is sometimes difficult to keep a balanced perspective and to remind oneself that most people are generally good but can commit evil acts. It is difficult for officers on the street to remember that their daily actions and good deeds positively affect the world in which we all live. Hillard embodied and demonstrated many of the finest qualities that police officers possess. He always felt most comfortable when he was talking to cops because, in the end, it was the cops whom he understood best, and he was never more enthusiastic than when he had the opportunity to welcome new Chicago police officers. In a speech to a class of graduating police recruits shortly before he retired, Superintendent Hillard said,

> As I look out on this room, I see a group of heroes in the making. I see a group of enthusiastic young people who have answered the call to serve others. And make no mistake about it, the deeds you perform over the course of your career will be heroic. Every arrest, every gun you seize, every citizen you help, every crime you solve will be the work of a hero. But you will not do it for the headlines, the glory, or the awards. You are in this profession because you have been called. And there is no higher calling. (Hillard, 2003b; also see Appendix A for Hillard's "Top Ten Tips" for New Chicago Police Officers.)

While it is true that only a few achieve sainthood, all men and women have the opportunity to live their lives in a saintly manner. Terry Hillard proved that. The men and women of law enforcement work on the streets of our cities to serve and protect mankind; they are our peace keepers; they are our saints in blue. In tribute to the fine example set by Terry Hillard and as an inspiration to all police officers who unselfishly serve throughout the world, the following hopeful prayer is offered:

> *Lord, make me an instrument of your peace.*
> *Where there is hatred, let me sow love;*
> *Where there is injury, pardon;*
> *Where there is doubt, faith;*
> *Where there is despair, hope;*
> *Where there is darkness, light;*
> *And where there is sadness, joy.*

Oh Devine master, grant that I may not so much seek to be
  consoled as to console:
To be understood as to understand;
To be loved as to love.
For it is in giving that we receive;
It is in pardoning that we are pardoned;
And it is in dying that we are born to eternal life.
                        – Prayer of St. Francis of Assisi

EPILOGUE

Since retiring on August 15, 2003, Terry Hillard has taken time to wind down and readjust to civilian life. The customary 14-hour work days are now in his past. His telephone never wakes him at 3:00 AM. He never has to be concerned with facing angry crowds or answering difficult questions in front of an inquisitive press corps. When the mayor wants to see him, he can rest assured that it is for personal reasons, not a citywide crisis. His life, once so public, is now private.

In addition to working on this book, Hillard has been engaged in consulting and teaching activities. He is cofounder of the consulting firm Hillard, Heintzle, LLC, which offers services related to strategic security. He also serves as a volunteer and board member for several not-for-profit organizations benefiting the Chicago community. He is active as an advisor to the Police Executive Research Forum and participates as a member of several other police-affiliated organizations.

Hillard retired to be with his family. Since retiring, he has enjoyed spending quiet time at home with Girl, Dana, Terri Lee, and Danae. Although eligible for retirement, Girl still works for the Chicago Public School District as an associate principal. Terry now tends to many of the household chores. Instead of marshaling the forces of the Chicago Police Department to solve a complicated string of homicides, he has to make sure that the laundry is done, the clothes are folded, the house is in order, and the groceries are stocked. He visits his mother often and enjoys spending time with his brothers, sisters, and friends, and he cooks for his family regularly and with great enjoyment.

On June 18, 2004, Dana Hillard graduated from the Police Training Institute at the University of Illinois and was sworn in as a police officer working for the Northwestern University Department of Public Safety. His father was the guest speaker at Dana's graduation ceremony, and his eyes filled with tears as he spoke of the pride he felt for his son and the other police officers in the class. Terri Lee has a master's degree and is completing doctoral work. She works in downtown Chicago. Danae is taking swimming lessons and waiting until she turns three so that she can take ballet. She also enjoys spending quality time with Papa.

In 2004, Chicago recorded the lowest number of murders in the city since 1965. Chicago's 448 murders in 2004 were less than the murders in both New

York City and Los Angeles and represent an astonishing 25% decrease from the 600 murders recorded in 2003.

Phil Cline, who was chief of detectives, and later first deputy superintendent in Hillard's administration, is now superintendent of Chicago Police. Cline has intensified the use of police intelligence information and has redeployed personnel to aggressively target hot spots of gang, drug, and gun activity. His strategy has proven effective – Chicago is no longer the murder capital of the United States.

Ron Huberman, the thirty-something patrol officer whom Hillard promoted to assistant deputy superintendent for his work on the CLEAR System is now mayor Daley's chief of staff.

The Chicago Housing Authority's Ten-Year Transformation Plan to tear down the poverty-stricken public housing complexes and integrate residents within mixed-income neighborhoods that offer better homes and opportunities for upward mobility is at its halfway point. The *Chicago Tribune* reports that of "the 4,600 residents relocated, three quarters of those are now concentrated in struggling, segregated communities such as Englewood, Roseland, and South Shore . . . and that . . . the migration has largely perpetuated economic and racial isolation" (Bebow & Olivo, 2005, p. 1).

The broad social problems associated with all large cities – substandard housing, unemployment, poverty, family disorganization, drug use, and a lack of educational opportunities – continue to plague a significant segment of Chicago's population.

In 2005, the Illinois Department of Corrections anticipates releasing 25,000 Chicago criminals from state prison. If statistics hold, more than half of those released will return to a life of gang involvement and crime and be rearrested and returned to prison within three years.

Currently, the national news media is obsessively reporting the story of Jennifer Wilbanks, the 32-year-old, caucasion, bride-to-be from Duluth, Georgia, who faked her own kidnapping to avoid getting married. In contrast, the story of Andre Crawford, who allegedly murdered 11 black females in Chicago, never made the national news.

Finally, and most importantly, the men and women of the Chicago Police Department continue to work diligently – risking their lives daily – to protect the good citizens of Chicago and the city they love.

Appendix A

SUPERINTENDENT HILLARD'S TOP TEN TIPS FOR CHICAGO POLICE RECRUITS

(In no particular order because they're all important.)

1. Stay in shape both mentally and physically. Maintain the discipline achieved at the academy throughout your career. You will need it.
2. Perform an act of kindness every day. Be the person your parents raised you to be.
3. Respect veteran officers. Use your ears more than your mouth. Listen to what venerable older officers have to say, and benefit from their wisdom.
4. Keep your family the most important part of your life. Career is important but not at the expense of your family. Find the good to balance the bad you will see every day, and share that good with your family.
5. Remember your training. You have a dangerous job. We care about you, so stick to what we have taught you. It will save your life.
6. Always respect the oath of office you have taken. You are the only one who can compromise your character. In the end, your honor and integrity make you who you are.
7. Wear your uniform proudly. It is a symbol of public trust and a tradition of honor.
8. Learn something new every day. Learn from your mistakes. You will make them, I promise, but make sure they are honest ones. Deserve and earn all of your promotions.
9. Treat citizens the way you would want a police officer to treat a member of your family.
10. Get home safely every day so each of you can be congratulated at the end of a long career.

Appendix B

VITA OF TERRY G. HILLARD

Summary of Education, Executive Training, Assignments, Awards, and Affiliations

Education

Honorary Doctorate of Law, Calumet College of St. Joseph, 2004
Honorary Doctorate of Public Service, St. Xavier University, 2002
Honorary Doctorate of Humanities, Lewis University, 2001
Chicago State University – Major: Corrections
   Degree: Master of Science – 1978
Chicago State University – Major: Corrections
   Degree: Bachelor of Science – 1976
Loop Junior College –Major: Criminal Justice
   Degree: Associate of Arts – 1973

Executive Training

Police Executive Forum – In Association with the Kennedy School of Training
   Management – 1997
Harvard University, North Andover, Massachusetts – 1997
F.B.I. National Academy – United States Department of Justice, Quantico,
   Virginia – 1984

Career Assignments

1998–2003	Superintendent of Chicago Police Department
1995–1998	Chief of Detective Division
1993–1995	Deputy Chief, Area Two, Patrol Division
1991–1993	Commander, 6th District, Patrol Division
1990–1991	Lieutenant, Narcotics Section (Special Enforcement)
1990–1990	Lieutenant, Gang Crimes South
1985–1990	Coordinator, Chicago Terrorist Task Force

1984–1985	Sergeant, Intelligence Section
1984–1984	Sergeant, 9th District, Patrol Division
1983–1984	Coordinator, Special Police Services, Mayor Harold Washington's Security Detail
1979–1983	Security Specialist, Special Police Services, Mayor Jane Byrne's Security Detail
1978–1979	Gang Crimes Specialist, Gang Crimes Unit
1977–1978	Police Officer, Gang Crimes South
1975–1977	Temporary Sergeant, 6th District, Patrol Division
1968–1975	Police Officer in Gang Crimes Unit, Area Two Task Force and the 2nd, 7th, and 18th Districts

Awards and Commendations

Police Medal
Superintendent's Award of Valor
Police Blue Star Award
Special Service Award, CAPS
Chicago Chamber of Commerce Award
19 Honorable Mentions
Leadership Award – PERF
Unit Meritorious Performance Award
Carter Harrison/Lambert Tree (honorable mention)
Five Department Commendations
General John Logan Chicago Patriot Award
Citizen Award of Appreciation, City of Chicago
Special Service Award, Democratic National Convention
FBI Director's Community Service Award

Military Awards

Achieved the rank of Sergeant E5 – U.S. Marine Corps 1963–1967
Presidential Unit Collection
Vietnam Service Medal
Good Conduct Medal
National Defense Service Medal
Republic of Vietnam Campaign Medal
Honorable Discharge

Affiliations

FBI National Academy Associates
NOBLE (National Organization of Black Law Executives)
International Association of Chiefs of Police

Major Cities Chiefs Association
Police Executive Research Forum
Illinois Association of Chiefs of Police
National Executive Institute Associates
South Suburban Chiefs of Police Association
Board of Trustees, St. Xavier University
Board of Directors, YMCA
Board of Directors, Special Olympics

RESOURCES AND BIBLIOGRAPHY

The City

Apple, R. W. (2004, August 4). Beyond the franks: There are other Chicago staples worth tasting. *New York Times* News Service. *The State Journal-Register*, p. 18.

Artner, A. G. (2004, July 18). Unfinished, but engaging, public art; "Cloud gate" and crown fountain intrigue. *Chicago Tribune*, p. 11.

Baker, R. M. (2004). The blue highway: A brief history of the blues. Retrieved April 14, 2004, from www.thebluehighway.com/history.html

Chicago Public Library. (2004). A chronological history of Chicago. Population of Chicago by decades: 1830–2000. Retrieved April 7, 2004, from www.chipublib.org/oo4chicago/ timeline/population.html

Chicago Housing Authority. (2004). *Change in Chicago over the past decade.* Retrieved April 6, 2004, from www.thecha.org/housingdevelopment

Chicago Historical Society and the Trustees of Northwestern University. (1996). *The queen of the west once more. The great Chicago fire and the web of memory.* Retrieved April 7, 2004, from www.chicagohs.org/fire/queen

City of Chicago. (2003). *Chicago fact book: Demographics.* Retrieved October 21, 2003, from www.ci.chi.il.us/plananddevelop/chgofacts/demo.html

Hedley, T. (2004). *The billy goat curse: How the "billy goat curse" got put on the Cubs.* Retrieved January 6, 2005, from www.mv.sherrard.us/headley/thecurse.html

Kamin, B. (2004, July 18). A no place transformed into a grand space; What was once a gritty, blighted site is now home to a glistening, cultural spectacle that delivers joy to its visitors. *Chicago Tribune*, p. 1.

Thigpen, D. E. (2005, April 15). Richard the second. *Time* magazine. Retrieved April 18, 2005, from www.time.com/magazine

Infamous Chicago Crimes

Altman, J., & Ziporyn, M. (1967). *Born to raise hell: The untold story of Richard Speck, the man, the crime, the trial.* New York: Grove Press.

Bergreen, L. (1994). *Capone: The man and the era.* New York: Simon & Schuster.

Breo, D. L., & Martin, W. J. (1993). *Crime of the century: Richard Speck and the murder of eight nurses.* New York: Bantam Books.

Court TV's Crime Library: Criminal Minds and Methods. *Born to raise hell.* Retrieved February 26, 2004, from www.crimelibrary.com/serial_killers/predators/speck/hell_3.html?sect=2

Court TV's Crime Library: Criminal Minds and Methods. *The manhunt.* Retrieved February 26, 2004, from www.crimelibrary.com/serial_killers/predators/speck/ manhunt_2.html?sect=2

Court TV's Crime Library: Criminal Minds and Methods. *Night of terror.* Retrieved February 26, 2004, from www.crimelibrary.com/serial_killers/predators/speck/ index_html

Enright, R. J. (1987). *Capone's Chicago.* Likeville, MN: Northstart Maschek Books.

Fischer, B. (1997). *John Dillinger: A short note.* Retrieved May 17, 2004, from http://home.swipnet.se/roland/dillinger.html

Fritsch, J. (2004, May 9). Psychologist has Gacy's brain in her basement. *Chicago Tribune,* pp. 1, 8.

Fussichen, K. (2003, April 13). *John Dillinger chronology. John Dillinger: Life and trials.* Available online at http://users.comkey.net/fussichen/otddill.html

Haunted Chicago. *Born to raise hell: The life and crimes of Richard Speck.* Retrieved May 17, 2004, from www.prairieghosts.com/speck.html

Haunted Chicago. *The Biograph Theater: The life and mysterious death of John Dillinger 2433 North Lincoln Avenue.* Retrieved May 17, 2004, from www.prairieghosts.com/dillinger.html

Immelman, A. (VSPA). (2002). Units for the study of personality in politics. Provisional psychological profile of the October 2002 Washington, DC-area sniper. Available online at www.csbsju.edu/vspa/research/sniper.html

Kobler, J. (1968). *Capone: The life and world of Al Capone.* New York: DaCapo Press.

Linder, D. (1997). *The confession of Nathan Leopold.* Retrieved January 11, 2005, from www.law.umkc.edu/faculty/projects/trails.leoploeb/leo_conf.html

Lohr, D. (2003, August 20). Richard Speck. *Crime Magazine and Encyclopedia of Crime.* Available online at www.crimemagazine.com/03/richardspeck,0820.htm

Lohr, D. (2004). Boy killer: John Wayne Gacy. *Crime Magazine and Encyclopedia of Crime.* Available online at www.crimemagazine.com/boykillergacy.htm

Lombardo, R. M. (2004). The genesis of organized crime in Chicago. Retrieved January 23, 2004, from www.ipsn.org/genesis.htm

Morrison, H., & Goldberg, H. (2004). *My life among serial killers: Inside the minds of the world's most notorious murderers.* New York: William Marrow/Harper-Collins Publishers.

Ramsey, M. (2004, July 19). Notorious Dillinger lives on in Chicago. *State Journal Register.*

Schoenberg, R. J. (1992). *Mr. Capone: The real–and complete–story of Al Capone.* New York: Morrow.

Smith, P. (1990, April 23). *Ransom kidnapping in America.* Available online at www.patterson-smith.com

Spiering, F. (1976). *The man who got Capone.* Indianapolis: Bobbs Merrill.

Wendt, L., & Kogan, H. (1953). *Big Bill of Chicago.* New York: Bobbs Merrill.

Up through the Ranks

Belluck, P. (1997, November 15). Top Chicago police official will retire over disclosure. *New York Times,* p. A8.

Choosing a Superintendent

Belluck, P. (1997, November 15). Top Chicago police official will retire over disclosure. *New York Times,* p. A8.

Carpenter, J., & Spielman, F. (1997, November 15). Top cop retires: Rodriguez cites series of setbacks, says he'll depart Dec. 1. *Chicago Sun-Times*, p. 1.

City's new top cop. (1998, February 19). *Chicago Sun-Times*, p. 25.

Commentary. (1998, February 19). *Chicago Sun-Times.*

Find the best possible top cop. (1997, November 19). *Chicago Tribune*, p. 24.

Fornek, S. (1997, November 17). Rodriguez can point to some bright spots. *Chicago Sun-Times*, p. 7.

Forty-nine applicants put in their names for police superintendent's post. (1998, January 20). *Chicago Tribune*, p. 3.

Jimenez, G., & Cone, T. K. (1997, November 17). Many officers saw writing on the wall. *Chicago Sun-Times*, p. 7.

Johnson, D. (1998, February 19). Popular detective will head Chicago police. A troubled department looking for leadership. *New York Times*, p. A-16.

Lead on, Superintendent Hillard. (1998, February 19). *Chicago Tribune*, p. 18.

Martin, A., & Mills, S. (1998a, January 18). Two ahead of pack for top police job: Daley mum on choice for superintendent. Chicago Tribune, p. 1.

Martin, A., & Mills, S. (1998b, February 2). Police board trims field in top cop search: 9 city police officials, state cop chief among 11 finalists for job. *Chicago Tribune*, p. 1.

Metsch, S. (1997, December 2). Top cop substitute criticized: Minority groups rip Daley over choice. *Daily Southtown.*

Metsch, S. (1998, February 19). Daley taps police superintendent: Hillard makes promise to remember the rank and file. *Daily Southtown.*

Mills, S. (1998, February 21). New police chief lays down the law: Hillard's plan still vague, but not his expectations. *Chicago Tribune*, p. 5.

Mills, S., & Martin, A. (1998, February 19). Daley makes cautious pick for top cop. *Chicago Tribune*, p. 1.

Roberts, M., & Spielman, F. (1997, December 12). Search for top cop closing in. *Chicago Sun-Times*, p. 6.

Rodriguez's legacy. (1997, November 16). *Chicago Sun-Times*, p. 49.

Sneed, M. (1998, February 20). Michael Sneed column. *Chicago Sun-Times*, p. 4.

Spielman, F. (1998a, February 7). Three city veterans to vie for top cop post. *Chicago Sun-Times*, p. 1.

Spielman, F. (1998b, February 8). Ramsey favorite for police superintendent. *Chicago Sun-Times*, p. 27.

Spielman, F. (1998c, February 13). Hillard gains support in competition for top cop. *Chicago Sun-Times*, p. 16.

Spielman, F. (1998d, February 17). Daley calls in 2 police finalists again. *Chicago Sun-Times*, p. 12.

Spielman, F., & Casey, J. (1997a, November 16). Top cop's exit puts pressure on Daley. *Chicago Sun-Times*, p. 1.

Spielman, F., & Casey, J. (1997b, November 16). Top cop's exit places mayor under the gun. *Chicago Sun-Times*, p. 6.

Spielman, F., & Roberts, M. (1998a, February 19). Hillard a man of the streets. *Chicago Sun-Times*, p. 6.

Spielman, F., & Roberts, M. (1998b, February 19). Hillard is top cop. *Chicago Sun-Times*, p. 1.

Taking Charge: The Challenge of the Superintendent

Attacking murder in Chicago. (2003, December 21). *Chicago Tribune*, p. 8.

Bowling, B. (1999, Autumn). The rise and fall of New York murder: Zero tolerance or crack's decline. *British Journal of Criminology, 39*(4), 531–554.

Brown, C. (2003, April). Chicago's star: Terry Hillard is the "windy city's" top cop. A rare combination of skills has put him on everyone's list of the best in the nation. *American Police Beat,* pp. 1, 58, 67.

Chicago Police Department. (1998). *Annual report.* City of Chicago.

Chicago Police Department. (2000). *Special report: Strengthening relations between police and minority communities: Ensuring accountability for effective policing in Chicago's diverse neighborhoods.* City of Chicago.

Chicago Public Library. (2004). *A brief history of the Chicago Police Department.* Retrieved January 26, 2004, from http://chipublib.org/oo4chicago/timeline/policedept.html

Huppke, R. W., & Heinzmann, D. (2004, February 1). Scourge of the city: Gangs, guns and drug dealing fuel city's cycle of violence. *Chicago Tribune,* pp. 1, 10–11.

Joanes, A. (2000, Spring). Does the New York City Police Department deserve credit for the decline in New York City's homicide rate? A cross-sectional comparison of police strategies and homicide rates. *Columbia Journal of Law and Social Problems, 33*(3), 265–304.

New York Attorney General's Office. (1999, December 1). *The New York City Police Department's "stop and frisk" practices: A report to the people of the state of New York.* State of New York.

Skogan, W. G., Steiner, L., & the Chicago Community Policing Evaluation Consortium. (2004, April). *CAPS: Community policing in Chicago, year ten. An evaluation of Chicago's alternative policing strategy.* Chicago: Criminal Justice Information Authority, State of Illinois.

The summer killing season. (2004, May 2). *Chicago Tribune,* p. 12.

White, M. D., Fyfe, J. J., Campbell, S. P., & Goldkamp, J. S. (2003, May). The police role in preventing homicide: Considering the impact of problem-oriented policing on the prevalence of murder. *Journal of Research in Crime and Delinquency, 40*(2), 194–225.

Will, G. (2003, September 28). *Los Angeles takes on crimes with cops.* Retrieved December 6, 2003, from www.townhall.com/columnists/georgewill/gw20030928.shtml

Policing Chicago Streets: Gangs, Guns, and Drugs

Carpenter, J. (1999, March 8). How gangs get guns: "Straw" buyers get weapons from suburbs. *Chicago Sun-Times,* p. 1.

Chandler, S. (2004, June 13). Gangs built on corporate mentality: Adopting best business practices permitted drug trade to flourish. *Chicago Tribune,* Section 5, pp. 1, 9.

Chicago Crime Commission. (1995). *Gang book 1995.* Available online at www.vilocity.net/~acekc/ccc%20gang%20book%20-%20main%20text.htm

Chicago Police Department. (2003). *Training manual: Gang awareness, narcotics and guns.* Chicago: Author.

Chicago Housing Authority. (2004, April 27). *Change. A brief history.* Available online at www.thecha.org/housingdevelopment

Curry, D. C., Maxson, C. L., & Howell, J. C. (2001, March). Youth gang homicides in the 1990s (OJJDP Publication #3). Washington, DC: U.S. Department of Justice: Office of Justice Programs.

Heinzmann, D. (2004, February 5). Homicide in Chicago: Scourge of the city. Gangs run drug pipeline from Delta to Chicago. *Chicago Tribune*, Section 1, pp. 1, 5.

Howell, J., & Decker, S. (1999, January). The youth gangs, drugs and violence connection. *Juvenile Justice Bulletin*. Washington, DC: U.S. Department of Justice: Office of Justice Programs.

Huff, R. C. (Ed.). (1996). *Gangs in America* (2nd ed.). Thousand Oaks, CA: Sage Publications.

Huppke, R. W. (2004, April 18). Homicide in Chicago: Scourge of a city. On streets, drug trade the only game in town. *Chicago Tribune*, pp. 1, 14–15.

Huppke, R. W., & Heinzmann, D. (2004, February 1). Homicide in Chicago: Scourge of the city. Shoot-first culture stalks streets of murder capitol. *Chicago Tribune*, p. 1, 10–11.

Main, F., & Sweeney, A. (2004, May 2). How this gun got into the hands of a little girl's killer. *Chicago Sun-Times*, pp. 1, 27, 29A.

Office of National Drug Control Policy. (2004, January). *Pulse check: National drug trends in drug abuse*. Washington, DC.

U.S. Attorney's Office, Northern District-Illinois. (1999). Initiative fact sheet, unpublished. As cited in Rosenthal, L. (2000). Gang loitering and race. *The Journal of Criminal Law and Criminology, 91*(1), 99–160.

U.S. Department of Justice: National Drug Intelligence Center. (2003, January). *National drug threat assessment 2003*. Johnstown, PA: Author. (Product No. 2003-QO317-001).

U.S. Department of Justice: National Drug Intelligence Center. (2004, April). *National drug threat assessment 2004*. Johnstown, PA: Author. (Product No. 2004-QO317-002).

U.S. Department of Justice: Office of Juvenile Justice and Delinquency Prevention (2003, April). *Highlights of the 2001 National Youth Gang Survey*. Washington, DC.

U.S. Department of the Treasury, Bureau of Alcohol, Tobacco, and Firearms. (2002). *Crime gun trace report (2000)*. Washington, DC: Author.

The Foundation of Chicago-Style Policing: Community, Information, Authority

Chicago Police Department. (2000). *Special report: Strengthening relations between police and minority communities: Ensuring accountability for effective policing in Chicago's diverse neighborhoods*. City of Chicago.

Pastore, R. (2004, February 15). Taking it to the streets: How Chicago Police Department used technology to fight crime and become the first grand CIO enterprise value award winner. *CIO Magazine* (5). Available online at www.cio.com/archive/021504/grand.html

Pearl, N. R., & Campbell, R. A. (2004, July). Building foundations/breaking barriers: Improving police-community partnerships. *Law Enforcement Executive Forum, 4*(4), 1–18.

Piquepaille, R. (2004, April 27). *Chicago police wins CIO magazine award*. Available online at http://radio.weblogs.comm/0105910/ 2004/02/22

Rosenbaum, D. P., & Lurigio, A. J. (1994). An inside look at community policing reform: Definitions, organizational changes, and evaluation findings. *Crime and Delinquency, 40*(3), 299–314.

Skogan, W. G., Steiner, L., & the Chicago Community Policing Evaluation Consortium. (2003, January). *Community policing in Chicago, years eight and nine: An evaluation of Chicago's alternative policing strategy and information technology initiative.* Chicago: Illinois Criminal Justice Information Authority, State of Illinois.

Skogan, W. G., Steiner L., & & the Chicago Community Policing Evaluation Consortium. (2004, April). *Community policing in Chicago year ten: An evaluation of Chicago's alternative policing strategy.* Chicago: Illinois Criminal Justice Information Authority, State of Illinois.

Trojanowicz, R., & Bucqueroux, B. (1990). *Community policing: A contemporary perspective.* Cincinnati, OH: Anderson.

The Media, the Police, and Major Cases

Alvord, V. (2003, January 5). Police pressured to call off chase. *USA Today.* Retrieved August 27, 2004, from www.usatoday.com/news/nation/2003-01-05-police-chases-x.htm

Belpedio, T. (2003, January 22). Toughen pursuit penalties. *Chicago Sun-Times.*

Chicago AP. (2000, January 31). Police charge man in serial killings, rape. Retrieved May 12, 2004, from www.beloitdailynews.com/100/lill31.htm

Chicago Police Board. (1998, March 12). *Police board upholds charge of excessive force in Mearday case: Officers to be discharged from department* (Press release). City of Chicago.

Chicago Police Department. (1998, September 4). Superintendent comments on the Ryan Harris case (Press release). City of Chicago.

Chicago Police Department. (2001, April 24). Statement from Superintendent Terry G. Hillard on the Miedzianowski decision (Press release). City of Chicago.

Chicago Police Department. (2002). *Annual report.* City of Chicago.

Chicago Police Department. (2003a, April 4). Press release on the death of Qing Chang. City of Chicago.

Chicago Police Department. (2003b, April 24). Remarks of Superintendent Terry G. Hillard: Vehicle pursuit policy press conference. City of Chicago.

Cook County State's Attorney's Office. (1998, September 4). Press release on the Ryan Harris case. Cook County, Illinois.

Dumas-Mitchell, A. (2001, March 7). Witnesses offer conflicting testimonies in Mearday Trial. *Chicago Defender*, p. 4.

Garcia, J. (2003, April 25). Police investigate allegations of excessive force in Cabrini disturbance. *ABC Channel 7 News Chicago.* Retrieved July 17, 2003, from http://abclocal.go.com/wls/news/042503_ns_cabrinidisturbance.html

Hanna, J. (2001a, March 8). Feared for life, Mearday says; Suspect in assault case says he was afraid when officers approached him. *Chicago Tribune*, p. 1.

Hanna, J. (2001b, March 9). Jury quickly acquits Mearday: Defendant hopes "the police will start to think before they react." *Chicago Tribune*, p. 1.

Hussain, R. (2003, January 6). 3 charged with murder in fatal crash. *Chicago Sun-Times*, p. 3.

Juvenile Justice. (1998). *What of juvenile justice? The botched investigation of the murder of Ryan Harris.* Retrieved April 13, 2004, from http://soivser.hyperchat.com/rainnn/chic.htm

Lighty, T. (2003, March 21). Last sentence in rogue cop case; Drug dealer tied to Miedzianowski gets 30-year term. *Chicago Tribune*, p. 3.

Lighty, T., & O'Connor, M. (2003, January 25). Rogue cop gets life; Drug ring dealer called betrayer of society, honest police. *Chicago Tribune*, p. 1.

Main, F. (2003a, January 4). Deadly end in police chase. *Chicago Sun-Times*, p. 3.

Main, F. (2003b, September 8). New rules put brakes on police chases. *Chicago Sun-Times*, p. 5.

Main, F., & Spielman, F. (2003, April 24). City restricts police chases, but not as much as some cities. *Chicago Sun-Times*, p. 16.

Meyer, G. H. (2003, January 6). Three charged with murder in fatal crash: Pregnant woman killed in chase. *Chicago Tribune*, p. 3.

Miller, S. L., & Wilson, T. (2000, February 1). Suspect glad he's caught; cops say taped confessions, DNA help make case. *Chicago Tribune*, p. 1.

Pallasch, A. M. (2003, January 8). Death in police chase may be "bank-breaker": Jury might award woman's family $20 mil., lawyer says. *Chicago Sun-Times*, p. 18.

Possley, M. (2001, January 27). Judge to permit testing of boy in Harris-case suit. *Chicago Tribune*, p. 5.

PursuitWatch.org. The campaign for safer and smarter police pursuits. Retrieved August 27, 2004, from www.pursuitwatch.org/media.htm

Rado, D. (2003, January 2). Pedestrian killed in chase mourned: Future was filled with promise, loved ones say. *Chicago Tribune*, p. 3.

Roberts, M. (1997, October 11). Brutality fallout enrages cop union. *Chicago Sun-Times*, p. 1.

Sadovi, C. (2003, January 7). "She liked the U.S. very much, even in China" husband of bystander killed in police chase shares memories. *Chicago Sun-Times*, p. 3.

Spielman, F., & Main, F. (2003, January 9). Police review chase policy: Hillard stops short of committing to make changes. *Chicago Sun-Times*, p. 4.

U.S. Attorney's Office, Northern District of Illinois. (1998, December 16). Chicago police officer among 12 charged in drug conspiracy (Press release). United States Department of Justice. Chicago.

Warmbir, S. (2001a, April 24). "Most corrupt" cop guilty in drug ring. Jury convicts former officer of teaming up with gang-bangers to smuggle $2 million in cocaine. *Chicago Sun-Times*, p. 1.

Warmbir, S. (2001b, April 25). Cop's bragging was his downfall. *Chicago Sun-Times*, p. 1.

Warmbir, S. (2003, February 8). Mistress of convicted cop gets 30 years in cocaine ring. *Chicago Sun-Times*, p. 4.

Wilson, T., & Ahmed, N. (2000, February 5). Serial killer suspect hid in plain view, cops say. *Chicago Tribune*, p. 1.

Dealing with a Night from Hell

Awareness comes at a very high price. (2001, May 10). *Chicago Sun-Times*, p. 39.

Caldwell, M. (2003, September 27). Russ killing by cop: Needs federal grand jury inquiry! *Chicago Defender*, p. 11.

Case 00-CH-06091. Serena Daniels, Carl Carter, Michael W. Williams, and Stafford Wilson, Petitioners vs. Police Board of the City of Chicago et al. Respondents. Opinion and Order, July 5, 2001, in the Circuit Court of Cook County, Illinois, County Department, Chancery Division. The Honorable Aaron Jaffe.

Devine, R. (2002, May 28). No charges in the Russ/Haggerty shootings. (Press release). Office of the Cook County State's Attorney.

Hillard, T. (1999a, June 17). Chicago city council police and fire committee hearings on the Russ/Haggerty shootings.

Hillard, T. (1999b, June 24). Chicago city council police and fire committee hearings on the Russ/Haggerty shootings.

Hillard, T. (1999c, July 12). Statement of Superintendent Terry G. Hillard (Press release). Chicago Police Department.

Hillard, T. (2000, February 11). Actions regarding the Russ case (Press release). Chicago Police Department.

Jackson, J. (1999, June 8). Rev. Jackson warns "People of goodwill must unite against new wave of terrorism": Civil leader calls for U.S. Justice Department to investigate police shooting (Press release). *Rainbow Push Coalition.*

Kass, J. (2001, May 9). Mayor plays caution card in settling suit. *Chicago Tribune*, p. 2.

Learning from the Haggerty case. (2001, May 9). *Chicago Tribune*, p. 26.

McLaughlin, A. (1999, June 23). When cops, not just white ones, kill. *The Christian Science Monitor.*

Mendell, D. (2003a, September 24). Russ' death blamed on cop's errors/shooting: Criminologist says incident mishandled. *Chicago Tribune*, p. 1.

Mendell, D. (2003b, September 26). Lawyers in Russ case paint different pictures of athlete. *Chicago Tribune*, p. 3.

Spielman, F., & Pallasch, A. (2001, May 8). An $18 million "lesson for city" family of LaTanya Haggerty settles case in which cop killed their daughter. *Chicago-Sun Times*, p. 1.

Strausberg, C. (2001a, May 29). $18 million to Haggerty family. *Chicago Defender*, p. 1.

Strausberg, C. (2001b, June 27). Finance panel oks $18 mil LaTanya Haggerty claim. *Chicago Defender*, p. 10.

Strausberg, C. (2002, May 29). No criminal charges in Haggerty, Russ shootings. *Chicago Defender*, p. 1.

Strausberg, C. (2003, October 20). City may appeal Russ $9.6 million verdict. *Chicago Defender*, p. 2.

The Life of Chicago Cops

Chicago Police Career Information. Retrieved February 12, 2005, from http://egov. cityofchicago.org

CIA. (2002, July 1). Interactive table of world nations. *World fact book.* Retrieved May 1, 2004, from www.mrdowling.com

Fraternal Order of Police, Chicago Lodge 7. (2004). About us. Retrieved December 6, 2004, from www.chicagofop.org/about_us.shtml

Goldfarb, D. (2004, June). *The effects of stress on police officers.* Available online at www.heavybadge.com/efstress.htm

Hepp, R., & Janega, J. (2001, July 6). Sad farewell to a brave cop: Mourners recall officer who made city "safer place." *Chicago Tribune*, p. 1.

Hillard, T. G. (1999a, January 13). Speech given at funeral services for Officer John Knight at St. Christina Church, Chicago.

Hillard, T. G. (1999b, March 16). Speech given at funeral services for officer James Camp. St. Philip Neri Catholic Church, Chicago.

Hillard, T. G. (2002a, March 22). Speech given at funeral services for Officer Donald Marquez. Moody Bible Institute, Chicago.

Hillard, T. G. (2002b, September 23). Speech given at funeral services for Officer Benjamin Perez. St. Daniel and Prophet Catholic Church, Chicago.

Kaiser, R. L. (1999a, August 15). Welcome to the deuce. *Chicago Tribune*, p. 1.

Kaiser, R. L. (1999b, August 17). You've fought long enough: The third of four parts. *Chicago Tribune*, p. 1.

Kaiser, R. L., & Kapos, S. (2001, August 21). Slain cop known as gentle giant. *Chicago Tribune*, p. 14.

Kass, J. (1998, August 27). Officer's funeral allows family, city to mourn together. *Chicago Tribune*, p. 3.

Kass, J. (1999, March 16). And you wonder why police officers become embittered. *Chicago Tribune*, p. 3.

Lynn, T. F. (2004, November). Police suicide, and stress: Facts and information. *Police Stress and Psychology*. Available online at www.policestress.com/_wsn?page2.html

Main, F. (2001, July 6). "He loved being the police": Hundreds of fellow officers turn out to honor Brian Strouse. *Chicago Sun-Times*, p. 7.

Mitchell, M. (2001, August 23). Senseless killing of cop leaves us asking "why." *Chicago Sun-Times*, p. 14.

Ninety Second Illinois General Assembly, Senate Resolution 0364.

Officer's wife grateful. (2001, August 26). *Chicago Sun-Times*.

Pallasch, A. M., & Wilson, T. (1998, August 25). Obituaries: Michael Ceriale, 26, model police recruit. *Chicago Tribune*, p. 9.

Remembering a slain officer and a little girl. (2001, August 23). *Chicago Defender*.

Saint Michael's House. A counseling service for police officers and their families. Retrieved November 11, 2003, from www.stmichaelshouse.org/about.htm

Schwab, L. (2004, August). Officer down: Helping fellow officers overcome depression. *PowerPoint* presentation to Illinois Sheriffs' Association.

Simpson, C., & Kaiser, R. L. (2001, August 31). Wounded cop's fight heartens doctors: Police join prayers for "fearless" pal. *Chicago Tribune*, pp. 1, 24.

Skogan, W. G., Steiner, L., & the Chicago Community Policing Evaluation Consortium. (2003, January). *Community policing in Chicago, year ten: An evaluation of Chicago's alternative policing strategy*. Chicago: Illinois Criminal Justice Information Authority, State of Illinois.

Sourcebook of Criminal Justice Statistics. (2002). Law enforcement officers killed in the United States, 1972–2002. Available online at www.albany.edu/sourcebook/pdf/t3175.pdf

Stratton, J. G. (1975, November). Pressures in law enforcement marriages. *Police Chief Magazine*, 44.

Sullivan, M. (1999, January 14). He was truly a hero. *Daily Southtown*.

Syle, H. (1978, Fall). The stress of police work. *Police Stress*, 7–8.

Violanti, J. M. (2004). *Dying from the job: The mortality risks for police officers*. Law Enforcement Wellness Association, Inc. Retrieved November 24, 2004, from www.cophealth.com/articles_dyng_a.html

Washington, S. (1999, March 11). Community mourns a slain officer. *Chicago Defender*.

Superintendent Hillard's Legacy: Accomplishment and Leadership

Brown, C. (2003, April). Chicago's star: Terry Hillard is the "windy city's" top cop. A rare combination of skills has put him on everyone's list of the best in the nation. *American Police Beat*.

Chicago Police Department. (2001). *Annual report*. City of Chicago.

Chicago Police Department. (1999/2000). *Biennial report.* City of Chicago.

Heinzmann, D., & Bush, R. (2003, April 20). Quiet leader, stormy tenure. *Chicago Tribune.* p. 1.

Jurkanin, T., Hoover, L., Dowling, J., & Ahmad, J. (Eds.). (2001). *Enduring, surviving, and thriving as a law enforcement executive.* Springfield, IL: Charles C. Thomas.

Public Building Commission of Chicago. (2000). History, Chicago Police Headquarters. Retrieved September 17, 2004, from http://pbcchicago.com/subhtml/police_hg.asp

Richards, C. (2003, April 23). 1-2 punch hits city, state hard. *Chicago Sun-Times,* p. 51.

Skogan, W. G., Steiner, L., & the Chicago Community Policing Evaluation Consortium. (2003, January). *Community policing in Chicago, years eight and nine: An evaluation of Chicago's alternative policing strategy and information technology initiative.* Illinois Criminal Justice Information Authority, State of Illinois.

Skogan, W. G., Steiner L., & & the Chicago Community Policing Evaluation Consortium. (2004, April). *Community policing in Chicago year ten: An evaluation of Chicago's alternative policing strategy.* Chicago: Illinois Criminal Justice Information Authority, State of Illinois.

The Decision to Retire

Bradley, B. (2003, April 19). Chicago police chief stepping down after 35 years with the force. *ABC 7 Chicago.* Available online at http://abclocal.go.com/wis/news/041803_ns_hillard.html

Hack, C. (2003, April 19). Chicago owes Terry Hillard a debt of gratitude: Top cop announces retirement. *Daily Southtown,* p. 1.

Heinzmann, D. (2003, March 7). Hillard's "confidant" on police force dies. *Chicago Tribune,* p. 3.

Heinzmann, D., & Bush, R. (2003, April 20). Quiet leader, stormy tenure. *Chicago Tribune,* pp. 1, 5.

Hillard, T. G. (2003a, March 18). Police recruit graduation address at Navy Pier.

Hillard, T. G. (2003b, June 5). Police recruit graduation address at Navy Pier.

Hillard, T. G. (2003c, August 15). To Chicago's police and citizens, a heartfelt thanks. *Chicago Sun-Times,* p. 51.

Marin, C. (2003, August 20). Leadership 101: You don't have to be showy to get noticed. *Chicago Tribune,* p. 21.

Pfleger, M. L., Rev. (n.d.). Voice of the people: Hail to the chief. *Chicago Sun-Times.*

Spielman, F., & Main, F. (2003, April 18). Hillard calls it quits: After 5 turbulent years, Chicago's top cop says, "I've done my time." *Chicago Sun-Times,* pp. 1, 6–7.

Spielman, F., Main, F., & Lawrence, C. (2003a, April 19). Outgoing Hillard draws praise from mayor, police. *Chicago Sun-Times,* p. 9.

Spielman, F., Main, F., & Lawrence, C. (2003b, April 20). Amid praise by Daley, aides, Hillard makes retirement official. *Chicago Sun-Times.*

Terry Hillard's legacy. (2003, August 14). *Chicago Tribune,* Section 1, p. 12.

Top cop deserves high praise. (2003, April 20). *Chicago Sun-Times,* p. 31.

Epilogue

Bebow, J., & Olivo, A. (2005, February 27). CHA fix fails to help ex-tenants: Former residents finding it difficult to fit in with their new neighbors. *Chicago Tribune,* Section 1, pp. 1, 14.

AUTHOR INDEX

A

Ahmad, J., 197, 228
Ahmed, N., 225
Altman, J., 219
Alvord, V., 141, 224
Apple, R.W., 8, 219
Artner, A.G., 219

B

Baker, R.M., 7, 219
Bebow, J., 214, 228
Belluck, P., 51, 53, 220
Belpedio, T., 143, 224
Bergreen, L., 219
Bowling, B., 73, 75–76, 222
Bradley, B., 207, 228
Breo, D.L., 219
Brown, C., 194–196, 222, 227
Bucqueroux, B., 93, 224
Bureau of Alcohol, Tobacco, and Firearms
  (*see* U.S. Department of the Treasury)
Bush, R., 199, 209, 228

C

Caldwell, M., 157, 225
Campbell, R.A., 94, 223
Campbell, S.P., 76, 222
Carpenter, J., 53, 87–88, 221–222
Casey, J., 53, 221
Central Intelligence Agency (CIA), 172, 226
Chandler, S., 79, 222
Chicago AP, 132, 224
Chicago Community Policing Evaluation
  Consortium, 93–94, 100–103, 108–110, 189,
  222, 224, 227–228
Chicago Crime Commission, 80, 222
Chicago Defender, 183, 227
Chicago Historical Society, 3, 219
Chicago Housing Authority, 10, 83–84, 219,
  222

Chicago Police Board, 224
Chicago Police Career Information, 166, 226
Chicago Police Department, 68–69, 72, 77,
  79–80, 95–99, 126, 134, 138, 140, 142, 146,
  186, 188, 222–224, 227–228
Chicago Public Library, 4, 219, 222
Chicago Sun-Times, 56, 63, 160, 180, 209, 221,
  225, 227–228
Chicago Tribune, 55, 64, 69, 77, 160, 209,
  221–222, 226, 228
City of Chicago, 4, 219
Cone, T.K., 53, 221
Cook County, Illinois
  Circuit Court, 154, 225
  State's Attorney's Office, 134, 146, 224
Court TV's Crime Library, 219–220
Curry, D.C., 222

D

Decker, S., 79, 81–82, 223
Devine, R., 152, 154, 225
Dowling, J., 197, 228
Dumas-Mitchell, A., 224

E

Enright, R.J., 220

F

Fischer, B., 220
Fornek, S., 53, 221
Fraternal Order of Police, 174, 226
Fritsch, J., 25, 220
Fussichen, K., 220
Fyfe, J.J., 76, 222

G

Garcia, J., 148, 224
Goldberg, H., 24–25, 220
Goldfarb, D., 172, 226
Goldkamp, J.S., 76, 222

229

SUBJECT INDEX